Up Against a Crooked Gospel

ETHICS AND INTERSECTIONALITY SERIES

Up Against a Crooked Gospel

*Black Women's Bodies
and the Politics of Redemption*

Melanie Jones Quarles

ORBIS BOOKS
Maryknoll, New York 10545

Founded in 1970, Orbis Books endeavors to publish works that enlighten the mind, nourish the spirit, and challenge the conscience. The publishing arm of the Maryknoll Fathers and Brothers, Orbis seeks to explore the global dimensions of the Christian faith and mission, to invite dialogue with diverse cultures and religious traditions, and to serve the cause of reconciliation and peace. The books published reflect the views of their authors and do not represent the official position of the Maryknoll Society. To learn more about Maryknoll and Orbis Books, please visit our website at www.orbisbooks.com.

Library of Congress Cataloging-in-Publication Data

Names: Jones Quarles, Melanie, author.
Title: Up against a crooked gospel : Black women's bodies and the politics
   of redemption / Melanie Jones Quarles.
Description: Maryknoll, NY : Orbis Books, [2024] | Series: Ethics and
   intersectionality | Includes bibliographical references and index. |
   Summary: "Explores how Black women have influenced and been influenced
   by the Black Church and US society"—Provided by publisher.
Identifiers: LCCN 2024017276 (print) | LCCN 2024017277 (ebook) | ISBN
   9781626985865 | ISBN 9798888660416 (epub)
Subjects: LCSH: African American women—Religious life. | Sex
   role—Religious aspects—Christianity. | African American churches.
Classification: LCC BR563.B53 J66 2024 (print) | LCC BR563.B53 (ebook) |
   DDC 277.30082—dc23/eng/20240521
LC record available at https://lccn.loc.gov/2024017276
LC ebook record available at https://lccn.loc.gov/2024017277

For the faith of my Grandmothers
Dedicated to Gertrude Foster and Adelaide Jones

Contents

Acknowledgments

Before entering graduate school, I engaged in a discernment activity with a Quaker Clearness Committee to give clarity about the scholarly life as a vocational pathway. One question has lingered from that session.

"What will you lose on this journey?"

Until that question, I had embarked on my journey with confidence and assurance of the numerous personal, professional, and academic gains of completing a doctoral program. I wrestled with the question of loss with silence at first, lamenting hesitantly about time. I could have never imagined the way loss would profoundly mark my graduate experience and, particularly, this project.

The death of my maternal grandmother, Gertrude Foster, during finals at the end of my first year shifted my research from a historical exploration of Black Baptist women to a womanist theo-ethical project on the complexity of Black women's bodies and character. I later endured the double-edged loss in the same year of my last living grandparent, LJ Foster, and my beloved father, the Reverend Dr. Michael Jones, rattling me to my core. The faith of my ancestors helped me finish my program and learn the hard lessons of surviving loss. This book emerges from the work I did in and have done since my graduate studies. It is a labor of legacy, love, and the work that my soul must have.

In Buddhist thought, "when the student is ready, the teacher will appear." I am gifted to be a millennial womanist scholar trained by womanist academicians. With my interests in African American religious history, Dr. Julia Speller guided me before I shifted to ethics and theology. My heart sings for my dissertation adviser, Dr. JoAnne Marie Terrell, who believed in me from the very beginning and nurtured the project that became this book as a patient midwife, coaching me through every difficult birthing pain. Terrell's invitation to perform a theological body scan of my life and story motivates me still. From the kitchen table to the public square, thank you for teaching me to find the meaning in loss that leads to life. I am incredibly blessed by the mentorship of Dr. Stacey M. Floyd-Thomas, who has remained a steady and sagacious guide from my time at Vanderbilt University Divinity School. Thank you, Dr. Stephanie Buckhanon Crowder, for engaging my early musings on Luke 13 and the narrative of the bent woman that anchors this project. Thank you, Dr. Christophe Ringer, for serving on my committee and being one of my fiercest interlocutors at critical times in my academic formation.

I am grateful to my fellow Chicago Theological Seminary (CTS) scholars and dear friends, Dr. Angela Parker, Dr. Jean Murphy, the late Dr. Jerrolyn Eulinberg, Dr. Teresa Smallwood, Dr. Malene Minor Johnson, the Reverend Thomas Ginter, Sherrie Phillips-Johnson, and the Reverend Benjamin Reynolds, who made CTS a breeding ground for cultivating our best ideas. To my "little" brother, the Reverend Quincy James Rineheart, may we continue to embody Black excellence in the church and academy while getting into good trouble.

Thank you to the administration, faculty, staff, and students at American Baptist College, Illinois Institute of Technology, Brite Divinity School, Seminary of the Southwest, and Union Presbyterian Seminary, who have opened doors for me to live fully into my gifts of scholarship, teaching, and administration. Leading the Katie Geneva Cannon Center for Womanist Leadership, teaching, and learning my greatest vocational joys.

My faith community, forever friends, and family embody the pillars who have helped me to stand tall, regardless. Every time I think of you, South Suburban Missionary Baptist Church, I thank God for you. In the words of my covenant uncle, Bishop Victor D. Agee, my circle is connected to my destiny. The Reverend Catina Parrish Clark remains a trusted confidante and faithful prayer partner during every season. Monique Gower, James McCreary, Dwight Jennings, the Joshua Generation—Minister Keisha Blount Nelson, Sakinah Hoyte, attorney Gerald Ashby Jr., Eric A. Smith II, and attorney Valencia Caroline Thurman—and the Wells Women—Dr. Eboni Marshall Turman, Dr. AnneMarie Mingo, Dean Neichelle Guidry, Dr. Alisha Lola Jones, Dr. Michele Watkins, Dr. Kimberly Russaw, and Dr. Stephanie Crumpton—have filled my life with genuine friendship, love, and laughter just when I needed it.

I belong to some good people and come from large families on my maternal—Fosters and Bradleys—and paternal—Joneses—lineages. Words cannot express the depth of my gratitude to my close relatives—David Jones, Carolyn Jones, Tamica Thomaston, NaKayla White, Carieon Smith—who gave me a soft place to land in a hostile world. My primary teacher for every discipline in life and faith is my mommy, the Reverend Dr. Annette Marie

Jones. Thank you for moving mountains so that I may excel at every phase of life. Both of my parents gave me their absolute best to ensure that I acquired the highest education and performed to the height of my abilities. I vividly remember my Dad spending hours in Christian bookstores as the consummate bibliophile and lifelong learner, scouring through countless volumes of theological and biblical scholarship. I will always count it as a privilege and an honor that I could finish the victory lap of this book in Daddy's office beside the numerous stacks of his most treasured possessions. May this work be a deposit into a legacy of fulfillment and flourishing.

When nothing else could help, love lifted me! I am honored to join the rich legacy of Quarles scholars through marital union in the line of Dr. Benjamin Arthur Quarles. I am abundantly blessed by the unwavering love of my husband and partner in life, love, and ministry, the Reverend De'Quon Antonio Quarles, who remains my biggest champion and pushes me to become my best self every single day.

God is the source of my strength and the strength of my life. To God be the glory for the marvelous things she has done. May these words and the meditations of my heart be acceptable in your sight, O Lord, My Strength and My Redeemer!

Abbreviations

AAR	American Academy of Religion
AME	African Methodist Episcopal Church
AMEZ	African Methodist Episcopal Zion Church
CEB	Common English Bible
CTS	Chicago Theological Seminary
EPI	Economic Policy Institute
KJV	King James Version
mGNT	Morphological Greek New Testament
NKJV	New King James Version
NRSV	New Revised Standard Version
RPC	The Rainbow PUSH Coalition
SBL	Society of Biblical Literature
SCLC	Southern Christian Leadership Conference
UCC	United Church of Christ
WTAL	Woman, Thou Art Loosed!

Introduction

"In Search of My Grandmother's Garden"

My maternal grandmother, Sweety Gertrude Foster, died of complications of an enlarged heart at the age of seventy-one years young on May 6, 2013. What began as a visit to the emergency room for stomach discomfort ended in her sudden demise. As I entered the hospital room to view and visit with her body after the fourth and final cardiac arrest, I noticed the most peculiar happening: my grandmother's crooked body laid straight (perfectly aligned) for the first time that I could remember. For folks who knew my grandmother, this was a sure sign that within moments of her passing she encountered embodied transformation (healing-restoration-liberation) because the crookedness of her spine would not allow her to lay her entire body down on her back for many years. I am certain that my grandmother was not born with a bent body because of the lasting photographs that reveal her body at multiple stages of her life standing erect, including my kindergarten graduation (at her age fifty; at my age five). Her spine began to bend considerably during my middle school and junior high years. The crookedness was noticeable at my graduation from elementary school (at her age fifty-nine; at my age fourteen) and terribly worse by my Divinity School graduation (at her age seventy; at my age twenty-five) just one year before her passing. I know all too well a woman of great virtue who suffered from a bent body.

I am haunted by the memory of my grandmother's story and three distinct and lingering images: (1) an erect body, (2) a bent/crooked body, and (3) a restored/transformed body. The photographs of an early erect body demonstrate my grandmother's crookedness as a temporal bearing that was enacted upon her body. The memory of my grandmother's bent body exposes the "unbearable weight" of the social tragedies of living as a poor, migrant, divorced Black churchwoman and domestic[1] that pressed her down.

---

[1] Born and reared in the South, Gertrude Foster spent her early years as a domestic nurturing white families in Memphis, Tennessee. When she migrated to Chicago in the 1960s,

The lasting image of her glorified body restored symbolizes hope and the potential for liberative transformation through an encounter with the Divine.

While rehearsing my grandmother's narrative, I could not help but notice the eerie correlation between her story and the unnamed woman with a bent condition in Luke 13:10–17. The bent woman's narrative parallels the story of my grandmother and the broader historical and contemporary narratives of the Black female body bent multiply by pervasive historical, social, and religious threats seeking to stifle her survival and liberation that are inextricably linked to attacks against Black women's moral agency. In the 1980s, exercising their moral and intellectual agency, Black women religious scholars adapted Alice Walker's four-part poetic framing of the "womanist"[2] definition, and birthed womanism as a critical approach in religious studies to take seriously the lived experiences of struggle and survival of Black women against multiple forces of oppression. I raise the narrative of the bent woman as ripe for womanist theo-ethical analysis because it brings to center stage the complexity of body and character.

---

she pursued the best available employment as a housekeeper at the downtown Hyatt Regency hotel. The 2,019-room Hyatt Regency is the largest hotel in the city of Chicago, employing more than eight hundred service workers. More recently, the National Labor Relations Board filed complaints against the hotel for unfair labor practices and failure to disclose surveillance of employees. The Hyatt expectation for housekeepers to clean thirty rooms in an eight-hour shift continues to debilitate the health of employees. Most notably, UNITE HERE, a labor union for hospitality workers, organized a "Hyatt Hurts" global campaign in 2012 alongside several leading organizations (e.g., the National Football League Players Association, AFL-CIO, National Organization of Women [NOW], and National Gay and Lesbian Task Force) to identify Hyatt as the "worst employer in the service industry" and address Hyatt's numerous labor abuses to employees. See Naomi Wolf, "Hyatt Hurts: Hotel Workers Organise Global Boycott for a Fair Deal," *The Guardian*, October 4, 2012, http://www.theguardian.com/commentisfree/2012/oct/04/hyatt-hurts-hotel-workers-boycott. Thousands of Hyatt workers initiated a strike in the fall of 2018 against the Hyatt Chicago properties to rally for year-round healthcare, especially during the winter "layoff" season because of reduced tourism and travel. See Alexia Elejalde-Ruiz, "Hyatt Reaches Contract Agreement with Striking Hotel Workers," *Chicago Tribune*, October 4, 2018, https://www.chicagotribune.com/business/ct-biz-hyatt-contract-hotel-strike-1005-story.html. My grandmother worked for Hyatt for roughly twenty years, enduring the hardships of insufferable workloads, low wages, and unequal access to healthcare. I explore the damages of Hyatt's labor practices in relation to my grandmother's bent condition later in the book.

[2]Drawing from the Black idiomatic expression "you actin' womanish," novelist Alice Walker in her collection of essays, *In Search of Our Mothers' Gardens: Womanist Prose*, penned the definition of the term "womanist" in efforts to name the distinctive political aims of African American women that existed outside of the white feminist scope in the 1980s. See Alice Walker, *In Search of Our Mothers' Gardens: Womanist Prose* (1983, repr., Orlando: Mariner Books, 2003), xi–xii.

The Emergence and Methods of Womanist Ethics

The works of womanist ethicists alongside womanist thinkers in theology, biblical studies, history, homiletics, and other disciplines within religion analyzing Black women's agency validate a progressive series of scholarly efforts engaged in the "doing of ethics" with Black women at its center for the last forty years. Ethics is the moral philosophy of the duties, obligations, virtues, and values that shape human life. As a discipline within religious studies, ethics takes up the *meaning-making* of human agency, human relationships, and human action.

Theological norming in Western constructions and the Black Church are often inimical to Black women's interests. Unlike dominant Western theologies and traditional Christian ethics that make "claims for gender-neutral and value-free inquiry as a model for knowledge,"[3] womanist theological ethics seeks to interrogate these aims through the "eyes of the 'least of these'"[4] and critique "theological constructions that negate the *wholeness* or full existence of women who deal with the realities of social injustice and multilayered oppressions."[5] The theological question at stake is, "What do womanists say about the God of their experiences, given their oppressive realities?" Womanist theo-ethical norming centers survival, liberation, and creative self-expression for Black women.

The central starting point of womanist theological ethics begins with trailblazing scholar Katie Cannon's "The Emergence of a Black Feminist Consciousness," wherein Cannon is first to source Alice Walker's term "womanist" to confront oppressive, hegemonic ideologies of racism, sexism, and classism that situate Black women's struggle and characterize Black women's biblical interpretation as valuable acts to "dispel the threat of death in order to seize the present life."[6] In her subsequent full-length text, *Black Womanist Ethics,* Cannon traces the moral agency of Black women from the antebellum period (as early as 1619) to the latter half of the twentieth cen-

---

[3]Katie Geneva Cannon, *Katie's Canon: Womanism and the Soul of the Black Community,* rev. and exp. twenty-fifth ann. ed. (Minneapolis: Fortress Press, 2021), 60.

[4]Stacey M. Floyd-Thomas, *Mining the Motherlode: Methods in Womanist Ethics* (Cleveland: Pilgrim Press, 2006), 7.

[5]Melanie Harris, *Gifts of Virtue, Alice Walker, and Womanist Ethics* (New York: Palgrave Macmillan, 2013), 50.

[6]Womanist ethicist Katie Geneva Cannon (1950–2018) was the first to adopt Walker's term in a published article within the academy of religion. From the standpoint of a womanist theological ethicist, Cannon's groundbreaking article frames the significance of biblical interpretation for Black churchwomen confronting oppression. Cannon, *Katie's Canon,* 29.

tury (roughly the 1980s). Her central thesis is to frame "how Black women live out a moral wisdom in their real-lived context that does not appeal to the fixed rules or absolute principles of the white-oriented, male structured society."[7] For Cannon, Black women are the oppressed of the oppressed, representing the "most vulnerable and the most exploited members of the American society."[8] Cannon takes up Black women's literary tradition as a re/source to engage the "living space" of Black women's complex and dynamic moral agency as well as her struggle for survival amid the tripartite oppression of racism/white supremacy, sexism, and classism/poverty.[9] By analyzing the life and literature of the quintessential twentieth-century anthropologist and folklorist Zora Neale Hurston, Cannon introduces three canonical virtues of Black women's moral wisdom: *invisible dignity, quiet grace,* and *unshouted courage.*[10]

In her 1994 article in the *Annual of the Society of Christian Ethics,* just a decade into published works in womanist ethics, Christian social ethicist Cheryl Sanders identified seven recurring themes associated with the discipline: "(1) spirituality, (2) theodicy, (3) ontology, (4) dialogue with black male and white feminist theologians, (5) biblical ethics, (6) biomedical ethics, and (7) black church relations."[11] Moreover, Sanders recognizes a tendency of womanist ethicists to resource mainly Black women activists and thinkers of the eighteenth and nineteenth centuries and challenges womanist ethicists to "use living black church women as both audience and resource for serious ethical reflection."[12]

Roughly twenty years later, Emilie Townes makes the case that womanist theology and ethics have evolved since early work in multiple ways, emphasizing

a model for black women's organizational strength; a critique of the black social stratification; advocacy for justice-based spirituality; the inclusion of ecological concerns; a concern for health care; a consideration of black sexuality; and the issue of work. Within this evolving character, womanist theology often melds theological and social

---

[7]Katie Geneva Cannon, *Black Womanist Ethics* (Atlanta: Scholars Press, 1988), 4.
[8]Cannon, *Black Womanist Ethics,* 4.
[9]Cannon, *Black Womanist Ethics,* 7.
[10]Cannon, *Black Womanist Ethics,* 7.
[11]Cheryl J. Sanders, "Womanist Ethics: Contemporary Trends and Themes," *The Annual of the Society of Christian Ethics* 14 (1994): 299–305.
[12]Sanders, "Womanist Ethics," 305.

scientific analysis with cultural studies, literary studies, and political economy and often addresses public policy issues affecting African American communities.[13]

In this book, I carve out another central theme in womanist theological ethics of embodiment and respond to ongoing calls to center the concerns of everyday Black women of faith in the academy, Black Church, and broader world.

Bent and Bended Language

In the four decades since its initial emergence, a womanist theo-ethical analysis is now methodologically interdisciplinary and, according to ecowomanist Melanie Harris, comprising dialogically three primary elements: "deconstruction (critique), description (mining), and construction (crafting)."[14] Womanist ethicist Stacey Floyd-Thomas, in her seminal work *Mining the Motherlode: Methods in Womanist Theological Ethics*, identifies womanist theological ethics through four key tenets: radical subjectivity, traditional communalism, redemptive self-love, and critical engagement.[15] Of the four tenets, redemptive self-love is the most essential for understanding how this book approaches embodiment and bendedness. Redemptive self-love is the act of undoing the separation between mind, body, and soul, revaluing the embodied moral virtue of Black women along the thinking-being-doing continuum.

While the term "bentness" is a word that describes the quality of being bent, I use "bendedness" in this book to align with its poetic tone in Black popular culture, the African American vernacular, and Black Church rhetoric. *Bendedness*, in my view, marks a physical condition as much as it signals a theological and moral predicament for Black women. Bendedness has emphasized one partner's desperate plea to restore the couple's love after wrongdoing in Boyz II Men's 1994 classic "On Bended Knee," and it has framed Colin Kaepernick's silent protest to resist racism and police brutality in this nation, "on bended knee." Furthermore, Black Christians often describe kneeling to God in prayer as "on bended knee." Bendedness holds

---

[13]Emilie M. Townes, "Womanist Theology," in *Encyclopedia of Women and Religion in North America*, ed. Rosemary Skinner Keller, Rosemary Radford Ruether, and Marie Cantlon (Bloomington: Indiana University Press, 2006), 1165.

[14]Harris, *Gifts of Virtue*, 50.

[15]Floyd-Thomas, *Mining the Motherlode*.

linguistic drama when pronouncing every syllable of the word while cap-
turing the full range of Black women's experiences of facing body-bending
oppression in an unjust world.[16]

As a millennial womanist theological ethicist, I grapple with the theo-
ethical implications of my grandmother's life and transition as paradigmatic
for a broader socio-historical reality facing Black women. The bending of my
grandmother's spine from back-bending domestic labor and body-crushing
oppression held moral indictments and physiological implications on her
body. I come to this work with deep questions that are not just personal
but also theo-ethical. Who or what contributes to the social phenomenon
of Black women's *bendedness* in body and character? How might Black
religion[17] be held responsible or accountable for such a bent condition?
Is freedom for Black women in religion and society possible in life before
death? What does it mean for Black women to employ their bodies to assert
agency and incite liberation?

Reading Black women's narratives alongside Scripture through womanist literary criticism in this book exposes ways traditional Christian
biblical interpretations may reflect and shape negative assumptions and
cultural stereotypes about Black women. Throughout this book, I adopt a
hermeneutics of parallel within "the female-centered tradition of African
American biblical appropriation" also named the "survival/quality-of-life
tradition of African American biblical appropriation" constructed by
womanist theologian Delores S. Williams in *Sisters in the Wilderness: The
Challenge of Womanist God-Talk* to read the biblical text alongside Black

---

[16]In her classic article "Characteristics of Negro Expression," folklorist Zora Neale Hurston
describes drama as the most notable characteristic of Negro expression reflected in active
and descriptive language within Black sacred culture. See Zora Neale Hurston, "Characteristics of Negro Expression," in *The Sanctified Church* (New York: Marlowe, 1998), 49–68.

[17]In line with Africana historian of religion Charles Long, I identify religion as "orientation—orientation in the ultimate sense, that is, how one comes to terms with the ultimate
significance of one's place in the world. The Christian faith provided a language for the
meaning of religion, but not all the religious meanings of the black communities were en-
compassed by the Christian forms of religion." Black Christianity is one expression of the
Black religious identity, but Long identifies "extra-church orientations" that have exhibited
"great critical and creative power" for Black people that are beyond Christianity. See Charles
H. Long, *Significations: Signs, Symbols, and Images in the Interpretation of Religion* (Aurora,
CO: Davies Group, 1999), 7. Black religion points to the meaning-making of Black people,
though not always explicitly Christian. While the focus of this book primarily addresses
Black religious expressions within Christianity, I use "Black religion" throughout to indicate
larger implications for Black religious traditions that play a paradoxical role in the liberation
and oppression of Black women, which is not limited to the Black Church.

women's experiences.[18] Williams describes at least two traditions of African American biblical appropriation: the liberation tradition and the survival / quality-of-life tradition. The first tradition represents "God the liberator of the poor and oppressed," who relates to men in their struggles for liberation as identified in spiritual songs, slave narratives, and Black sermons and is illustrated in biblical stories, characters, and dramas involved in the liberation struggle.[19] Williams names the exodus story of the Hebrew people, prophetic accounts of God's deliverance (e.g., Shadrack, Meshack, and Abednego; Daniel in the lion's den), and Jesus's announcement of his ministry and witness in Luke 4 as Hebrew and Christian testament examples sourced by Black male theologians to validate God's liberation as a biblical paradigm.

For Williams, the second tradition within African American cultural sources "emphasized female activity and deemphasized male authority."[20] Williams points to the story of Hagar in Genesis 16 and 21 as a biblical account passed down through generations of African American sources to frame a biblical paradigm of survival/quality of life. Furthermore, Williams interprets the narrative of Hagar as a source to confront Black women's surrogacy in the church and society. Similarly, I interpret Luke 13:10–17 and the story of the bent woman as another sacred narrative whereby Black women may easily locate and identify themselves. The bent woman in Luke 13:10–17 parallels Black women facing bendedness by multidimensional oppression in an imperialist white capitalist heteropatriarchal world and a Black Church tradition that sustains them, that they sustain, and that, paradoxically, devalues their virtue.

The Black Church: A Double Edged-Sword?

Black religious scholars describe the Black Church as "the single most autonomous Black institution in North America."[21] The term "Black Church" links to the evolution of the Du Boisian construction of "The Negro Church" as familial, the center of social life, a theater of amusement,

---

[18]Delores S. Williams, *Sisters in the Wilderness: The Challenge of Womanist God-Talk* (Maryknoll, NY: Orbis Books, 1993), 6.

[19]Williams, *Sisters in the Wilderness*, 6.

[20]Williams, *Sisters in the Wilderness*, 6.

[21]Stacey M. Floyd-Thomas et al., eds., *Black Church Studies: An Introduction* (Nashville: Abingdon Press, 2007), 7.

and a political nucleus for Black people.[22] There is scholarly tension about whether the nomenclature of "Black Church" may simply refer to African American denominational churches or congregations. Lincoln and Mamiya identify the Black Church by the historically Black mainline denominational churches—National Baptist Convention U.S.A. Inc., National Baptist Convention of America, Progressive National Baptist Convention, Inc., African Methodist Episcopal Church, African Methodist Episcopal Zion Church, Christian Methodist Episcopal Church, and Church of God in Christ—and the rising tide of numerous independent African American reformations across Baptist, Methodist, and Pentecostal Protestant lines. Some Black religious scholars understand the Black Church to include African American congregations within historically white denominations, including Roman Catholicism, the Episcopal Church, Presbyterians, United Methodists, and Congregationalists. Others recognize nondenominational churches that are "Black" in nature concerning leadership, aesthetics, worship style, preaching, spiritual formation, and cultural traditions as also belonging to the Black Church. I identify the Black Church by all three distinctions: (1) mainline African American denominations and historically Black independent churches, (2) African American congregations in predominantly white denominations, (3) nondenominational churches with majority Black congregations and worship styles. I also consider African American faith communities or Black religious expressions outside of the Christian tradition—the Nation of Islam, Ifa traditions, etc.—that overlap with the Black Church concerning the sins of sexism, classism, and homophobia.

The origin of the Black Church traces back to the antebellum South, where enslaved Africans gathered in free worship in the "hush harbors" (i.e., brush arbors) as an invisible institution.[23] Religious historian Albert Raboteau,

---

[22]See these works to underscore critical valuations of this terminology: William Edward Burghardt Du Bois, *The Negro Church* (Atlanta: Atlanta University Press, 1903); C. Eric Lincoln and Lawrence H. Mamiya, *The Black Church in the African-American Experience* (Durham, NC: Duke University Press, 1990); Eddie Glaude Jr., "The Black Church Is Dead," HuffPost, April 28, 2010, https://www.huffpost.com/entry/the-black-church-is-dead_b_473815; Juan Marcial Floyd-Thomas, *Liberating Black Church History: Making It Plain* (Nashville: Abingdon Press, 2014); Evelyn Brooks Higginbotham, *Righteous Discontent: The Women's Movement in the Black Baptist Church, 1880–1920* (Cambridge, MA: Harvard University Press, 1993).

[23]Religious historian Albert Raboteau describes hush harbors as the meeting of the enslaved in "secluded places—woods, gullies, ravines, and thickets" to avoid detection by slaveholders, escape danger, and encounter the Divine. Albert J. Raboteau, *Slave Religion:*

in his pioneering historical account *Slave Religion: The Invisible Institution of the Antebellum South*, chronicles the authentic religious experience of the enslaved as secretive and beyond the gaze of slaveholders. According to Raboteau, "From the abundant testimony of fugitive and freed slaves it is clear that the slave community had an extensive religious life of its own, hidden from the eyes of the master. In the secrecy of the quarters or the seclusion of the brush arbors ('hush harbors') the slaves made Christianity truly their own."[24] The early formation of the Black Church emerged as a resistance movement in what Pulitzer Prize–winning novelist Toni Morrison describes as "the Clearing," where the enslaved sought to escape a vicious American slaveocracy cradled in white supremacist ideology and Christian complicity.[25] By the late eighteenth and early nineteenth centuries, the exodus of Black Christians out of segregated white Christian churches on the basis of racism and into public Black sacred orders marked the formation of the Black Church as a visible institution.

While the shift to a visible Black Church provided institutional autonomy and *free* worship for Black people to convene in respectable, racially homogeneous spaces, many newly established Black churches espoused white hierarchies, class stratification, and gender and sexual inequity. The nineteenth-century narrative of Jarena Lee, the first authorized Black woman preacher in the African Methodist Episcopal Church (AME)—who petitioned AME founding bishop Richard Allen for eight years before receiving license to preach and was never granted ordination during her lifetime—is a classic example of this popular phenomenon. The appropriation of Western assaults against Black women's bodies in the Black Church manifest by refusing to ordain Black women, discrediting their labor, and ignoring their leadership and activism.

I argue the Black Church proffers a double-edged sword concerning

---

The *"Invisible Institution" in the Antebellum South*, updated ed. (New York: Oxford University Press, 2004), 232.

[24]Raboteau, *Slave Religion,* 212.

[25]In Morrison's *Beloved,* the Clearing represents the hallowed place carved out in the thick of the woods where the enslaved gathered to escape white control, even if only temporally. The Clearing is where Black people from the elder to the younger could exercise the full range of their emotions (dance, cry, laugh, grasp for breath) and love their bodies and flesh wholly against a (white) hostile world "yonder." The Clearing affirmed and revered Black women's spiritual leadership in the form of "Baby Suggs, holy." The Clearing opened space for diverse Africana religious expressions and worship styles of lament, embodied movement, and celebration that defied white evangelical Christian norms. See Toni Morrison, *Beloved* (New York: Knopf, 1987), 98.

Black women that boasts a gospel of liberation for Black people, but also participates in preserving Black women's oppression. To date, Black women represent the largest majority of Black churchgoers; the largest religious group of the Black community remains Black Christians. Today's millennial and younger generations resist the cultural and spiritual dominance of the Black Church largely because of its intracommunal harm toward Black women, low-income, incarcerated, and LGBTQ-identified persons and its failure to embody the gospel of liberation it proclaims in word and deed.[26] I am the daughter of the Black Church reared in the tradition since birth and a third-generation ordained Black Baptist clergywoman with pastoring parents from both my maternal and paternal lineages. My critique of the Black Church in this book is rooted in a womanist prophetic call for the institution that nurtured my grandmother's faith and my existence as a thinking woman of faith to live into the best version of its moral witness and break the oppressive bonds that ensnare Black women's bodies and lives.

Living in a "Crooked Room"

In the face of prevailing images that contort Black women's bodies and character in society and the Black Church, Black women exist in a "crooked room"[27] with few to no options to escape misrecognition. Political scientist Melissa Harris-Perry, in her groundbreaking work *Sister Citizen: Shame, Stereotypes, and Black Women in America*, argues that Black women in America "fully embody" the struggle for recognition, which is the "nexus of

---

[26]See Melanie C. Jones, "Who's Saving Whom?: Black Millennials and the Revivification of Religious Communities," in *Religion, Race, and COVID-19: Confronting White Supremacy in the Pandemic*, ed. Stacey M. Floyd-Thomas, Religion and Social Transformation (New York: NYU Press, 2022), 54–77; Megan Jordan, "Millennials Aren't Skipping Church, the Black Church Is Skipping Us," *The Black Youth Project* (blog), December 31, 2019, http://blackyouthproject.com/millennials-arent-skipping-church-the-black-church-is-skipping-us/; Maya King, "The Black Church Can Engage More Black Millennials by Bringing Politics Back into the Pulpit," *The Black Youth Project* (blog), September 29, 2017, http://blackyouthproject.com/the-black-church-can-engage-more-black-millennials-by-bringing-politics-back-into-the-pulpit/; Olivia Smarr, "Which Black Lives Matter to the Black Church?," *The Black Youth Project* (blog), February 24, 2015, https://blackyouthproject.com/which-black-lives-matter-to-the-black-church/.

[27]Melissa V. Harris-Perry, *Sister Citizen: Shame, Stereotypes, and Black Women in America; [for Colored Girls Who've Considered Politics When Being Strong Isn't Enough]* (New Haven, CT: Yale University Press, 2011), 28.

human identity and national identity."[28] Perry locates the "slanted images of the crooked room as the problem of recognition."[29] The effects of America's crooked room, in Perry's schema, results in three significant damages for Black women: "shame, suffering, and unequal policy outcomes."[30]

Similar to the Lukan woman who is doubly bent and unable to stand up straight, the compounding assaults against the Black woman expose her body as bent doubly, triply, quadruply . . . multiply as her body exists further away from the privileged, white, male, heterosexual, able-bodied norm. Such a normative gaze confines and disgraces Black women's character in an imperialist white supremacist capitalist heteropatriarchal world and, tragically, *reincarnates* in Black religiosity. Seemingly, attention to Black women's agency is important for womanist theological ethics to redeem Black women's human virtue, and also to reveal the embodied power that Black women possess to unbend their lives, institutions, and world.

Luke 13:10–17: Woman, Thou Art Loosed?

Biblical scholars have ignored the Luke 13:10–17 account and the story of the remarkable woman. According to biblical scholar Mikeal Parsons, only two scholarly articles addressed this pericope by 1987.[31] While feminist biblical interpreters have taken up the prominence of women in Luke,[32] several feminist scholars focus the bulk of their criticism on interpretations of the uninvited woman (Lk 7:37–50), the sisterhood strife of Mary and Martha (Lk 10:38–42), the woman in the parable of the lost coin (Lk 15:8–10), the widow seeking justice (Lk 18:1–5), and the poor widow (Lk 21:1–4). It is

---

[28]Harris-Perry, *Sister Citizen,* 4.

[29]Harris-Perry, *Sister Citizen,* 35.

[30]Harris-Perry, *Sister Citizen,* 251.

[31]Parsons references biblical scholar M. Dennis Hamm's 1987 article that cites two preceding articles by J. Wilkinson and L. Milot. Dennis Hamm, "The Freeing of the Bent Woman and the Restoration of Israel: Luke 13:10–17 as Narrative Theology," *Journal for the Study of the New Testament* 10, no. 31 (January 1987): 23–44; John Wilkinson, "Case of the Bent Woman in Luke 13:10–17," *The Evangelical Quarterly* 49 (October 1977): 195–205; Louise Milot, "Guérison d'une femme infirme un jour de sabbat: l'importance d'une comparaison (Luc 13,10–17)," *Sémiotique et bible* 39 (1985): 23. See Mikeal Carl Parsons, *Body and Character in Luke and Acts: The Subversion of Physiognomy in Early Christianity* (Grand Rapids: Baker Academic, 2006), 83.

[32]The *Feminist Companion Series to Luke* edited by Amy Jill Levine does not include an article devoted solely to the narrative of the bent woman in Luke 13:10–17. See Amy-Jill Levine, ed., *A Feminist Companion to Luke* (London: Sheffield Academic Press, 2002).

likely that some feminist biblical scholars have discounted this passage because literalist interpretations can enable violent, anti-Jewish claims against the Sabbath and glorify ableism.[33] To date, no Black or womanist biblical scholar has published sustained interpretations of this text.

Although engagement of Luke 13:10–17 remains limited in biblical scholarship, the narrative of the bent woman is a celebrated sacred text in the Black Church tradition, bearing a similar significance for Black women as the story of Hagar. On one end, Black televangelists, as popular as Bishop T. D. Jakes and the Woman Thou Art Loosed (WTAL) movement,[34] have employed this text in preaching, teaching, and cultural media as a source for theologizing and pathologizing Black women's experience. Most notably, Black feminist religious theorist and cultural critic Tamura Lomax's *Jezebel Unhinged: Loosing the Black Female Body in Religion and Culture* traces and critiques the damaging implications of Jakes's interpretation of Luke 13:11–12 and the WTAL that situate Black women's bodies as sites of sin and weak character.[35] On the other, Black churchwomen continue to return to this text as a sacred narrative for relief and remedy. The woman in Luke attains full bodily restoration and promotion by Jesus to a more virtuous distinction in her community, but this happens only through a confrontation with the powers that oppose her freedom. My aim is to interpret Luke 13:10–17 beyond the pale of "another" woman being simply rescued by Jesus, but toward the woman whose bent body signals her oppression and whose agency confronts a bent socio-religious system that denies her liberation and restoration. In line with Williams, who suggests that God's response to Hagar in Genesis 16 and 21 is God's response to Black women struggling to survive in the wilderness,[36] I utilize a hermeneutics of parallel to make possible the freedom of living unbent and the revaluing of her virtue in the community that the woman experiences in Luke 13:10–17 for contemporary Black women in society and Black religion.

---

[33]See Elisabeth Schüssler Fiorenza, "Lk 13:10–17: Interpretation for Liberation and Transformation," *Theological Digest* 36 (1989): 303–19; Julia Watts Belser and Melanie S. Morrison, "What No Longer Serves Us: Resisting Ableism and Anti-Judaism in New Testament Healing Narratives," *Journal of Feminist Studies in Religion* 27, no. 2 (October 30, 2011): 153–70.

[34]See T. D. Jakes, *Woman Thou Art Loosed!: Healing the Wounds of the Past*, 2nd ed. (Shippensburg, PA: Destiny Image, 2011).

[35]See Tamura A. Lomax, *Jezebel Unhinged: Loosing the Black Female Body in Religion and Culture* (Durham, NC: Duke University Press, 2018). I engage Lomax's Black feminist cultural criticism of Jakes more fully later in the book.

[36]Williams, *Sisters in the Wilderness*, 5–9.

Mapping the Body of the Project

Chapter 1, "The 'Body Proper' in Black Religious Thought," discusses the body as locus and problem in Western philosophy and Christian theology. I take up ancient concepts of body-soul dualism and mind-body dualism as perennial concerns and engage the modern "turn to the body" in philosophy and theology. This chapter begins by examining Western philosophical and Christian theological valuations of the body. The chapter moves to unearthing embodiment as a central category in Black religious thought as a response to the hegemonic marking of the Black body and Black female body by imperialist white supremacist heteropatriarchy and Black religious respectability. I analyze what is at stake when the body is a central locus in Black religious scholarship and demonstrate how Black and womanist religious scholars Kelly Brown Douglas, Anthony Pinn, M. Shawn Copeland, and Eboni Marshall Turman contribute to this continuum.

Chapter 2, "Near the Cross: Womanist Christology between Suffering and Salvation," engages the Christology-centered scholarship of four leading womanist theologians: Jacquelyn Grant, Kelly Brown Douglas, Delores S. Williams, and JoAnne Marie Terrell. This chapter probes the suffering of Black women through the perspective of domestic work and the burdens of sacrifice, surrogacy, and strength in society and the Black Church. Gospel writers record a number of unlikely faithful followers at the site of crucifixion when the "chosen twelve" male disciples were scattered. Many women were at the foot of the cross because of life-changing encounters experienced through the liberating life and ministry of Jesus Christ. The cross harbors a double-ended narrative within the Christian story as a symbol for Jesus's violent death at the hand of imperial and coercive powers and a revelation of liberation through at-one-ment with God. The chapter interrogates the salvific significance of Jesus's crucified body and relationship to the suffering of the vulnerable in the face of political execution and religious exclusion. Womanist Christology locating Black women not on the cross but near an "empty" cross recognizes the suffering Black women endure by multidimensional oppression and the potential for radical transformation with God.

The third chapter, "Our Saviors Are Ourselves, Part One: The Burden to Save Democracy," lays bare the undue expectation for Black women to *save* America as they struggle for full recognition and citizenship through voting, the most fundamental right of democracy. This chapter traces the bloody history of suffrage and the political disenfranchisement of Black women despite the rise to one of the largest voting blocs in America in recent elections. I return to Melissa Harris-Perry's notion of the crooked room to address the problem of misrecognition for Black women on the US political scene and the political damages by stereotypes that constrict Black women's agency. America's default to Black women to clean up its ugly political messes reinscribes a salvific burden with no recompense.

Chapter 4, "Our Saviors Are Ourselves, Part Two: Redeeming the Soul of the Black Church," affirms the salvation of Black women as double-edged with political and spiritual implications. Any vision of Black liberation and freedom that evades Black women is no liberation at all. This chapter exorcises Black theology and the Black Church for ignoring Black women's contributions to the spiritual and prophetic redemption of the Black community. Moreover, the Black Church's occupation with the business of saving Black women illuminates Black women not only living in a crooked room but up against a crooked gospel. This chapter explicates the promise of womanist perspectives on sin, suffering, and salvation in the quest toward a womanist theo-ethical vision of co-partnership with God to redeem Black women. While Black women take an active role in salvation, a return to the hermeneutics of sacrifice is necessary for Black women to avoid sacrificing ourselves as a pitfall to the salvation of the Black Church.

Chapter 5, "Hitting a Straight Lick with a Crooked Stick: A Womanist Reading of Luke 13:10–17," engages interpretations of Luke 13:10–17 in biblical scholarship and contemporary Christianity. I critically engage interpretations of this text largely missing in biblical scholarship and interpret the text through what Delores Williams names as a womanist hermeneutics of parallel by situating Black women's experience alongside the Lukan account. Popular interpretations ground a theology of moral contempt espoused most notably by the Bishop T. D. Jakes's WTAL movement for Black women, which I seek to analyze and interpret against the grain, utilizing the exegetical pathways of womanist biblical scholars Stephanie Buckhanon Crowder and Renita J. Weems, and the womanist virtue theories of Katie Geneva Cannon. My grandmother's story contextualizes Black women's connection to the Luke 13 woman beyond the troubling lens of Black women's flawed moral character and shame.

The sixth and final chapter, "Turning the World Right Side Up," restates the problem, the contribution of this project to Black religious thought and womanist theological ethics, and further implications for this study. I employ the narrative from my (grand)mother's garden to ground this book within a backdrop of the multitraumatic experiences of an everyday Black churchwoman and expose the thick location of the problem of bendedness for Black women against multidimensional oppression. Some enduring questions remain: How do Black women live unbent lives? What Black religious and cultural spaces are upright enough to empower Black women to live freely and without constraint? How might Black women foster a "right side up" world for our future and children? The aim of this project is to recognize Black women as the embodied moral agents who bear the substance necessary to confront multidimensional oppression in religion and society, and, ultimately, "turn the world right side up, again and again."[37]

---

[37]I am drawing upon the highly contested speech attributed to Black abolitionist Sojourner Truth. Truth did give an extemporaneous unnamed speech at the 1851 Woman's Rights Convention in Akron, Ohio. As an eyewitness in the crowd, abolitionist Marius Robinson published a version of the speech in the *Anti-Slavery Bugle* titled "On Woman's Rights" on June 21, 1851, just a few weeks after the speech was given. White abolitionist Frances Dana Baker Gage published a different version of that speech in the New York *Independent* on April 23, 1863, and the National Anti-Slavery Standard on May 2, 1863, that shifted Truth's vernacular from a New York low-Dutch accent to a southern Black slave accent, misrepresenting Truth's authentic voice and serving the agenda of the suffrage and early woman's movement to further distinguish white women from Black women. Historian Nell Painter was first to draw attention to the differences of these speeches in historical record in her classic biography of Sojourner Truth. See Nell Irvin Painter, *Sojourner Truth: A Life, a Symbol* (New York: W. W. Norton, 1996). The Library of Congress Headlines and Heroes feature and the Sojourner Truth Project continue to expose the truth about the nuances between the two versions of the speech. See Malea Walker, "Sojourner Truth's Most Famous Speech | Headlines & Heroes," Library of Congress, April 7, 2021, https://blogs.loc.gov/headline-sandheroes/2021/04/sojourner-truths-most-famous-speech. Leslie Podell, "The Sojourner Truth Project," Sojourner Truth Project, accessed April 7, 2024, https://www.thesojourn-ertruthproject.com. In both Robinson's and Gage's versions of the speech, Truth speaks to women turning the world right side up again. According to Robinson, Truth confesses, "Well if woman upset the world, do give her a chance to set it right side up again." Marius Robinson, "Women's Rights Convention. Sojourner Truth," *Anti-Slavery Bugle*, June 21, 1851. In a popular version introduced by Gage, Truth maintains, "If de fust woman God ever made was strong enough to turn de world upside down all alone, dese women togedder (and she glanced her eye over the platform) ought to be able to turn it back, and get it right side up again! And now dey is asking to do it, de men better let 'em." Sojourner Truth, "Woman's Rights," in *Words of Fire: An Anthology of African-American Feminist Thought*, ed. Beverly Guy-Sheftall (New York: New Press, 1995), 36.

1

The "Body Proper" in Black Religious Thought

Christianity inherited from Plato the notion of the soul as the seat of salvation, relegating the body to an inferior position as the source of sin.

—Kelly Brown Douglas[1]

The Black female body, because it was the conduit through which enslavement passed to her descendants, was historically deemed the ground zero site for the propagation of Black inferiority.

—Brittney C. Cooper[2]

The human body is a living paradox made up of intense contradictions. What the body senses and feels juxtaposed to what one perceives and how one behaves or acts illuminates the enigmatic realities of embodiment. As the corporate body (the body as a whole; sum of its parts) works together, its members function increasingly apart. A body of bodies further magnifies and problematizes theo-ethical and anthropological concepts of freedom, responsibility, identity, alterity, time, memory, rationality, and corporeality. The political nature of the body is double-sided, representing, on one end, the multifaceted factors that influence individual bodies identifying with larger bodies—and, on the other, the philosophical implications of what it means for an individual to control her body.

---

[1] Kelly Brown Douglas, "Black and Blues: God-Talk/Body-Talk for the Black Church," in *Womanist Theological Ethics: A Reader*, ed. Katie G. Cannon, Emilie Maureen Townes, and Angela D. Sims, Library of Theological Ethics (Louisville, KY: Westminster John Knox Press, 2011), 113–31.

[2] Brittney C. Cooper, *Beyond Respectability: The Intellectual Thought of Race Women* (Urbana: University of Illinois Press, 2017), 20.

Western philosophy and theology situate the body as both a central locus and a problem.[3] Ancient philosophers, beginning with Plato, articulated human goodness as a virtue of the soul rather than the body or materiality. In Plato's framework, the soul is immortal, representing the spiritual force that guides the mind and body and possesses the ability to apprehend the world of forms. The body, however, is a spiritless entity that is trapped in the material world, remains in a constant state of flux, and is destined to die. Thus, the soul is in constant opposition over (or conflict within) the body. Even while it is housed within a body, the soul must dominate the body to escape to the purest knowledge. For Plato, the body becomes a site of passion and desire, and a threat to the social order. Canadian philosopher Carol Collier describes an ancient discussion of the body and soul at war in Plato's early works, which reduces the body to an "obstacle in the soul's search for knowledge."[4] Since the soul is the principle of life, living a moral life builds up the soul not the body.

Whereas Plato's student Aristotle valued the body and soul as they work together and recognized the body and senses as a starting point for knowledge of nature and the Divine, some Gnostics, influenced by Platonic philosophy, maintained that those who sought escape to the eternal realm were the purest philosophers who were most capable to rise to divinity. Persons who were devoted to the life of the intellect were lower than the purest group but capable of redemption. Persons given to matters of the material (i.e., expressions of passions) were doomed morally for destruction. Gnostic adoption of Plato's cosmology sparked controversy by Neoplatonists, most notably Plotinus, who criticized the Gnostics for misinterpreting Plato by conflating the sensible, material world with evil.

Though the body is central to Christian identity in doctrines and practices—for example, baptism, the incarnation, Eucharist, Resurrection, worship, prayer, fasting, and meditation—the relationship between the body

---

[3] My initial ruminations about the problem of the body in Western philosophy and theology began in an earlier book chapter. See Liz Alexander and Melanie C. Jones, "When Caged Bodies Testify: African and African-Descended Women's Memoirs as Sacred Texts," in *Unraveling and Reweaving Sacred Canon in Africana Womanhood*, ed. Rosetta E. Ross and Rose Mary Amenga-Etego (Lanham, MD: Lexington Books, 2015), 51–68. I extend these claims and build upon that work in this chapter.

[4] Carol Collier, *Recovering the Body: A Philosophical Story* (Ottawa: University of Ottawa Press, 2013), 27. It should be noted that Collier does discover a glimpse of another framing of the body as a source of the knowledge of nature and the Divine articulated by the voice of a woman in Plato's dialogues that she later explores through the lens of philosopher Baruch Spinoza.

and the Christian moral life remains ambivalent. Christian theologians as early as the Apostle Paul employ the metaphor of the "body of Christ" as the locus for Christian "hierarchy and harmony" with Christ as the head of the church. Influenced by both Platonic and Gnostic thought, Paul, in some writings, also associates the body and flesh with that which keeps one from attaining spiritual vitality.[5] Paul adopts Plato's dualism emphasizing death or denial of the body (and even more so flesh) as the path toward a spiritual life in early writings.

Some scholars suggest that Augustine of Hippo furthers this rupture by linking the corruptibility of the body to sexual pleasures and passions. Womanist theologian Kelly Brown Douglas argues that Augustine drew heavily upon the work of both Plato and Paul, forming a "Platonized Christianity." Augustine maintained that "the body with its passions" (i.e., sexual desires) contributes to "humanity's fallen state" and "was to always be subjugated to the soul with its rationality."[6] While later writings emphasize an interest to wrestle with the unity of the body and soul, Augustine's *Confessions* elevated the soul to the site of reason and the body to a lascivious enigma whose passions must be tamed and controlled.

Medieval philosopher Thomas Aquinas exemplifies another tradition in Christian thought that sought to integrate Aristotle's valuing of form and matter to know the Divine. What Plato imagined as forms, Aquinas distinguishes as God in Christian theology. In Thomistic thought, revelation represents knowledge that only God can give. The highest truths of Christian theological beliefs, such as the incarnation and Trinity, cannot be understood by reason alone but require revelation from God. Human reasoning mediated through the body gives humans the ability to know God and perceive God's revelation; reasoning is also necessary for faith. Collier points out that Aquinas's revaluation of the body as necessary for the knowledge of God informs Christian conceptions of the resurrection of the body: that the soul lives beyond the death of the body to the material world, but must ultimately be perfected and rejoined with the body in the fullness of time and upon the Great cosmic reunion between the Divine and humanity.[7] Together, Augustine and Aquinas illuminate contradicting Christian theological conceptions of the body as an impediment to the

---

[5] Paul articulates this dualism between the salvation of the Spirit and the sin of the body and flesh throughout Romans 7 and 8.

[6] Kelly Brown Douglas, *What's Faith Got to Do with It?: Black Bodies/Christian Souls* (Maryknoll, NY: Orbis Books, 2005), 35.

[7] Collier, *Recovering the Body*, 88.

Christian moral life and a source necessary for knowledge of the Divine.[8]

While Plato's body-soul dualism emphasized one aspect of probing and reducing the body in Western thought, the work of Enlightenment philosopher René Descartes unmasks a second aspect of separation between the psyche and the body or mind-body dualism. The Cartesian Latin maxim *cogito ergo sum*—"I think therefore I am"—articulates a mind-over-matter logic as the human mind is the site of rationality, seat of reason, and better capable than the body to rule against doubt because the senses are deceptive.[9] Descartes elevates the essence of the (hu)man self by arguing that true (hu)manity rests on one's ability to rationalize using the mind and invalidates the linkage between consciousness and embodiment. The body becomes, for Descartes, simply a machine. Descartes's mind-body dualism "represents the beginnings of the modern 'self,' detached from its body and from nature," which scholars signal as a shift away from the Divine and toward hierarchical mechanisms of control of other bodies to build up the enlightened self.[10]

From these Western philosophical and theological traditions, classical theorizing of the body does not signify a repression of body talk, but rather an "obsession" or preoccupation with the body that has resulted in hyper-surveilling, taming, and controlling of *certain* bodies. One key example is the relationship between the sexes from the primordial to the present that distinguished different biological and physiological characteristics between men and women to determine which characteristics reinforce patriarchal rule over women's bodies. Scripting and reducing the body to carnality in classical Western thought established a destructive grounding for modern oppression rooted in binary essentialisms in religion and society. In most systems, normative bodies are elevated to constituents of the mind, and nonnormative, subjugated bodies are often depersonalized and diminished to materiality (i.e., mind/body = man/woman, mind/body = Europe/Africa, mind/body = white people/Black bodies, mind/body = straight/queer, and so on). Moreover, negation of a bodily identity (e.g., skin color) or function of materiality remains at the center of why certain populations of bodies face subjugation.

In ancient caste systems, some believed people were born into serfdom

---

[8]It should be stated that Aquinas's revaluing of the body and soul does not equate to equal valuation of the sexes. Aquinas also adopts Aristotle's flawed reproductive biology to identify women as inferior and defective.

[9]See René Descartes, *Discourse on Method and Meditations on First Philosophy*, trans. Donald A. Cress (Indianapolis: Hackett, 1980).

[10]Collier, *Recovering the Body*, 141.

or peasantry because they lacked the ability to think or behave as people of higher social stature. In more contemporary sexist systems of oppression, women-identified or nonbinary persons endure marginalization because their bodies, gender identities, and gender expressions exist outside the patriarchal order. In a racist system, persons of color face oppression because their bodies fall short of a supremacist standard of racialized whiteness. In an ablest system, persons with disabilities confront discrimination because their bodies do not fit within an able-bodied societal norm. In heteronormative systems, the first argument against LGBTQ-identified persons is a biological one, whereby queer sex and gender trans-formations are deemed unnatural or an intolerable manipulation of the body. Poststructuralist philosophers and critical theorists, namely Michel Foucault and Judith Butler, expose ways that contemporary assaults against nonnormative bodies signal a turn to theorizing the body as a mode of moral discourse to engage relevant questions: "Why are certain bodies intelligible (or unintelligible) within power discourses?" "Whose body(ies) matter?"[11]

Black Women's Body Politics

The vicious torture and brutal enslavement of African peoples in the belly of slave ships through the Middle Passage and into the New World coupled with horrifying racial logics stripped Black bodies of gender differentiation.[12] Black feminist literary critic Hortense Spillers, in "Mama's Baby, Papa's Maybe: An American Grammar Book," skillfully narrates this tale:

That [New World] order, with its human sequence written in blood, *represents* for its African and indigenous peoples a scene of *actual* mutilation, dismemberment, and exile. First of all, their New-World, diasporic plight marked *a theft of the body*—a willful and violent (and unimaginable from this distance) severing of the captive body from its motive will, its active desire. Under these conditions, we lose at least

---

[11]See Michel Foucault, *The History of Sexuality. 1: An Introduction* (New York: Vintage Books, 1990). Judith Butler, *Bodies That Matter: On the Discursive Limits of "Sex,"* Routledge Classics (New York: Routledge, 2011).

[12]I originally developed ideas in this section in an earlier published article. See Melanie C. Jones, "The Will to Adorn: Beyond Self-Surveillance, Toward a Womanist Ethic of Redemptive Self-Love," *Black Theology* 16, no. 3 (September 2, 2018): 218–30, https://doi.org /10.1080/14769948.2018.1492303.

gender difference *in the outcome*, and the female body and the male body become a territory of cultural and political maneuver, not at all gender-related, gender-specific.[13]

In efforts to weaken the African subject, the grammar of anti-blackness functioned to impair the will and ungender the Black body. From the view of the captive community, Spillers articulates that the body represents the site and "space, at which point of convergence biological, sexual, social, cultural, linguistic, ritualistic, and psychological fortunes join."[14] However, the coming together of these faculties faces interference by imposed meanings that the captors place upon the captive body. For Spillers, the New World order marked the captive Black body by "irresistible, destructive sensuality," diminishing the Black body to "a thing becoming *being for* the captor," "otherness," and "powerlessness."[15] Even so, before there were Black bodies there was Black flesh. Spillers further distinguishes the *body* as marked by the discursive inscriptions that bear the weights of imposed meaning and forces of control, and *flesh* as "that zero degree of social conceptualization that does not escape concealment under the brush of discourse, or the reflexes of iconography."[16] Any moral project seeking to liberate the captive and render Black bodies intelligible must attend to reconstituting the fleshy fragments, reconnecting the body faculties, and reconstructing conceptions of Black identity, humanity, sexuality, and gender difference. What, then, must we say about Black women's body politics?

Western culture saturated within the mechanics of the Euro-American normative gaze mischaracterizes the Black female body. Early European discovery accounts of African civilizations and peoples marked Black women's bodies by polarizing contradictions: repulsive and alluring, hypersexual and asexual, grotesque and exquisite. The implications of these dualities ensnared the Black female body within two equally oppressive domains—as an obsession of the modern world and the very materiality that the Western social order craves to possess.

Black feminist theorist Beverly Guy-Sheftall presents the narrative of Saartije Baartman as an iconic example for framing the Euro-American obsession-possession dialectic that emerges from European travelers' first

---

[13]Hortense J. Spillers, "Mama's Baby, Papa's Maybe: An American Grammar Book," *Diacritics* 17, no. 2 (1987): 64, https://doi.org/10.2307/464747, 67.

[14]Spillers, "Mama's Baby, Papa's Maybe," 67.

[15]Spillers, "Mama's Baby, Papa's Maybe," 67.

[16]Spillers, "Mama's Baby, Papa's Maybe." 67.

encounters with African women on precolonial African soil as early as the fifteenth century. Saartije Baartman (often referred to as Hottentot Venus by her onlookers), was a South African "Khoikhoi" woman born in 1790 bearing a shapely round figure that would have been natural to her cattle-herding Indigenous community. She was exhibited and trafficked with an animal trainer while forced to sing and dance for white onlookers, often nude or scantily dressed, for public and private "freak shows" in London and Paris during the early nineteenth century. Following Baartman's death in 1815 in her mid-twenties, European anatomist Leopold Cuvier studied, examined, and dissected her. Cuvier also commissioned Baartman's portraiture and physical remains—namely her skeleton and genitalia—to be secured—remains placed in a jar—and put on display at the Musée de l'Homme (Museum of Man) until 1974. Following the petition of the Griqua National Council and former South African president Nelson Mandela to the French government in 1994, Baartman's remains were finally repatriated and returned to South Africa in 2002, roughly two hundred years after her death. Guy-Sheftall argues,

> This example also underscores a recurring theme in the "body dramas" that Black women experience. Being Black and female is characterized by the private being made public, which subverts conventional notions about the need to hide and render invisible women's sexuality and private parts. There is nothing sacred about Black women's bodies, in other words. They are not off-limits, untouchable, or unseeable.[17]

Baartman's tragic narrative unmasks this double-dealing exchange, with European men conceiving African women's curvaceous bodies both as desirable objects available for sexual pleasures and undesirable silhouettes perpetually on display to be mocked by public disdain.

The Euro-American preoccupation with Black women's bodies historically functioned to fixate the character of Black women in the Western moral imagination as other, indecent, lascivious, vile, and the "antithesis of virtuous, European women."[18] The "rape dancing"[19] of enslaved African

---

[17]Beverly Guy-Sheftall, "The Body Politic: Black Female Sexuality and the Nineteenth-Century Euro-American Imagination," in *Skin Deep, Spirit Strong: The Black Female Body in American Culture*, ed. Kimberly Wallace Sanders (Ann Arbor: University of Michigan Press, 2002), 18.

[18]Guy-Sheftall, "The Body Politic," 21.

[19]I am pointing to the colonial practices of "dancing the slave" when slaveholders sought

women by European men on slave ships across the Middle Passage, forced impregnation, and exploiting of Black bodies on the auction block fortified the Black female body and her sexuality as trapped between property and pleasure. The obsession-possession duplexity of the Black female body reproduced and heightened in North America during the antebellum period when enslaved women and girls were visualized as machines: fieldworkers, breeders, "coerced surrogates,"[20] domestics for white households as well as their own, nurturers for white babies as well as their own, and playmates for any range of pleasures. As Guy-Sheftall asserts,

> Slave women were also victims of their reproductive capacity since they were encouraged and even forced to breed like animals. They were also the South's perpetual wet nurses providing from their breasts milk for Black and white babies alike. In other words, it was the exploitation of the Black woman's body—her vagina, her uterus, her breasts, and also her muscle—that set her apart from white women and that was the mark of her vulnerability.[21]

As North American enslaved women and girls were overworked and hypersexualized, the hegemonic imagination fashioned white women and girls as the ultimate standard of femininity, innocence, and charm.[22] Long after

---

to keep the enslaved healthy and profitable while traveling at sea by dancing on slave ships in the Middle Passage. Many enslaved African women experienced rape by European men during the dance, which uncovers the heightened brutality upon the Black female body coupled with captivity, reproductive labor, and the stripping of human dignity because of the Transatlantic slave trade. Ironically, dance on slave ships and later in African American culture also revealed early resistance strategies and spiritual strategies to combat multifarious forces of subjugation. See Sowande' M. Mustakeem, *Slavery at Sea: Terror, Sex, and Sickness in the Middle Passage* (Urbana: University of Illinois Press, 2016); Katrina Hazzard-Gordon, *Jookin': The Rise of Social Dance Formations in African-American Culture* (Philadelphia: Temple University Press, 2010).

[20] Term coined by womanist theologian Delores Williams. See Delores S. Williams, "Black Women's Surrogacy Experience and the Christian Notion of Redemption," in *Cross Examinations: Readings on the Meaning of the Cross*, ed. Marit Trelstad (Minneapolis: Fortress Press, 2006), 19–32.

[21] Guy-Sheftall, "The Body Politic," 30.

[22] American historian Barbara Welter first articulated "the cult of true womanhood" or a prevailing value system for the white middle and upper classes that marked the virtues of white women as piety, purity, submission, and domesticity. Numerous "women's magazines, gift annuals and religious literature of the nineteenth century" verified and reinforced these religious and cultural mores for the ideal (white) woman. See Barbara Welter, "The Cult of

slavery, the pervasiveness of the obsession-possession bifurcation magnified in stereotypes and tropes functioned to disregard Black women's bodies and character by typifying Black women as desexualized matriarchs: Mammy and Aunt Jemima; sexual savages: Jezebel and Sapphire; and second-rates: Topsy-Turvy.

Unable to ascend to the "cult of true womanhood"[23] reserved for white women, Black women have long suffered denigration rooted in ideas of innate amorality, immorality, and wantonness. By the turn of the twentieth century, during the early women's and social purity movements—and what historian Rayford Logan called the "nadir of America's race relations"[24]— Black women's body politics were saturated in Victorian and Edwardian ideals and biblical codes of modesty. In an earlier article, "The Will to Adorn: Beyond Self-Surveillance, toward Redemptive Self-Love," I trace this social history of the Reconstruction and Black Migration era and its linkage to Black women's respectability politics that inform a contemporary policing and surveilling culture against Black women in religion and society.[25]

In "Women's Oppression and Lifeline Politics in Black Women's Religious Narratives," Delores Williams provides another layer, arguing that Black women's oppression reflects multidimensional assaults on Black women's sexuality, psychology, and morality. Williams suggests,

> The Afro-American woman's oppression is distinct from that of the Anglo-American woman. The Afro-American woman's sexuality, pro-creative powers, even her capacity to nurture, are appropriated by the white ruling class, providing economic benefits and personal comforts for white men and women. This continual violence, physical and psychological, destroyed the bodies and spirits of many black women.[26]

True Womanhood: 1820–1860," *American Quarterly* 18, no. 2 (1966): 151–74, https://doi.org/10.2307/2711179.

[23]Welter, "The Cult of True Womanhood," 151.

[24]Rayford W. Logan, *The Negro in American Life And Thought: The Nadir, 1877–1901* (New York: Dial Press, 1954), 52–53. Logan marks the period following the Civil War as the lowest point in America's southern race relations with rampant lynching, legal discrimination, and anti-Black violence. Later historians like John Hope Franklin push this argument beyond the turn of the twentieth century and into the 1920s. Such a nadir may have spawned the Great Migration for some Black southerners to move north in hopes for a better life.

[25]Jones, "The Will to Adorn."

[26]Delores S. Williams, "Women's Oppression and Lifeline Politics in Black Women's Religious Narratives," *Journal of Feminist Studies in Religion* 1, no. 2 (1985): 59–71.

Utilizing Black women's classic literary works, such as Zora Neale Hurston's *Jonah's Gourd Vine* and *Their Eyes Were Watching God*, Margaret Walker's *Jubilee,* and Alice Walker's *The Color Purple*, Williams implicates white men, Black men, and white women as the "authors of Black women's oppression," whereby a web of vicious systems exists not only to violate Black women's bodies but also to break the *spirit* of Black women.[27] Black feminist cultural theorist bell hooks names this political matrix of oppression as "imperialist white supremacist capitalist patriarchy" to trace the intersecting and "interlocking systems that work together to uphold and maintain cultures of domination" in the particular context of the United States.[28] Such a framing links the multidimensional assaults against Black women's bodies historically to the Euro-American colonizing of African peoples and cultures, white supremacist logics that presume "white is right" coupled with anti-blackness, economic exploitation for the comfort of the dominant class, and conventional gender-based hierarchies that inscribe heteronormativity.

Womanist Methods for Doing Body Ethics

With Stacey Floyd-Thomas, I value three primary research methods for doing womanist theological ethics in this book: literary analysis, the sociology of Black liberation, and the historiography of Black women. First, through literary and textual analysis, womanist ethicists source Black women's literature as a "repository of black women's moral wisdom . . . and privileged site for the exploration of black female empowerment that would otherwise be overshadowed by the suffering as a result of the forces of white, capitalist, patriarchal systems."[29] Womanist virtue ethics, in particular, analyzes literature that conveys what is said about Black women and what Black women say about themselves as an effort to redeem the virtues of Black womanhood that have been considered vices by normative ethical concepts and ideals. Novels, poetry, short stories, speeches, autobiographies, biomythographies, and self-accounts represent sacred texts that Black women use to tell the truth of their experiences and correct jaded

---

[27]Williams, "Women's Oppression and Lifeline Politics," 60, emphasis mine.

[28]bell hooks, *Writing beyond Race: Living Theory and Practice* (New York: Routledge, 2013), 4.

[29]Stacey M. Floyd-Thomas, *Mining the Motherlode: Methods in Womanist Ethics* (Cleveland: Pilgrim Press, 2006), 11.

assumptions about their character and identity. This book weaves narrative storytelling of Black women and literary works by Black women to counter pervasive Western cultural and religious representations of Black women that conceal their moral virtue.

Second, addressing multidimensional oppression entails sociological analysis that informs womanist theological ethics with empirical research about the social landscape of Black people and the struggles impacting Black women's lives. In line with feminist ethicist Beverly Wildung Harrison, womanist ethicists beginning with Katie Geneva Cannon adopt and adapt the "Dance of Redemption" as a methodological pathway to map "how patterns *form* values that *inform* context" through seven steps: conscientization, historical socioethical analysis, examining the theological resources, norm clarification, clarifying strategic options, annunciation/celebration, and re-reflection/strategic action.[30] This book explicates the economic, political, and spiritual burdens injuring Black women's bodies and souls, while employing choreosomatic approaches of redemption to move Black women from death to life. Furthermore, the book takes a cue from what Black feminist theorist Brittney Cooper names as "embodied discourse" wherein Black intellectual women like Anna Julia Cooper "forged their understandings of Black racial identity and Black freedom upon the terrain of the very visible Black and female body" to unearth Black women's bodies beyond burden but toward virtuous possibilities of truth-telling, justice-seeking, and wisdom-bearing.[31]

Third, emancipatory historiography does the necessary work of "mining the motherlode," excavating Black women's moral wisdom from the underside of history. This pathway seeks to dismantle the dominant narratives not by "*revisionism*," but "*revivification*," which is an "ongoing attempt to write black women's lives, experiences and morality back into the larger story."[32] Womanist ethicists employ this method through theoretical analysis, systemic analysis, cultural disposition, and collective action. At its core, this project retells the hidden and underrecognized stories of unnamed women in Scripture, poor Black migrant and domestic women like my grandmother, and Black women historical and contemporary figures whose contributions

---

[30]Floyd-Thomas, *Mining the Motherlode*, 83.
[31]Brittney C. Cooper, *Beyond Respectability: The Intellectual Thought of Race Women*, Women, Gender, and Sexuality in American History (Urbana: University of Illinois Press, 2017), 3–4.
[32]Floyd-Thomas, *Mining the Motherlode*, 106.

illuminate Black women's indelible significance to the moral, spiritual, and political witness of the Black Church and broader American context, even in the face of misrecognition.

Building upon Floyd-Thomas, I use these three methods and contribute a fourth-wave millennial womanist methodological pathway, which I identify as popular aesthetics that integrates popular culture and aesthetics.[33] My

---

[33] I first coined the term "millennial womanism" in response to the 2014 Pew Research report about the shifting American religious landscape with the rise of the "nones" because of the growing millennial generational cohort identifying as religiously unaffiliated. See Pew Research Center, "America's Changing Religious Landscape," Pew Research Center, Religion & Public Life Project, May 12, 2015, https://www.pewresearch.org/religion/2015/05/12/americas-changing-religious-landscape/. Millennial womanism builds upon the foundation of womanist foremothers and clarifies the particular experiences that Black millennial women bring to the womanist paradigm in efforts to connect faith and justice as digital natives committed to Black women's flourishing through prophetic activism online and on the line. Alongside Liz S. Alexander, we spearheaded a 2017 digital forum featuring twenty contributors to engage the unique womanist epistemological and methodological framework from a millennial lens. We first identified millennial womanism as "a contemporary framework that makes space intentionally for doing womanist work in the age of social media, black lives matter and say her name movements, mass incarceration, religious pluralism, a kaleidoscope of gender and sexual identities, and multi-dimensional realities of oppression (i.e. at the crossways of race, gender, sexuality, class, abilities, religion, etc.), to name a few." In its initial phase, these ten core concerns guide millennial womanist inquiry: "seeks the freedom and flourishing of Black women and girls as a non-negotiable; advocates for radical expansiveness (not simply inclusivity) that values community; moves beyond respectability politics with an intentional call for recognition and reciprocity; unapologetically strives for healing and wholeness of mind, body, spirit, and soul; embraces all things divine within and outside of traditional ecclesial communities and religious traditions; demands transformative justice (dismantling multi-dimensional systems of oppression + calling for restorative justice); invests in cross sector collaboration that gathers diverse voices, skills, talents and abilities in social justice advocacy and prophetic ministry; fosters intergenerational bonds to transfer and translate sacred wisdom with elders and younger generations; recognizes social media as a methodological resource for womanist work and witness; creates sacred platforms to do ministry and advocacy without waiting for traditional institutions to receive us." See Melanie C. Jones and Liz Alexander, "#MillennialWomanism," .base: Black Theology Project, May 30, 2017, https://btpbase.org/millennialwomanism/. While debates remain about the continuities and contributions across the waves of womanist religious thought, millennial womanism finds its home in fourth-wave womanism with recognition of millennial invention and manipulation of social media and other digital technologies as a popular and primary method for meaning-making and movement-shaping that merge the sacred and the prophetic. See EbonyJanice, *All the Black Girls Are Activists: A Fourth-Wave Womanist Pursuit of Dreams as Radical Resistance* (New York: Row House Publishing, 2023). At the same time, millennial and fourth-wave womanists recognize popular technologies especially in the form of social media are not value neutral, presenting death-dealing chal-

interest in aesthetics employs what Floyd-Thomas describes as critical engagement to think philosophically about the "history of the present" while centering Black women's human agency as mediated through the body and encountered with the Divine.[34] In essence, popular aesthetics takes up the deeper meaning of the moment to uncover the hidden histories through cultural criticism that frame what is seen in the present. This pathway takes interest in how Black women's bodies and relations to other beings inform culture and construct selves. Popular culture in the modes of the Black arts as well as media, film, digital and technocultural artifacts, social media, and political commentary in news and other forms of journalism emerge in this book as valuable sources for engaging Black women's embodied moral wisdom that have yet to be fully explored in womanist theological ethics.[35]

Theorizing the Black Body in Black Religious Thought

While there is much talk about Black bodies in our contemporary era in the academy and wider culture, Black religious thinkers move discussions beyond singular notions of the "body proper" (a physical form that exists as a singular biological unit with an individual psyche) to engage the discursive inscriptions levied against Black bodies and the dynamic ways Black people exercise freedom and meaning-making through their bodies. Four major Black religious thinkers who turn to the body ground my thinking

---

lenges of surveillance, hypervisibility, predatory invasion, and unequal access that require critical engagement to uncover the dangers even as we attend to their uses. I begin discussion about this phenomenon in Melanie C. Jones, "Who's Saving Whom?: Black Millennials and the Revivification of Religious Communities," in *Religion, Race, and COVID-19: Confronting White Supremacy in the Pandemic*, ed. Stacey M. Floyd-Thomas, Religion and Social Transformation (New York: NYU Press, 2021), 54–77. Popular aesthetics represents a first step to begin naming a fourth-wave womanist methodological pathway that may be useful for current and future waves to attend to these challenges.

[34]French philosopher Michel Foucault uses the term "history of the present" in an early section of *Discipline & Punish* but does not fully interpret its meaning. Some scholars link "history of the present" with Foucault's interest in genealogy to critique the contemporary or expose hidden meaning that the present may be trapped within. See *Discipline & Punish: The Birth of the Prison*, trans. Alan Sheridan (New York: Vintage Books, 1995).

[35]I build upon Emilie Townes's *Womanist Ethics and the Cultural Production of Evil* and Monique Moultrie's *Passionate and Pious: Religious Media and Black Women's Sexuality*, which represent pivotal texts integrating cultural studies in womanist ethics. See Monique Nicole Moultrie, *Passionate and Pious: Religious Media and Black Women's Sexuality* (Durham, NC: Duke University Press, 2017).

of Black "embodiment" and "enfleshment" in Black religious discourse and contribute to my conception of *bendedness* facing Black women.

Womanist systematic theologian Kelly Brown Douglas's body of work remains the most pivotal to my development as a womanist theological ethicist and this project with her critical theological analysis of the paradoxical nature of the Black body and Black faith. Black religious scholar Anthony Pinn's work offers a Black humanist perspective that informs the aesthetic dimensions of the Black body in Black religious studies that is essential to this project. Catholic systematic theologian M. Shawn Copeland adds to this discussion a perspective of the body through the lens of theological anthropology that brings into closer view theological engagement of Black women's bodies and freedom. Womanist theological ethicist Eboni Marshall Turman unveils the moral problem of enfleshment from Christian conciliar traditions to the twentieth-century Black social gospel to emphasize the incarnational linkages between Black women and the Divine.

Body as a Tool for Salvation

Kelly Brown Douglas presents the Black body as the guilty body developed during enslavement and fortified in contemporary manifestations of Stand Your Ground law and culture. Douglas argues, in *Stand Your Ground: Black Bodies and the Justice of God*, America's grand narrative of Anglo-Saxon exceptionalism that undergirds white supremacist theo-ideologies rendered the Black body as guilty. American chattel slavery frames a starting point that sanctioned the total occupation of Black bodies as white property. Chattel, for Douglas, signifies that Black people did not own their bodies and had no rights. Black bodies held value for the slaveocracy with skilled free labor, but the conventional buying and selling of Black bodies from riverbanks to auction blocks distinguish Black bodies not as "cherished property" but "valued commodity."[36] Douglas traces the alignment of natural law theory and the Anglo-Saxon myth heralded by proslavery gospelers to sustain theo-ideological justification for the chattel Black body as a sinful body whose freedom would not only upend the social order but also pose a "threat to God."[37] The hypersexualization of the Black body supported the sexual exploitation of white slaveholders while placing guilt on the

---

[36]Kelly Brown Douglas, *Stand Your Ground: Black Bodies and the Justice of God* (Maryknoll, NY: Orbis Books, 2015), 54.

[37]Douglas, *Stand Your Ground*, 60.

stereotyped lusty, lascivious Black bodies depicted as violent (not violated) and prone to sin. Douglas writes,

> The very construction of the black body as an uncontrollable beast, given its hypersexualized nature, means this body must be controlled. Indeed, as natural law theology contends, control of this body is for the common good. A free black body is tantamount to a wild body on the loose. So, once again, a free black body is, according to the productions of America's exceptionalist narrative, quintessentially a dangerous Black body.[38]

The free Black body that pursues existence outside of white control is regarded as dangerous; thus, the apparatus of criminalization becomes necessary to discipline and punish the guilty Black body to regain white authority.

Douglas offers the body as a "tool for salvation, not an impediment."[39] God-talk is body talk when considering the relationship between the Black body and the embodied Christ. Jesus as Christ, in Douglas's framework, embodies a paradoxical crossroads theology as *fully human* and *fully divine*.[40] Jesus's life and ministry reveals the "sacred relevance of the human body at the same time that it signals the very real significance of the body to all interactions." [41] Christianity's Christological paradox creates problems for Christian acceptance of racialized, sexualized, Black, and blues bodies. A "Platonized Christianity" that polarizes Jesus Christ's twofold makeup (divine vs. human) pits the body against the soul and ultimately places human sexuality in contempt. As Douglas maintains, "It is Jesus as the incarnate One that invalidates oppressive forms of Christianity and thus allows for black women and men to affirm a Christian identity at the same time that

---

[38]Douglas, *Stand Your Ground*, 70.

[39]Douglas, "Black and Blues," 129.

[40]The term "paradox" is significant to Douglas's constructions because it maintains two distinct existences coming together, but this relationship is not antagonistic. Dualism conceives two opposing sides that are at war with the other. Paradox affirms differences that have the potential to complement or work together rather than against the other. Douglas suggests, "What a paradox and a dualism hold in common is the acknowledgment of difference entering into relationship. Where they diverge is in how that relationship of difference is construed. A paradox does not dictate the terms of the relationship; a dualism does. Hence, a paradoxical relationship can be mutual or reciprocal. A dualistic relationship, by definition, does not exhibit such complementary qualities. It is for this reason that Christianity's Christological core should be principally regarded as a paradox, not a dualism." Douglas, *What's Faith Got to Do with It?*, 20.

[41]Douglas, "Black and Blues," 129.

their bodies are ravished in the name of Christianity."[42] The paradoxical nature of Black faith is "born in the cauldron of oppression and giving witness to the freedom of God."[43] While sexuality demonstrates what it means to be fully human and relation to other humans and the Divine, Douglas critiques the Black Church for reinscribing "hyperproper sexuality" (sex as good for procreation) to control Black bodies and confine Black freedom.[44] If the Black Church rejects diverse genders and sexualities, then it commits violence to itself and validates white supremacist theo-ideologies that blame Black bodies for white sin.

Bodies in Motion Creating Meaning

In his salient sketch of Black religion, *Terror and Triumph*, Black religious scholar Anthony Pinn takes up the body as site, sign, space, and soundtrack characterizing the "religious nature of the black experience."[45] Pinn argues, "The body represents the major site of contestation, the space in which terror is manifested."[46] Enslavement and continuing dehumanizing assaults on Black humanity narrate the terrorizing of Black bodies as America's religion. Whereas the Black body is inscribed by the discursive productions of American terror that seek to control, Black bodies script creative narratives of expression that pursue liberation, which is the recognition of full humanity. Liberation requires attention to a "certain style or rhythm by which the process of struggle for new ontological and existential status unfolds."[47] In other words, what do Black bodies do to create counter-meaning and perhaps even counterworlds? Here, presentation of the body through stylization and aesthetics becomes essential for the making of new being and becoming.

Pinn contributes a "hermeneutics of style" as a mode of interpretation in Black religious studies "with style understood as the ebb and flow of the black creative impulse and the values and sensibilities that direct the historical movement of black bodies and interests."[48] From dressing up in Sunday's best for church to strolling in high glitz and glam down the streets in parades to the ballroom scene in LGBTQ night cultures, Black people putting the Black body on display through expressive and decorative cultures,

---

[42]Douglas, *What's Faith Got to Do with It?*, 105.

[43]Douglas, *Stand Your Ground*, 164.

[44]Douglas, "Black and Blues," 128.

[45]Anthony Pinn, *Terror and Triumph* (Minneapolis: Augsburg Fortress, 2003), 146.

[46]Pinn, *Terror and Triumph*, 142.

[47]Pinn, *Terror and Triumph*, 140.

[48]Pinn, *Terror and Triumph*, 141.

visual arts, and literature articulate a stylistic resistance to the objectification of Black bodies. For Pinn, "Cultural production forces a confrontation with ethics and moral sensibilities"[49] to discern meaning and interrogate implications. Pinn raises the "ethics of perpetual rebellion" for "bodies in motion" as a "continuing concern with liberation from dehumanization" that focuses less with the "product," but the "process."[50]

Body as Sacrament

In *Enfleshing Freedom: Body, Race, and Being*, M. Shawn Copeland pays close attention to the Black body through the lens of theological anthropology. Copeland outlines Christian entanglement with slavery in the Atlantic world as early as the fifteenth century, wherein the matter of Christian conversion established conflicting ideas about whether to save the "savage" Black body through baptism and fellowship into Christian community or wield the Bible to "legitimate and sanctify the bondage of Black bodies."[51] In effort to maintain a "master-slave hierarchy," the latter "advocated a Christianity that sought to unmake the God-image in Africans, to render them servile, docile, and acquiescent to a divine ordination of their subjugation to whites."[52] Copeland raises Black women's bodies as ground zero during enslavement for objectification as "property, production, reproduction, and sexual violence."[53] Not only did Black women endure heavy labor on the fields, but Black women's bodies "labored in the making of the material of plantation," breeding the seed to fertilize the plantation economy while being diminished to "body parts: parts that white men used for pleasure; parts that white men manipulated and sold for economic profit; parts that literally were coerced to nurse the white racist supremacy."[54] Copeland traces Black women's embodied freedom during enslavement through acts of resistance, subversion, and redemption. Though objectified, Copeland attends to the ways Black women exercised subjectivity by "freeing the mind" and stealing education, "freeing the Spirit" and stealing away to encounter communion with others and the Divine in the wilderness, and "redeeming the body" by risking their lives to escape to freedom through the Underground Railroad

---

[49]Pinn, *Terror and Triumph*, 153.

[50]Pinn, *Terror and Triumph*, 153.

[51]M. Shawn Copeland, *Enfleshing Freedom: Body, Race, and Being* (Minneapolis: Fortress Press, 2010), 28.

[52]Copeland, *Enfleshing Freedom*, 28.

[53]Copeland, *Enfleshing Freedom*, 29.

[54]Copeland, *Enfleshing Freedom*, 38.

or underground economies.[55] Copeland attends to rituals of healing and reclamation practiced by enslaved women that resisted objectification and recovered a love of Black flesh.

Copeland presents the body as a sacrament, a mediator of God's grace given to humanity to be in solidarity with others and divinely connected to the creative Triune God. Jesus, as the Word who became *flesh*, symbolizes a marked body subjugated by the Roman imperial order of his day and marked by sex (maleness) and sexuality (queer body) as he emphasized a ministry of solidarity that welcomed the "inclusion of new and 'other' bodies at the table."[56] Copeland commands the church to revalue "the flesh of the church" because "the flesh of the church is the flesh of Christ."[57] Copeland argues that the broken bodies of enslaved Black women alongside Jesus's crucified broken body reveal concretely "the freedom of the human subject."[58] The sacramental presence of Christ in the Eucharist is a "countersign" to sin, particularly the violence and dehumanization of the Black body, and a call to solidarity.[59] Eucharistic living builds solidarity among difference in community and magnifies the liberating essence of the body of Christ. Copeland interprets freedom as a verb rather than a noun, which bears rhetorical significance as freedom becomes less of a fixed attainment and more of a dynamic helix of possibilities that exists for Black women's bodies both within and beyond time and space.

Body as God-Incarnate

In *Toward a Womanist Ethic of Incarnation: Black Bodies, the Black Church, and the Council of Chalcedon*, Eboni Marshall Turman brilliantly outlines early scripting of the body in Christian conciliar traditions and debates about the relationship between Jesus and God. For Turman, the Council of Chalcedon rightly settled this dilemma, presenting Christ as fully human and fully divine, but the Western Christian church did not carry this belief into practice in word and deed. Turman argues that a "(mis)conception of *bodily integrity*" that follows Christian communities makes churches often

unable to escape the circularity of human oppression because they are rooted in a narrative that *seemingly* suggests that the body that defies

[55]Copeland, *Enfleshing Freedom*, 38–42.
[56]Copeland, *Enfleshing Freedom*, 61.
[57]Copeland, *Enfleshing Freedom*, 81.
[58]Copeland, *Enfleshing Freedom*, 128.
[59]Copeland, *Enfleshing Freedom*, 127.

normative wholeness must be *dehumanized* and choreographed to adhere to a specific narrative, one that ascribes to a binary hierarchy of sorts that too often divinizes certain kinds of flesh, while demonizing others.

Thus, for Turman, a return to the theory of Chalcedon marks hope to "advance against the restrictive politics of Incarnation."[60]

Turman critiques the Black Church for denying the bodies and souls of Black women. Turman "claims that the politics of identity that are at stake in the confession of Christ Incarnate, and the controversy that gave birth to American liberal religion, are of the same substance as the problem of enfleshment primarily caused by the American binary racial hierarchy and chiefly delineated in Dubois's theory of double consciousness."[61] Turman critiques the "problem of enfleshment" for Black life by analyzing civil rights leader Benjamin Mays's project of "making men" harnessed at the University of Chicago and employed at Morehouse College. Turman links Mays's problematic moral project while president of Morehouse College as an example of "how" the Black Church, particularly the cadre that champions a Black social gospel, becomes a liberative space for mostly male leaders and an oppressive space for Black churchwomen and nonnormative bodies. Turman calls the Black Church as a form of the body of Christ to live up to its full potential by "dismantling the binary hierarchy of personhood that informs its moralscape."[62] Turman presents the womanist logic of incarnation as a mediating ethic between *kata sarka* (what happens to Black women's bodies) and *en sarki* (what happens in Black women's bodies). Turman's womanist ethic of incarnation "recognizes the potentiality of black women's bodies as the image of the broken body of Christ in the world, and thus, black women as the very incarnation of ('enfleshment') of hope for the black church of the twenty-first century."[63]

A Bent Body Politic

Drawing from Douglas, Pinn, Copeland, and Turman, I attend to the body as revelation and redemption. Black women's bodies bear the weight

[60]Eboni Marshall Turman, *Toward a Womanist Ethic of Incarnation: Black Bodies, the Black Church, and the Council of Chalcedon* (New York: Palgrave Macmillan, 2013), 38.

[61]Turman, *Toward a Womanist Ethic of Incarnation*, 5.

[62]Turman, *Toward a Womanist Ethic of Incarnation*, 159.

[63]Turman, *Toward a Womanist Ethic of Incarnation*, 49.

of multidimensional assaults that hold deep historical memory and tell the story of a vicious religious and Western social order. The sacramentality of the bent condition illustrates Black women's bodies as the broken body of Christ, divinely embodied (made in the image of God) and uniquely positioned to confront the crooked moralscape of Black Church and the broader America. Black women's bodies in motion resist objectification as Black women become subjects who work in solidarity with Jesus in their quest for salvation, liberation, and redemption.

2

Near the Cross

Womanist Christology between Suffering and Salvation

> *My grandmother witnessed to a faith that was born at the foot of the cross. Black faith is, therefore, a paradox.*
> —Kelly Brown Douglas[1]

My grandmother, at age seventy-one, went to the emergency room with mild nausea and shallow breathing. Over the span of four days, my grandmother's condition worsened, with lowering blood pressure and ultimately a bowel obstruction in the kidneys that reduced blood flow to her heart, causing her unexpected demise. My grandmother lived with an enlarged heart for over thirty years; no one suspected when she elected to go to the hospital for care that her transition was nigh. After four cardiac arrests, my grandmother expired at 10:25 am on May 6, 2013. Following a day of gut-wrenching grief, my family and I began to make funeral arrangements to remember her life and celebrate her legacy. We chose an ivory pearl and gold casket to bury my grandmother with the double cross emblem on all four corners and an interior pillow inscription, "May the Work I've Done Speak for Me."[2] I knew then that laying her body near the cross signified something more than a badge of honor to remember my grandmother as a good Christian woman of faith. Since contemplating the recurring image of the "double-crossed" cross as a revered marker of the Christian faith and a

---

[1] Kelly Brown Douglas, *Resurrection Hope: A Future Where Black Lives Matter* (Maryknoll, NY: Orbis Books, 2021), 183.

[2] Sullivan Pugh, "May the Work I've Done Speak for Me," in *The New National Baptist Hymnal*, ed. K Morris (Nashville: Triad Publications, 1977), 399.

symbol of Jesus's violent death and suffering holding my grandmother "up" on all four sides, I have wrestled with the question, "What does it mean for a Black woman to remain near the cross?"

Gertrude Foster was a Black woman raised in the South who served as a domestic worker to white families during her early years in Memphis, Tennessee. After becoming pregnant with my mother, her eldest child, she migrated to Chicago in the 1960s to accompany my grandfather, LJ Foster. The decision to start a family and raise her children in Chicago meant that she had to forgo her educational endeavors in her early twenties. The dreams of a better life in the urban North deferred quickly because of Chicago's failing labor market and what sociologist William Julius Wilson names as "the social deterioration of ghetto neighborhoods" in the 1960s.[3] Within ten years of moving to the Englewood neighborhood on the South Side of Chicago,[4] her second child and firstborn son died young and her marriage

---

[3] William Julius Wilson, *When Work Disappears: The World of the New Urban Poor* (New York: Vintage Books, 1997), 4.

[4] The Englewood neighborhood formed with the settlement of German and Irish migrants at the railroad crossing known as Junction Grove in the 1850s. At the turn of the twentieth century, new housing construction encouraged the separation of classes. The population reached a height of more than eighty-six thousand and developed a booming shopping district at the intersection of Sixty-Third and Halsted. The Great Depression devastated the Englewood business market, real estate declined, and white flight escalated. Englewood shifted from 2 percent Black in the 1940s to 96 percent Black by the 1970s. The building of the Dan Ryan Expressway eliminated housing for Englewood residents and Chicago authorities disinvested in the Englewood neighborhood, leaving houses and shops to decay. Sears and Wieboldt's, the two major anchor stores, pulled out, and the shopping district struggled as Chicago opened new markets closer to white residents in Evergreen Park and Ford City. By the early 2000s, the social deterioration of Englewood increased the crime rate to one of the highest in the country as residents in Chicago's neighborhood struggled to survive. Chicago launches a campaign to restore Englewood every decade with some success like the rebuilding of the Kennedy King Community College at Sixty-Third and Halsted. Chicago's renewed interest to restore Englewood in recent times is directly linked to the landlocked status of Chicago's Hyde Park neighborhood near the University of Chicago and affluent white residents pushing farther south and closer to the Dan Ryan Expressway for quick access to downtown Chicago. See Encyclopedia of Chicago, 2005, s.v. "Englewood," http://www.encyclopedia.chicagohistory.org/pages/426.html; John R. Schmidt, "Englewood, Past and Present," WBEZ Chicago, May 31, 2012, https://www.wbez.org/stories/englewood-past-and-present/a434694c-8793-492e-a713-5882faf4c5da; Elise De Los Santos, "Flashback: Englewood's Shopping District Rivaled That of the Loop—but It Fell Victim to Rise of Suburban Malls, White Flight," *Chicago Tribune*, December 25, 2020, https://www.chicagotribune.com/history/ct-opinion-flashback-englewood-shopping-district-20201225-yhhq3t4j6rfp5o44ofxqcszjqa-story.html.

with my grandfather ended in divorce. She lived as a single mother raising two children while working odd jobs with mediocre pay to make ends meet for her growing family.

In the mid-1980s, Gertrude found the best available employment for Black women of her experiences as a room attendant at the downtown Hyatt Regency Hotel in Chicago, where she worked diligently as a housekeeper for over twenty years before being forced to retire because of debilitating health. For more than a decade, numerous legal cases have condemned Hyatt as the "worst employer of the hotel services industry" and, particularly, the largest Hyatt property Hyatt Regency Chicago for unfair labor practices, low wages, and increased surveillance of workers.[5] The laborious domestic work of bending to clean floors, make beds, and attend to guests caused reduced blood flow to her legs, injuring her veins and causing osteoporosis in her spine, resulting in her enduring the final years of life "slumped over." Through all of her health challenges and life adversities, she never complained, but held close to her faith in God and belief in Jesus Christ. She served as a church mother for children, young and old, who desired mothering. Although she suffered with physical ailments and unrelenting social oppression, her struggles could not keep her from offering sincere hospitality by welcoming family and friends into her home for a fine meal every Sunday. When we walked into the intensive care unit during her final hour, I observed at the moment of her death that her once crooked body laid straight, signaling embodied transformation (healing-restoration-liberation).

While I could not develop a coherent reason as to why I supported the cross insignia on my grandmother's casket, other than it "felt" right, I believe there is rich Christological meaning that encompasses both her unrelenting faith in Jesus Christ and her experience of unjust suffering in the sign of the cross. For her transformed body to remain near the cross, a symbolic image of Jesus's death, and her spirit to experience rest with Christ provides profound insight into Jesus Christ's eternal presence with Black women who have suffered, always. This chapter makes the following moves. First, I ground the narrative of my grandmother within the broader story of Black women's suffering through the lens of domestic labor in the urban North and denied labor in the Black Church. Second, I articulate the

---

[5]Naomi Wolf, "Hyatt Hurts: Hotel Workers Organise Global Boycott for a Fair Deal," *The Guardian*, October 4, 2012, http://www.theguardian.com/commentisfree/2012/oct/04/hyatt-hurts-hotel-workers-boycott.

significance of women at the cross who witness and share in the suffering of Jesus. For many Black Christian women, Jesus Christ *really* matters because Jesus knows all about their troubles and Jesus heals all their troubles both now and in the eschatological future. Third, I turn to womanist Christology to explore the relationship of Jesus Christ, Black women, and the significance of the double-edged cross as a Christian symbol. I explicate the Christological implications of Black women remaining near the cross by engaging four pioneering womanist theologians—Jacquelyn Grant, Delores Williams, Kelly Brown Douglas, and JoAnne Marie Terrell—and contemporary considerations. I develop a womanist Christological typology to locate their differing theological positions and unique viewpoints concerning the meaning of the cross for Black women's experiences. Last, I argue that the crucifixion of Jesus disavows the suffering of Black women, but it is not the whole story as Black women belong among the first to witness the power of Resurrection.

"May the Work I've Done Speak for Me"

May the work I've done speak for me
May the work I've done speak for me
When I'm resting in my grave, there is nothing that can be said,
May the work I've done speak for me.[6]

"May the Work I've Done Speak for Me" is a popular gospel song within the Black Church tradition that is often sung at funeral services or used in obituaries to recognize the significant contributions of a loved one to a family and community, especially in a world that denies the work and labor of the oppressed.[7] The song references the deceased "resting in the grave"

---

[6]Pugh, "May the Work I've Done Speak for Me."

[7]African American gospel music marks "a form of euphoric, rhythmic, spiritual music rooted in the solo and responsive church singing of the African American South." "African American Gospel," Library of Congress, https://www.loc.gov/collections/songs-of-america/articles-and-essays/musical-styles/ritual-and-worship/african-american-gospel. A gospel song is often recognized by its repeated refrain and infusing of rhythm and blues. As a descendent of African American spirituals, the genre of gospel gained notoriety in the mid-1930s with the emergence of performer-songwriters Charles Albert Tindley of Philadelphia, John W. Work of Tennessee, and Thomas A. Dorsey of Chicago, the father of gospel music, who linked with Mahalia Jackson to develop the musical style. Womanist ethnomusicologist Alisha Lola Jones describes gospel singing as "worshipful, erotic, and sensual activity for

with a sense of confidence that the fruit of their labor no matter how small will live well beyond their years. My grandmother's bendedness and suffering as a Black woman are directly related to her work as a domestic in the South nurturing white families and as a housekeeper in the urban North.

Hyatt Hurts and Black Women's Domestic Labor

The Hyatt company we know today was founded in 1957 by Chicago lawyer Jay Pritzker, who bought the Hyatt House motel next to the Los Angeles International airport (LAX) on a napkin deal; Jay and his brother Donald catapulted the business to a public North American six-hotel chain in the late 1960s. By the early 2000s, Hyatt and Hyatt International "still owned by the Pritzker family and still based in Chicago . . . together operated or licensed and employed about 80,000 people around the world. In the Chicago area, the companies had about 3,500 workers."[8] The average workday at Hyatt hotels for housekeepers requires cleaning thirty rooms a day in an eight-hour shift, which translates to roughly four rooms per hour or one room every fifteen minutes. As a result, Hyatt housekeepers report the highest injuries of hotel service workers, declaring the back-bending work as physically and financially disabling.[9] The exponential expansion of the Hyatt empire in the last fifty years unmasks an increasing corporate interest to widen its reach that often rests upon the backs of workers to assume its influence. Hyatt represents the quintessential American story of manifest destiny as a religious ideal that fosters neoliberal capitalist assaults on the vulnerable to sustain the rich—one of America's wealthiest families—and prey on the poor.[10] President Barack Obama nominated Penny Pritzker as

---

both performers and listeners in which fire and desire are ignited through the process of encountering God. . . . The *telos* of setting the atmosphere is to fulfill participants' expectations to have a tangible encounter with God during the worship experience." Alisha Lola Jones, *Flaming? The Peculiar Theopolitics of Fire and Desire in Black Male Gospel Performance* (New York: Oxford University Press, 2020), 1. A popular rendition of this song was released by gospel artist Shirley Caesar in 1973. See Shirley Caesar and Caesar Singers, "The Invitation," *May the Work I've Done Speak for Me* (New York: HOB Records, 1973).

[8] Encyclopedia of Chicago, s.v. "Hyatt Hotels Corp.," 2005, http://www.encyclopedia.chicagohistory.org/pages/2712.html.

[9] "Hyatt Housekeepers in 8 Cities File Injury Complaints with OSHA," UNITE HERE!, November 9, 2010, https://unitehere.org/press-releases/hyatt-housekeepers-in-8-cities-file-injury-complaints-with-osha/.

[10] See a fuller treatment of manifest destiny as America's civil religion in Kelly Brown Douglas, *Stand Your Ground: Black Bodies and the Justice of God* (Maryknoll, NY: Orbis Books, 2015), 90–132.

the US secretary of commerce, naming the Hyatt heiress one of the most successful business leaders at the height of a global Hyatt workers strike in 2013, which forced her resignation from the Hyatt board to sever her ties with an ongoing labor dispute. The rise of Democrat J. B. Pritzker, son of Donald Pritzker, to the office of Illinois governor in 2019 may further expose the entanglement of corporate influence and political corruption in a neoliberal era. As of March 31, 2024, the Hyatt hotel corporation head-quartered in Chicago boasts more than twenty brands, and "1300 hotels and all-inclusive properties in 78 countries across six continents."[11]

On July 23, 2012, Hyatt workers (under the union organizing banner of UNITE HERE) and allies (the AFL-CIO, the NFL Players Association, the National Organization of Women, the National Gay and Lesbian Task Force, Netroots Nation, Interfaith Worker Justice, and other entities) launched a global boycott campaign, dubbed "Hyatt Hurts," to raise awareness of Hyatt's numerous labor abuses. While Hyatt workers had pursued protest efforts in the past, this campaign quickly escalated to one of the largest ef-forts in the history of worker rights in America. Hyatt workers identified the Hyatt giant as the "worst employer in the hotel industry," denying basic worker rights to employees and prohibiting workers' unions. Social justice organizations like Interfaith Worker Justice supported the global boycott of Hyatt hotels in 2012 for five major reasons:

> 1) Hyatt housekeepers clean dangerously high number of rooms . . . resulting in some of the highest injury rates for a major hotel chain, 2) Hyatt is shifting its core work to perma-temps, 3) Hyatt refuses to remain neutral as non-union workers organize, 4) Hyatt can choose to be a high road employer, 5) Hyatt workers and their unions have asked for support.[12]

---

[11]Taylor Borden, "The Hyatt Story: How a Packed LAX Motel and a $2.2 Million Offer Scribbled on a Napkin Spawned One of the World's Biggest Hotel Empires," *Business Insider*, February 13, 2020, https://www.businessinsider.com/how-hyatt-hotel-empire-was-created-pritzker-family. "Hyatt's Growth Momentum Continues with Record Global Pipeline of 129,000 Rooms," June 3, 2024, https://investors.hyatt.com/news/investor-news/news-details/2024/Hyatts-Growth-Momentum-Continues-With-Record-Global-Pipeline-of-129000-Rooms/default.aspx.

[12]Interfaith Worker Justice announced its closure on January 31, 2021. Its archives and resources were transferred to the Interfaith Network for Worker Solidarity, a project of Georgetown University's Kalmanovitz Initiative for Labor and the Working Poor. This quote comes from a document originally published as Interfaith Worker Justice, "Support Global Boycott of Hyatt Hotels." Mark Pattison, "Interfaith Worker Justice closes, to give resources to

Through subcontracting work to temp agencies and reducing hours, Hyatt cut corners to avoid fulfilling required employee benefits (i.e., health insurance, paid time off, sick days, etc.) to full-time staff housekeepers. Hyatt housekeeper Francine Jones described her experience of injury in 2010 after laboring at Hyatt for over nineteen years as a domestic worker. Jones laments, "I live with chronic pain in my back and knees from all the heavy lifting and bending I do to change beds, scrub floors and toilets, and push heavy furniture around to vacuum. I wake up at night because of the pain, and I need two hands to even just hold a coffee pot."[13] Hyatt's failure to integrate back-saving mops, fitted sheets, or support for lifting heavy luxury mattresses to reduce employee harm illuminates a sustained interest in corporate efficiency over worker injury. Moreover, Hyatt's retaliation against employees for seeking unionization by turning the heat lamps on Chicago workers during a heat wave further reveal Hyatt's maltreatment and abuse to domestic workers.[14]

Initiated by Chicago Theological Seminary doctoral student Carolyn Roncolato and diverse religious scholars in the fall of 2012, I joined the letter-writing campaign and call to action urging the American Academy of Religion (AAR) and Society of Biblical Literature (SBL) to join the global boycott of Hyatt during its 2012 Annual Meeting in Chicago. AAR and SBL decided it was cost prohibitive to break the Hyatt contract at close to eight hundred thousand dollars but opted to relocate attendees who desired to stay at other hotels while also shifting base operations to the Hilton and moving most meetings away from the Hyatt.[15] Some religious scholars organized an Interfaith Sabbath Walk in front of the Hyatt McCormick hotel in downtown Chicago to march in solidarity with Hyatt workers.[16]

Georgetown arm," *National Catholic Reporter* online, January 4, 2022, https://www.ncronline. org/news/justice/interfaith-worker-justice-closes-give-resources-georgetown-arm.

[13]Andrew Stern, "Hotel Workers File Complaints against Hyatt," Reuters, November 9, 2010, https://www.reuters.com/article/hyatt-housekeepers-idCNN0911835120101109.Stern.

[14]In 2011, Hyatt workers at the Park Hyatt Chicago claimed Hyatt placed heat lamps on protestors during a Chicago heat wave as a scare tactic to discourage unionization. See Julie Wernau and Wailin Wong, "Hyatt Turns Up Heat on Picket Line," *Chicago Tribune*, July 21, 2011, https://www.chicagotribune.com/business/ct-xpm-2011-07-21–chi-hyatt-turns-up-heat-on-picket-line-201107210story.html.

[15]See Lillian Daniel, "Inconvenient Solidarity: Religion Professors Support a Hotel Boycott," *Christian Century*, November 1, 2012, https://www.christiancentury.org/article/2012-11/inconvenient-solidarity.

[16]Interfaith Worker Justice, *Interfaith Sabbath Walk for Justice at Hyatt*, accessed July 21, 2021, https://www.youtube.com/watch?v=Pelb87GAeeQ.

The dissent of religious scholars encouraged the AAR and SBL boards to establish a Joint Task Force to review its labor policies. SBL, in alignment with AAR, identified four principles to guide future labor deliberations: "1) transparency with constituents about labor disputes, 2) minimize the financial impact to boycotted properties by negotiating attrition rates, 3) lower programming in affected hotels, 4) and honor contracts."[17] Here, "big business" stifled sustained solidarity with the vulnerable despite the exorbitant financial risks even within the religious academic establishment.

"Domestic workers are one of the fastest growing workforces in our country," Senator [now Vice President] Kamala Harris (D-CA) announced to Congress in 2019.[18] The 2007 US Bureau of Labor Statistics reported 1.8 million domestic workers in the hotel industry.[19] The Economic Policy Institute (EPI), according to the Domestic Workers Chartbook 2022, maintains there are now more than 2.2 million domestic workers in the US workforce.[20] The US Census Bureau notes, "Women represent the largest majority of domestic workers at 88.6%. Hispanic or Latina (40.5%), Black (21.5%), Asian American or Pacific Islander (8.8%), and Native American (2.2%) women represent 73% of domestic workers," in a UNITE HERE 2021 report.[21] In 1920, 40 percent of domestic workers were Black women.[22] In 1960, 60 percent of employed Black women in the South were domestic

[17]Society of Biblical Literature, "SBL/AAR Joint Task Force on Labor Policy Minutes," November 18, 2012, https://www.sbl-site.org/assets/pdfs/JLPTF_111812_minutes.pdf.

[18]"Senator Kamala Harris (D-CA) and Congresswoman Pramila Jayapal (WA-07) Introduce National Domestic Workers Bill of Rights," *National Domestic Workers Alliance* (blog), July 15, 2019, https://www.domesticworkers.org/press-releases/senator-kamala-harris-d-ca-and-congresswoman-pramila-jayapal-wa-07-introduce-national-domestic-workers-bill-of-rights/.

[19]Susan Buchanan et al., "Occupational Injury Disparities in the US Hotel Industry," *American Journal of Industrial Medicine* 53, no. 2 (February 2010): 117, https://doi.org/10.1002/ajim.20724.

[20]Asha Banerjee, Katherine deCourcy, Kyle Moore, and Julia Wolfe. "Domestic Workers Chartbook 2022: A Comprehensive Look at the Demographics, Wages, Benefits, and Poverty Rates of the Professionals Who Care for Our Family Members and Clean Our Homes," Economic Policy Institute, November 22, 2022, https://www.epi.org/publication/domestic-workers-chartbook-2022/.

[21]UNITE HERE, "Playing Dirty: The Hotel Industry's Plan to End Daily Room Cleaning Would Cost Women of Color Billions," June 14, 2021, https://unitehere.org/press-releases/playing-dirty-the-hotel-industrys-plan-to-end-daily-housekeeping-would-cost-women-of-color-billions/.

[22]Jacquelyn Grant, "The Sin of Servanthood: And the Deliverance of Discipleship," in *A Troubling in My Soul: Womanist Perspectives on Evil and Suffering*, ed. Emilie Maureen Townes (Maryknoll, NY: Orbis Books, 1993), 205.

workers. Today, roughly one in five domestic workers are Black women. An analysis of the shifting landscape of the domestic service industry throughout the twentieth century reveals Black women increasingly pushed out of an industry once ranked among the best available work for Black women. Such pervasive anti-blackness unveils that both corporations and middle- to upper-class households remain slower to hire Black women domestic workers in favor of immigrant women and non-Black women of color. A groundbreaking study in the 2010 *American Journal of Industrial Medicine* titled "Occupational Injury Disparities in the US Hotel Industry" reports "hotel employees have higher rates of occupational injury and sustain more severe injuries than most other service workers."[23] Housekeeping requires high physical labor, and housekeepers suffer most injuries in their "upper extremity . . . followed by back injuries and lower extremity injuries,"[24] as reported to the Occupational Safety and Health Administration (OSHA). On the economic front, maids and housekeepers live as the working poor, earning a mean hourly wage of $13.47 and a mean annual wage of $28,010, according to the May 2020 US Bureau of Labor Statistics.

Motivated by the Hyatt Hurts campaign and other union boycotts, the Domestic Workers Coalition passed and Republican governor Bruce Rauner signed into law the Illinois Domestic Worker Bill of Rights (HB 1288) in 2016 to grant domestic workers rights to a state minimum wage, human rights protections, one day of rest in seven days for workers employed above twenty hours per week, and fair wages for women and minorities. EPI reports that "nine states (California, Connecticut, Hawaii, Illinois, Massachusetts, Nevada, New Mexico, New York and Oregon) and the cities of Seattle and Philadelphia have passed Domestic Workers Bill of Rights" in 2019.[25] In 2024, domestic workers bills of rights have passed in 11 states, 2 major cities, and the District of Columbia. Though introduced to Congress by Senator Kamala Harris and Congresswoman Pramila Jayapal (D-WA) in 2019, a national Domestic Bill of Rights has yet to be passed. The absence of basic employment protections for mostly women of color domestic workers

---

[23]Buchanan et al., "Occupational Injury Disparities in the US Hotel Industry," 117.

[24]Buchanan et al., "Occupational Injury Disparities in the US Hotel Industry," 119.

[25]Julia Wolfe et al., "Domestic Workers Chartbook: A Comprehensive Look at the Demographics, Wages, Benefits, and Poverty Rates of the Professionals Who Care for Our Family Members and Clean Our Homes," Economic Policy Institute, May 14, 2020, https://www.epi.org/publication/domestic-workers-chartbook-a-comprehensive-look-at-the-demographics-wages-benefits-and-poverty-rates-of-the-professionals-who-care-for-our-family-members-and-clean-our-homes/.

exacerbates employment discrimination through racial oppression, sexual harassment, unfair wages, and heavy workloads. The strikes, protests, and contract debates within the last twelve years between Hyatt and union and fair labor organizations such as UNITE HERE in Chicago uncover the ongoing labor challenges that Hyatt workers have endured spanning back as far as my grandmother's tenure during the 1980s to the early 2000s at the peak of Hyatt's growth.[26] As early as 1988, the Equal Employment Opportunity Commission ruled that Hyatt hotels practiced racial discrimination toward Black women by banning cornrows.[27] The grooming codes functioned not only to reduce Black women's bodies as objects of production but also to regulate their bodies—how they work, move, behave, and dress.

The suffering of Black women through domestic labor is not a new history. The primary objective of the slaveocracy in the antebellum era was to employ enslaved and indentured workers as free laborers to sustain agribusiness and households. Enslaved Black women were forced to labor in both the field (men's work) and the house (women's work) for white slaveholding families. During the Reconstruction era, domesticity marked the fourth cardinal virtue in what feminist historian Barbara Welter describes as "the cult of true womanhood" instituted to establish distinct gender roles between American men and women.[28] While white men dominated the public square as "the movers, the doers, the actors," white women were expected to be "the passive, submissive responders" whose primary sphere of influence and place of protection was the home.[29] Welter utilizes nineteenth-century literature, magazines, and religious pamphlets to emphasize the cultural depictions of the "true woman"—pious, pure, submissive, and domestic— as too vulnerable, innocent, and weak in character to contend with forces outside the home. Welter describes, "In the home women were not only the highest adornment of civilization, but they were supposed to keep busy at morally uplifting tasks. Fortunately most of housework, if looked at in true womanly fashion, could be regarded as uplifting."[30] The cult of domesticity succeeded in characterizing the proper roles for white middle-class women,

---

[26] UNITE HERE, "Chicago Hotel Workers Ratify Local Contract with Hyatt Hotels," August 8, 2013, http://www.unitehere1.org/2013/08/chicago-hotel-workers-ratify-local-contract-with-hyatt-hotels/.

[27] Jim Schachter, "EEOC Says Hyatt Showed Bias in Its Ban on Cornrows," *Los Angeles Times,* May 17, 1988, https://www.latimes.com/archives/la-xpm-1988-05-17-fi-2915-story.html.

[28] Welter, "The Cult of True Womanhood," 151.

[29] Welter, "The Cult of True Womanhood," 159.

[30] Welter, "The Cult of True Womanhood," 164.

reserving the home as the white women's domain, and distinguishing Black women as inferior in a post–Civil War period. White women gained control over Black domestic women, creating enmity between mistress and maid. The presence of maids in the home gave mistresses (mostly white women) the luxury to attain Victorian ideals while reserving unwanted, laborious work—cleaning, laundering, ironing, cooking, rearing children, etc.—for Black women.

Domestic labor engendered a subordinate social class for Black women that was fraught with danger to their personhood. Black feminist historian Darlene Clark Hine, in her classic article "Rape and the Inner Lives of Black Women," argues that the noneconomic reason for Black female migration was "a desire to achieve personal autonomy and to escape both from sexual exploitation from inside and outside of their families and from the rape and threat of rape by white as well as Black males."[31] The pervasive threat of rape alongside economic devastation discloses Black women's discrete interest in migrating from the South to the North despite limited opportunities for employment.

> Black women's work was the most undesirable and least remunerative of all work available to migrants. As late as 1930 a little of over three thousand Black women, or 15 percent, of the Black female labor force in Chicago were unskilled and semiskilled factory operatives. Thus, over 80 percent of all employed Black women continued to work as personal servants and domestics. . . . Given that many Black women migrants were doomed to work in the same kinds of domestic service jobs held in the South, one wonders why they bothered to move in the first place.[32]

Except for factory work, Black women migrating to the urban North did not encounter new work opportunities or roles. Domestic and clerical work were the only available "legitimate" choices for Black women in both the North and the South. Even in urban cities like Chicago at the turn of the century, the conditions of domestic work were not ideal for Black women. Black historian Cynthia Blair outlines the social-sexual forces shifting Black women's labor at the height of Chicago's "most explosive growth" in *I've Got to Make My Livin': Black Women's Sex Work in Turn-of-the-Century Chicago.*

---

[31]Darlene Clark Hine, "Rape and the Inner Lives of Black Women in the Middle West," *Signs* 14, no. 4 (1989): 914.

[32]Hine, "Rape and the Inner Lives of Black Women," 913.

Blair describes, "The obstacles African American women faced in their efforts to find employment, make a living, and at the same time defend their independence and dignity within the urban wage system pushed some to look elsewhere for their money."[33] Blair makes the case that some women resisting low-wage "legitimate" work turned to underground economies of sex work and prostitution to make a living on their own terms. While whites and Black "respectables"[34] deemed sex work as disrespectable and illegitimate, explicit binaries between service versus sex work for Black women through the lens of moral versus immoral when recognizing Black women's work motivated complex strategies of resistance to navigate multidimensional oppression. In line with Hine and Blair, Black migrant women fled to the urban North to escape social-sexual domination of their bodies and to seize greater autonomy of their identities. Moving north gave Black women the semblance of a better life with latitude to protect their bodies and control their sexuality.

Black women hiding their interior lives helped to guard their public "work." Hine names a "culture of dissemblance" as a resistance strategy that some Black women used to counter prevailing assumptions about their bodies and sexuality. According to Hine,

> In the face of the pervasive stereotypes and negative estimations of the sexuality of Black women, it was imperative that they collectively create alternative self-images and shield from scrutiny these private empowering definitions of self. A secret, undisclosed persona allowed the individual Black woman to function, to work effectively as a domestic in white households, to bear and rear children, to endure the frustration-born violence of frequently under- or unemployed mates, to support churches, to found institutions, and to engage in social service activities, all while living within a clearly hostile white, patriarchal, middle-class America.[35]

---

[33]Cynthia M. Blair, *I've Got to Make My Livin': Black Women's Sex Work in Turn-of-the-Century Chicago* (Chicago: University of Chicago Press, 2010), 22.

[34]I am pointing here to a "politics of respectability" as defined by historian Evelyn Brooks Higginbotham as Black churchwomen and their institutions sought moral uplift for Black people through public, respectable categories of work, dress, and behavior to counter salacious stereotypes of Black women and foster greater acceptance by whites. Evelyn Brooks Higginbotham, *Righteous Discontent: The Women's Movement in the Black Baptist Church, 1880–1920* (Cambridge, MA: Harvard University Press, 2003), 185–230.

[35]Hine, "Rape and the Inner Lives of Black Women," 916.

Secrecy aided Black women in thwarting the constant threat of rape in their own homes and white homes. Black migrant women's agency to refuse living in white homes while working to resist predators[36] often meant they had to lead double lives as daughters, wives, and mothers and maintain two households. Black domestic women were caught in a multidimensional, antagonistic bind to conceal their lives while carrying the weight of their communities and caring for white families. In *Labor of Love, Labor of Sorrow: Black Women, Work, and the Family from Slavery to Present*, American historian Jacquelyn Jones further argues that Black women "served as primary or supplementary breadwinners in their households, and unlike white women, they took home wages nearly equal to those of their menfolk. The progress of African Americans as a group was clearly linked to the job status of black women, and thus discrimination encountered by wives and mothers in the workplace was a crucial factor in inhibiting the upward mobility of their families."[37] Black women's work was essential to the economic survival of the Black community. Despite their sexual vulnerability, Black migrant domestic workers, especially those who hoped for social advancement in the urban North as the "promised land," bore the burdens of sacrifice, surrogacy, and strength by accommodating a subordinate status with longer hours and lower pay to "uplift" their communities and expand opportunities for future generations. Even Black women who took the few factory and clerical jobs outside the service industry encountered this tension as they were pushed to the "bottom," which describes the lowest positions among their poor white and immigrant counterparts.

Black women employed as servants and subordinates to sustain white comfort and leisure is a recurring narrative in popular culture. Based on the 1936 novel by Margaret Mitchell, the widely acclaimed 1939 film *Gone with the Wind* made history as the highest-grossing film, earning over $3 billion.[38] A lackluster love and war drama that boasts nostalgia of a racist,

---

[36]Predatory encounters for Black domestic women may include unwanted sexual advances from men and complications between white mistress and Black maid in the workplace of the home.

[37]Jacqueline Jones, *Labor of Love, Labor of Sorrow: Black Women, Work, and the Family from Slavery to the Present* (New York: Basic Books, 2010), 132.

[38]Following the appeal of Academy Award–winning filmmaker John Ridley in an *LA Times* op-ed, HBO removed *Gone with the Wind* from its streaming network HBO Max at the height of #BlackLivesMatter 2020 protests in the wake of George Floyd's murder because it failed to align with Warner Media's values. HBO announced interest to add a disclaimer to the film including its "racialized depictions" upon its return to the network. The film was

slaveholding South and false depictions of Blacks pleased with servitude catapulted to national prominence as "a barometer of America's race relations in the 1930s and 1940s."[39] Black women characters became central to the story as maid (Butterfly McQueen) and Mammy (Hattie McDaniel) dramatized an undying love for the O'Hara family while rejecting their own. Kathryn Stockett's 2009 debut novel, *The Help*, tells another fictional story of African American domestic workers in the South who achieved *dissemblance* by separating their lives from their care of white families during the 1960s. Told from the perspective of a white woman journalist, the novel was a sweeping sensation, earning a spot on the *New York Times* Bestseller List for more than one hundred weeks by August 2011. The comedic highlight of the story is a Black maid (Octavia Spencer) who is denied access to the indoor restroom of the white family where she works and later retaliates with a "mess" chocolate pie. America's infatuation with these made-up stories about the oppressive conditions of domestic work that it created for Black women reinforces and validates the subordination of Black women as normative. The glorification of Black women as "the help" is sustained in popular culture through the Academy's celebration of Hattie McDaniel (1939)[40]—the first Black woman to win an Oscar—and later Octavia Spencer (2012) in the same supporting roles. Both films validate the Mammy stereotype, which limits Black women's bodies and roles to nurturing white identity at the expense of self-sacrifice. The exploitation of Black women's domestic labor magnifies the Mammy trope when Black women become respectable under the normative gaze only if they remain as what Delores

---

replaced two weeks later with an opening video to invite viewers to engage the film in its historical context. See John Ridley, "Hey, HBO, 'Gone With the Wind' Romanticizes the Horrors of Slavery. Take It off Your Platform for Now," *Los Angeles Times*, June 8, 2020, https://www.latimes.com/opinion/story/2020-06-08/hbo-max-racism-gone-with-the-wind-movie; Daniel Victor, "HBO Max Pulls 'Gone With the Wind,' Citing Racist Depictions," *New York Times*, June 10, 2020, sec. Business, https://www.nytimes.com/2020/06/10/business/media/gone-with-the-wind-hbo-max.html. Todd Spangler, "HBO Max Restores 'Gone With the Wind' with Disclaimer Saying Film 'Denies the Horrors of Slavery,'" *Variety*, June 24, 2020, https://variety.com/2020/digital/news/gone-with-the-wind-hbo-max-disclaimer-horrors-slavery-1234648726/.

[39]Leonard J. Leff, "'Gone With the Wind' and Hollywood's Racial Politics," *The Atlantic*, December 1, 1999, https://www.theatlantic.com/magazine/archive/1999/12/gone-with-the-wind-and-hollywoods-racial-politics/377919/.

[40]Though Hattie McDaniel earned an Academy Award, she was not welcomed to attend the premiere of the film because it was held at a whites-only theater in Atlanta, Georgia. Later, the Ambassador Hotel in Los Angeles permitted McDaniel to attend the Twelfth Academy Awards, but at a segregated table away from her castmates.

Williams names, "perpetual mother figures—religious, fat, asexual, loving children better than themselves, self-sacrificing, giving up self-concern for group advancement."[41] I turn next to the denial of Black women's labor in the Black Church.

The "Backbone" of the Black Church

The visible Black Church fortified the hegemonic interest in subduing Black women by disciplining Black women's bodies and silencing their voices. Labor within the visible Black Church aligned with Victorian and Edwardian gender roles and rigid biblical household codes (*Haustafeln*) that ordained a separate and unequal status for Black women. Black men were compelled to lead; Black women were compelled to serve. Any attempts to shift the gender roles concerning the work of faith were deemed as threats to the socio-religious order of the Black Church. In *The History and Heritage of African American Churches: A Way out of No Way*, historian L. H. Whelchel argues that the nineteenth-century Black Church governing structures imitating Western beliefs limited the roles of Black women and provided unequal acceptance of their service and skill in relation to their male counterparts.

> The Black Church divide from White churches was purely a racial separation. Blacks wanted their own space to worship amongst their own racial culture, but they left with the same non-liberative doctrine, hierarchical structures and beliefs. After the African traditional practices were systematically suppressed, slave masters began to impress upon their slaves their Western Christianity which excluded women from the vocation of ministry.[42]

The story of Jarena Lee, the first authorized Black woman preacher in the African Methodist Episcopal Church (AME)—who petitioned AME founding bishop Richard Allen for eight years before receiving license to preach in the AME Church—is a classic nineteenth-century example of this phenomenon. After leaving the historically white Episcopal Church, Lee sought respite and recovery in the congregational assembly of her people at

---

[41]Delores S. Williams, *Sisters in the Wilderness: The Challenge of Womanist God-Talk* (Maryknoll, NY: Orbis Books, 1993), 70.

[42]L. H. Whelchel, *The History and Heritage of African-American Churches: A Way out of No Way* (St. Paul, MN: Paragon House, 2011), 18.

the Mount Bethel AME Church in Philadelphia, only for Allen to revoke her God-ordained call to preach because of church polity. Allen's dismissal could not stop Lee's persistence as she pursued itinerant preaching and lived into her vocational service even without recognition. Allen's decision to license Lee came only after Rev. Richard Williams could not finish his sermon and Jarena Lee experienced the spiritual urge to deliver a fiery preached message extemporaneously to the assembled. Though Lee preached for more than twenty years up and down the Eastern Seaboard with a glorious following, the AME Church refused Lee's ordination during her lifetime and failed to ordain women to preach as elders until 1960 (roughly 140 years later). Lee's narrative further reveals Black women pushing against the bounds of subjugation since the origin of the Black Church.

The dismissal of Black women's work remains at the center of the Black Church tradition. At the turn of the twentieth century, Black sociologist W. E. B. Du Bois documents the devaluing of Black women's contributions to the institutional development of the Negro Church in *Darkwater: Voices from within the Veil*:

> As I look about me today in this veiled world of mine, despite the noisier and more spectacular advance of my brothers, I instinctively feel and know that it is five million women of my race who really count. Black women (and women whose grandmothers were black) are today furnishing our teachers they are the main pillars of those social settlements we call churches and they have with small doubt raised three-fourths of our church property.[43]

The Black women's club movement provides a significant example of Black women working to secure the institutional Black Church through a "politics of respectability."[44] At the helm of dissemblance, Black clubwomen employed increasingly "respectable" strategies of resistance to raise the moral, educational, and economic stature of the Black community in every possible way. Black clubwomen appealed to three significant aims: (1) countering negative images of Black women's sexuality, (2) developing resources to

---

[43]W. E. B. Du Bois, *Darkwater: Voices from within the Veil* (Mineola, NY: Dover Publications, 1999), 179.

[44]I am returning here to Evelyn Brooks Higginbotham's articulation of the "politics of respectability" for Black Baptist clubwomen. In a later chapter, I make the case that the challenge of respectability mirrors disciplining power for Black women that remains restricting and confining.

support Black women's legitimate work, and (3) building autonomous institutions (e.g., educational, religious, social) that improved the quality of Black life. Although denied opportunities to preach, Black clubwomen upheld the social and prophetic witness of the Black Church by organizing clubs and auxiliary groups and funding initiatives to uplift Black people while simultaneously confronting the social injustices of rape, lynching, voter suppression, and racial segregation.

In *Labor of Faith: Gender and Power in Black Apostolic Pentecostalism,* Africana studies scholar Judith Casselberry argues for a different example of apostolic Black women advocating a "politics of righteousness" that carried the emotional labor of the Black Church.[45] Praying, tarrying, wailing, warfare, anointing, and laying on of hands represent spiritual works performed by women to fight against the social forces of oppression and sustain the Black Church, while maintaining holiness notions of women's submission and obedience. Womanist sociologist Cheryl Townsend Gilkes best describes Black women's indispensability on multiple fronts: "If it wasn't for the women, then there would be no church."[46] The cultural and spiritual prominence of the Black Church is directly related to Black women—their blood, sweat, tears, and coin. Black women's work remains essential to the viability and vitality of the tradition.

Consequently, the Black Church has played a dual role: as a place of relief from the woes of a hostile white world, and as a proponent of Black women's suffering through the exploitation of Black women's labor and activism. Black women's suffering of subordination manifests not only in society but also in the Black Church. The heavy burdens of sacrifice, surrogacy, and strength weigh on the backs of Black churchwomen, injuring their bodies and spirit.

Black women bear the burden of sacrifice in the Black Church. The Black Church as a spiritual home for Black people relies upon the employment of "traditional Black women's work," including the domestic tasks of cleaning, cooking, sewing, and other caretaking needs that Black women fulfill. Though intended for white women, the Black Church replicates the social order of the cult of domesticity by raising Black men as the "the movers, the doers, the actors" and denigrating Black women as "passive, submis-

---

[45]Judith Casselberry, *The Labor of Faith: Gender and Power in Black Apostolic Pentecostalism* (Durham, NC: Duke University Press, 2017), 105.

[46]Cheryl Gilkes, *If It Wasn't for the Women . . .: Black Women's Experience and Womanist Culture in Church and Community* (Maryknoll, NY: Orbis Books, 2001), 54.

sive responders."[47] Black women as Welter describes are determined to be too weak in character to do the "public work" of the Black Church. What constitutes men's work in the Black Church is preaching, pastoring, and maintaining property, which elevates the social status of Black men in the community. The positions of pastor, preacher, sexton, executive officer, and lead musician represent male-dominated roles with paid wages. Women's work in the Black Church includes assisting, supporting, and complementing Black men, which maintains a submissive and sacrificial posture for Black women. The positions of first lady, usher, nurse, deaconess, secretary, clerk, cook, and even soloist often exist as unpaid labor in the Black Church. The Black Church expects Black women to offer their work as a freewill sacrifice and reasonable service. Though Black women are likely more skilled through educational training than Black men for leadership in the Black Church, only few if any at all exceptional Black women are recognized as senior pastors, bishops, apostles, and executives.

Black women bear the burden of surrogacy in the Black Church. From slavery to freedom, Delores Williams suggests that Black women have navigated two surrogate roles: "that of substituting female power and energy for male power and energy, and that of mammy."[48] Most Black Baptist and Methodist churches assign women's work (i.e., women's ministry, women's council, missionary society) to parallel auxiliary organizations within the church, but these women's groups in no way usurp traditional male authority in the Black Church. For Pentecostal, Sanctified, and Apostolic churches, the balance of power between women and men bears a range of possibilities depending on the tradition's understanding of women's proper role or place. Gilkes asserts, "These varieties of shared power or of access to authority reflect the range of positions church mothers occupy."[49] The Mammy is not only a popular trope but also marks a religious image for Black churchwomen. In *When and Where I Enter: The Impact of Black Women on Race and Sex in America*, Black feminist historian Paula Giddings describes the power-broking of Mammy figures between two conflicting worlds:

When some figures, such as mammies on the large plantations, were able to extend their domain to the master's house, they often became the "broker" between the slave community and Whites—thus increasing the Black woman's influence. The Black woman's "power," however,

[47]Welter, "The Cult of True Womanhood," 159.
[48]Williams, *Sisters in the Wilderness,* 73.
[49]Gilkes, *If It Wasn't for the Women,* 73.

still derived from her functionalist roles rather than from influence in traditional male domains. But it was power nonetheless.[50]

The benevolent Church Mother resembles such a brokering power as "overseer" of women's work who exists between conflicting spheres of Black men and women in the Black Church. The Church Mother may receive opportunities to participate in traditional men's work of preaching, teaching, and leading in some churches, earning popularity and prominence across genders. However, the Church Mother earning respect within the religious community does not necessarily shift the power relations between Black men and Black women, nor does she assert more prominent leadership roles for Black women. The enslaved Mammy received more power than other Black women but virtually kept the slaveocracy intact. One may argue that the Church Mother's power upholds or at least does not threaten the hierarchy or patriarchy of the Black Church.

Black women bear the burden of strength in the Black Church. Jacqueline Jones provides insight into the experiences of Black working women during the Great Migration who sought the Black Church as a refuge to lift their spirit and recover southern communal connectedness displaced by their move to the urban North.

> In the sanctuary, women entered a world divorced from worldly cares; there they prayed together for the souls of wayward husbands and rebellious children, all those who had, in the words of one wife, "forgotten to stay close to God" and were therefore bound for destruction. Smaller ghetto churches in general showed a pronounced lack of interest in social-welfare issues during this period; they offered heavenly, not earthly, salvation. Their exhortations for the faithful to resist temptation appealed most strongly to the women who served as the foundation of community stability and order. Some migrants linked women's strong religious faith, as evidenced by church-going, to their ability to withstand the trauma of moving north and surviving in a strange new place.[51]

Migrating Black women went to Black churches for rescue (and sometimes escape) and received no support to confront social ills, coupled with scold-

---

[50]Paula Giddings, *When and Where I Enter: The Impact of Black Women on Race and Sex in America* (New York: W. Morrow, 1984), 58.

[51]Jones, *Labor of Love, Labor of Sorrow*, 160.

ing theologies[52] that blamed Black women for their efforts to provide for the Black community. The labeling of Black women's strength as a product of faith ignored their desires to not simply be caretakers but to be cared for. The myth of the StrongBlackWoman, as extensively examined by womanist practical theologian Chanequa Walker-Barnes, frames Black women with nowhere to turn to lay their burdens down. "Absent the spiritual sanction to grieve, African American women have no choice but to retreat to a position of stoicism, the form of emotional repression so common among StrongBlackWomen."[53] Whether by respectability (clubwomen) or righteousness (sanctified women), Black women carrying the Black Church and community by social or spiritual service feed the belief that Black women must bear the yoke alone.

The burdens of sacrifice, surrogacy, and strength work together to justify Black women's servanthood in the Black Church. Womanist theologian Jacquelyn Grant most explicitly critiques this sin of servanthood in Christianity that maintains service and servitude as virtues for faithfulness to God. Because "service and oppression for Blacks go hand in hand," Grant describes service as a disempowering and "overspiritualized" notion that has no import for Black women without concrete dismantling of oppressive social forces.[54] When assessing the histories of domestic service and subjugated roles in the Black Church, "African American women have been the 'servants of the servants.' "[55] For Grant, Black women are the "backbone" of the Black Church, with a particular emphasis on "back" to interrogate the Black Church practice of keeping Black women in the background, thus disgracing Black women's work and service.[56] The threat of sexual exploitation is ever-present in the Black Church and functions to keep Black women "on their backs." Furthering attention to the back, the Black Church

---

[52]I identify scolding theologies within the preaching and teaching by mostly Black men and some Black women that situate Black women within a theology of contempt and a confining moralscape of damned-if-you-do and damned-if-you-don't. See Melanie C. Jones, "The Will to Adorn: Beyond Self-Surveillance, toward a Womanist Ethic of Redemptive Self-Love," *Black Theology* 16, no. 3 (September 2, 2018): 218–30, https://doi.org/10.1080/14769948.2018.1492303.

[53]Chanequa Walker-Barnes, *Too Heavy a Yoke: Black Women and the Burden of Strength* (Eugene, OR: Cascade Books, 2014), 144.

[54]Grant, "The Sin of Servanthood," 209.

[55]Grant, "The Sin of Servanthood," 200.

[56]Jacquelyn Grant, "Black Theology and the Black Woman," in *Words of Fire: An Anthology of African-American Feminist Thought*, ed. Beverly Guy-Sheftall (New York: New Press, 1995), 325.

justifies the silencing of Black women's voices and exploiting of their bodies through faulty biblical interpretations and damaging theologies that pose Black women as the problem, not acknowledging that the very institution denies their humanity. Black women exercise a labor of love for a Black Church that does not always love Black women. Grant shifts the theological conversation from servanthood to the language of discipleship. "The church does not need servants as oppressively conceived of and experienced by man; the church needs followers of Christ—disciples."[57] If Christian service equates to subordination, then perhaps Black women may look to the "deliverance that comes through discipleship."[58]

> *The work I've done seems so small,*
> *Sometimes it seems like, seems like nothing at all,*
> *But when I stand before my God*
> *I want to hear Him say, "Well done,"*
> *May the work I've done speak for me.*[59]

Many Women Were There:
A Sisterhood of Faithful Disciples at the Cross

My affirmation of my grandmother being buried with the crest of the empty cross on all four sides is hinged on Gospel stories that reveal the presence of Jesus's most faithful followers—women—near the cross during Jesus's crucifixion. Followers of Christ were often called disciples in Scripture. The chosen Twelve represent featured male characters who traveled with Jesus from place to place during his life and ministry. The Gospel accounts also record named and unnamed women followers who encountered Jesus through healings, miracles, and meals and faithfully supported Jesus's endeavors spiritually, physically, and financially. Luke 8:1–3 records,

---

[57]Grant, "The Sin of Servanthood," 216.

[58]Grant, "The Sin of Servanthood," 216. Grant does acknowledge that the language of discipleship may not be enough to dismantle oppression and continues this discussion in relation to theological anthropology that I will discuss in the next chapter. See Jacquelyn Grant, "Servanthood Revisited: Womanist Explorations of Servanthood Theology," in *Black Faith and Public Talk: Critical Essays on James H. Cone's Black Theology and Black Power*, ed. Dwight N. Hopkins (Waco, TX: Baylor University Press, 2007), 126–37.

[59]Pugh, "May the Work I've Done Speak for Me."

Soon afterwards he went on through cities and villages, proclaiming and bringing the good news of the kingdom of God. The twelve were with him, as well as some women who had been cured of evil spirits and infirmities: Mary, called Magdalene, from whom seven demons had gone out, and Joanna, the wife of Herod's steward Chuza, and Susanna, and many others, who provided for them out of their resources.

Women followers of Jesus came from diverse socioeconomic backgrounds and varied experiences—from the wealthy Joanna, wife of a royal official, to Mary, Jesus's mother, who struggled to secure a room for his birth. Although these women were not given special titles and are often underrecognized in Scripture, they followed Jesus during his birth, life, and ministry and even to the cross to witness the final moments of life for a man they loved deeply. Today's interpreters cannot deny the intimacy of Jesus's encounters with women, but Jesus resisted exploitation. The women cared for Jesus enough to suffer violence with him near the cross. All four Gospel writers record women followers present at Jesus's death on the cross (Mt 27:55–56; Mk 15:40–41; Lk 23:49; Jn 19:25b–27).

Mark's account identifies a large group of women "looking from a distance" during Jesus's crucifixion. Mark 15:40–41 names "Mary Magdalene, Mary the mother of James, Salome, women who followed Jesus, women who ministered to Jesus, and women who traveled with Jesus up from Jerusalem" in the record of those near the cross. Mark describes these women not as passive followers only receiving from Jesus but also as ministering to Jesus. These women held intimate encounters, meaningful connections, and unbreakable bonds with Jesus. Mary Magdalene and Mary the mother of Joses in Mark 15:47 were watching attentively and waiting cautiously to see exactly where Jesus was laid. The women cared for their loved one by anointing Jesus's body with spices and arriving early to the tomb to ensure Jesus was never alone.

Matthew's account describes the presence of many women near the cross, both named and unnamed, watching from a distance.

Many women were also there, looking on from a distance; they had followed Jesus from Galilee and had provided for him. Among them were Mary Magdalene, and Mary the mother of James and Joseph, and the mother of the sons of Zebedee. (Mt 27:55–56)

With the use of the word "many"—"πολύς"—the writer of Matthew illustrates a large gathering of faithful women followers near Jesus at the crucifixion. These women watched Jesus mature from birth, encouraged his ministry, witnessed his miracles, supported his travels, anointed his body, received his healing, and carried his gospel message. Despite the torment of watching a man they loved suffer state-sanctioned death, the women stayed and suffered with him.

John's Gospel provides a narrative of Jesus addressing one of his most faithful followers on the cross, his mother:

> Meanwhile, standing near the cross of Jesus were his mother, and his mother's sister, Mary the wife of Cleopas, and Mary Magdalene. When Jesus saw his mother and the disciple whom he loved standing beside her, he said to his mother, "Woman, here is your son." Then he said to the disciple, "Here is your mother." And from that hour the disciple took her into his own home. (Jn 19:25b–27)

John 19:25b–27 is a popular text (the Third Word) used in Seven Last Words services observed on Good Friday in the Black Church tradition to remember the seven sayings of Jesus recorded in Scripture. Most Black sermonic interpreters use the Johannine passage to humanize Jesus and signal his concern for his mother's survival and safety in the comfort of the beloved disciple. While some scholars debate the identity of the beloved disciple as possibly John, Mary Magdalene, or another close follower, the presence of the "Marys" indicate that women were close enough to the cross to suffer with Jesus during a crucial moment. Jesus's concern about the needs of women followers through his sayings on the cross reveals Jesus's concern for women today, especially the most vulnerable.

Luke presents two groups of women present at Jesus's crucifixion: the daughters of Jerusalem (23:26–31) and the women of Galilee (23:49). A multitude follows Jesus as he walks with Simon of Cyrene, an outsider, who is seized by Roman rule to carry the cross and bear the burden with Jesus. In *Simon of Cyrene: A Case of Roman Conscription*, womanist biblical scholar Stephanie Buckhanon Crowder interprets the inclusion of Simon of Cyrene in the Gospel of Luke by two primary functions: "1) He represents those oppressed by addressing the Roman social history of compulsion and 2) He represents different approaches to the Gospel of Jesus Christ."[60] Crowder makes the case that Simon as depicted by Luke was not a disciple of Jesus

---

[60]Stephanie R. Buckhanon Crowder, *Simon of Cyrene: A Case of Roman Conscription*, Studies in Biblical Literature 46 (New York: P. Lang, 2002), 50.

but "forced to act because of Roman conscription."[61] Similar to Simon, Luke includes the daughters of Jerusalem to narrate a distinct account from Matthew and Mark that signals oppression and opens the social world of Luke. Jesus hears the cries of the wailing women, who were likely professional mourners weeping for him, and warns these women not to weep.

> As they led him away, they seized a man, Simon of Cyrene, who was coming from the country, and they laid the cross on him, and made him carry it behind Jesus. A great number of the people followed him, and among them were women who were beating their breasts and wailing for him. But Jesus turned to them and said, "Daughters of Jerusalem, do not weep for me, but weep for yourselves and for your children. For the days are surely coming when they will say, 'Blessed are the barren, and the wombs that never bore, and the breasts that never nursed.' Then they will begin to say to the mountains, 'Fall on us'; and to the hills, 'Cover us.' For if they do this when the wood is green, what will happen when it is dry?" (Lk 23:26–31)

The writer does not make it clear whether the daughters of Jerusalem were disciples. Perhaps the daughters of Jerusalem knew of Jesus's ministry, witnessed his miracles, and felt the devastation of his immanent death. So, they wept for him, and Jesus turned to them to lament their suffering. Jesus's warning to the daughters of Jerusalem signals a deliberate act to recognize their plight in the wake of terror, even on the journey to his demise.

Though Luke does not single out names of the women—as do Matthew, Mark, and John—the women of Galilee in Luke 23:49 represent the faithful disciples of Jesus who play a role in the Passion narrative. Readers of Luke may interpret the women of Galilee as including the "women cured of evil spirits and infirmities" and the named women in Luke 8:1–3: Mary called Magdalene; Joanna the wife of Chuza, Herod's steward; and Susanna. These women were early disciples of Jesus who traveled with him proclaiming the good news and participated in service διακονέω (*diakoneō*) to Jesus and the chosen Twelve. New Testament scholar Ben Witherington III denotes discipleship as a central theme in Luke. "Women are a continuing theme and example used by Luke as he tries to teach the qualities of a true disciple—one who is loyal and faithful to Christ through trials and joy; one who witnesses to the person and work of Christ; one who serves the Lord and the

---

[61]Crowder, *Simon of Cyrene,* 69.

brethren freely from their own means, and so on."[62] Feminist biblicists Jane Schaeberg and Sharon Ringe in *The Women's Bible Commentary* interrogate the mutuality of the work or service of the women when depicted in Luke 8 as deferential to the male disciples. "The women are cast in a nonreciprocated role of service or support of the males of the movement. Since in Luke-Acts, the Twelve are the major witnesses and leaders, these women's role is subordinate. The wording of 8:2–3 implies that they are acting out of gratitude of being healed, unlike the Twelve."[63] The women of Galilee were devoted to Jesus despite their unequal treatment in relation to the male disciples. Jesus granted these women something greater for their service in Luke: healing and redemption. Even after the large crowd fled, repenting and beating their breasts at the site of an innocent Jesus crucified in Luke 23:48–49, the women of Galilee stood watching the scene at a distance.

The presence of a multitude of faithful women disciples near Jesus during the crucifixion is significant given the likely absence and scattering of the chosen Twelve. The Passion narratives convey the disciples facing threats to their lives and livelihood in the moments leading up to Jesus's crucifixion. Judas lamented his act of betrayal and hung himself, missing the crucifixion (Mt 27:3–10). Peter denied his relationship with Jesus three times (Mt 26:69–75). Peter's presence at the cross would have raised suspicion by onlookers and placed his life in jeopardy. Though Scripture is ambiguous about the presence of the male disciples at the crucifixion, many of the disciples likely scattered given Jesus's arrest by Roman soldiers and subsequent public trials (Mt 26:47–56). The Gospel of John's mentioning of the "beloved disciple" in John 19:25b–27 may imply that few—maybe one, if any at all—of the Twelve were present at the cross. Nevertheless, many women were there. Though unpopular, numerous, and unnamed, a large assembly of women followers were near the cross to witness Jesus's suffering in its most brutal form. Mary Magdalene is the archetype of a faithful disciple who is mentioned in all four Passion narratives as one who stayed with Jesus until the very end. Some of the women were so faithful to Jesus and his mission that they did not leave Jesus's body after he gave up his last breath. While Joseph of Arimathea offered a resting place (a borrowed

---

[62]Ben Witherington III, "On the Road with Mary Magdalene, Joanna, Susanna, and Other Disciples—Luke 8:1–3," in A Feminist Companion to Luke, ed. Amy-Jill Levine, 133–40. (New York: Sheffield Academic Press, 2002), 134.

[63]Jane Schaberg and Sharon H. Ringe, "Gospel of Luke," in *Women's Bible Commentary*, ed. Carol A. Newsom, Sharon H. Ringe, and Jacqueline E. Lapsley, 3rd ed., 20th ann. ed. (Louisville, KY: Westminster John Knox Press, 2012), 506.

tomb) for Jesus's body, the Synoptics suggest that women either anointed his body for burial or watched near the tomb where Jesus's body laid (Mt 27:57–60; Mk 15:42–47; Lk 23:50–56).

Women suffering with Jesus through his crucifixion, death, and burial is also the story of Jesus's faithful followers becoming the first to witness and herald the hope of divine Resurrection. The Gospel writers (Mt 28:1–10; Mk 15:1–8; Lk 24:1–12; Jn 20:1–18) record that women were the first to discover a risen Jesus and the first to tell the good news of the Resurrection, which is the "bedrock of the Christian faith."[64] From this perspective, the suffering of Jesus *and* women becomes temporal, and the Resurrection becomes eternal. The double cross images at the four corners of my grandmother's casket represent not only the suffering that she endured but also that, in her body remaining near the cross, she joins the faithful assembly of disciples who will tell the story of embodied transformation. I move to womanist Christology to ground my musings within the God-talk of Black women.

Womanist Christology: A "Cross" Examination

When womanist foundational voices, namely Katie Cannon, Jacquelyn Grant, Delores Williams, Clarice Martin, and Renita Weems, began confronting sexism in Black liberation theology and the Black Church and racism in feminist theology in the 1980s, they also faced the challenge of speaking in new tongues and refining God-talk for Black women. In her classic 1979 article "Black Theology and the Black Woman," Jacquelyn Grant is the first to bring Black liberation theology to the carpet by examining its theological objective of liberation for Black people in the work of James Cone and exposing its failure to move toward full liberation by invisibilizing Black women. Grant draws from Swiss theologian Karl Barth's use of "self-test" in theology as a resource for Black theology to construct a similar self-inquiry to measure its intentions by its practice. Grant argues, "If, as I contend, the liberation of black men and women is inseparable, then a radical split cannot be made between racism and sexism. Black women are oppressed by racism and sexism. It is therefore necessary that black men and women be actively involved in combating both evils."[65] Grant affirms that racism and sexism will both need to be core concerns of Black theology

---

[64]Schaberg and Ringe, "Gospel of Luke," 510.
[65]Grant, "Black Theology and the Black Woman," 326.

to address the full experience of oppression in the Black community. Later, in her groundbreaking *White Women's Christ, Black Women's Jesus: Feminist Christology and Womanist Response*, Grant argues that feminist theology failed its task of liberating women by dismissing nonwhite women. "Feminist theology is inadequate for two reasons: it is *white* and *racist*."[66] It is white because it only addresses white women's experiences and racist because it claims to discuss all women's experiences, thus eclipsing the experiences of Black women in particular. In Grant's view, "Womanist theology begins with the experiences of Black women as its point of departure" to construct theologies that advocate prophetically against multidimensional oppressive systems and interpretations.[67]

Delores Williams developed a Christian womanist theological method in her 1987 article "Womanist Theology: Black Women's Voices," advocating four primary intentions: (1) a multidialogical intent—to speak to/ with/for multiple communities across social, political, and religious lines; (2) a liturgical intent—"critique the thought/worship/action of the Black Church"; (3) a didactic intent—"teach new insights about moral life with an eye for justice and survival of poor women, children and men"; and (4) a "commitment both to reason and to the validity of female imagery and metaphorical language in the construction of theological statements."[68] The question "Who do you say God is for Black women?" is at the core of womanist theology. Williams extends the womanist theological definition in her full-length volume:

> Womanist theology is a prophetic voice reminding African-American denominational churches of their mission to seek justice and voice for all their people, of which Black women are the overwhelming majority in their congregations. Yet, this prophetic voice is concerned about the wellbeing of the entire African-American community, female and male, adults and children. . . . Womanist theology attempts to help black women see, affirm, and have confidence in the importance of their experience and faith for determining *the character of the Christian religion* in the African-American community. Womanist theology challenges all oppressive forces impeding black women's struggle for

---

[66] Jacquelyn Grant, *White Women's Christ, Black Women's Jesus: Feminist Theology and Womanist Response* (Atlanta: Scholars Press, 1989), 195.

[67] Grant, *White Women's Christ, Black Women's Jesus*, 205.

[68] Delores S. Williams, "Womanist Theology: Black Women's Voices," *Christianity and Crisis* 47, no. 3 (March 2, 1987): 66–70.

survival and for the development of a positive, productive quality of life conducive to women's and the family's freedom and well-being. Womanist theology opposes all oppression based on race, sex, class, sexual preference, physical ability, and caste.[69]

At multiple intersections of Black women's experiences, womanist theology constructs transformative God-talk that rejects the subordination of Black women, Black men, and other vulnerable populations while simultaneously advocating for critical theological shifting and careful ethical practice that resists all forms of oppression in the academy, church, and society.

Womanist scholars interrogating theological categories with Black women at the epistemological center soon developed a progressive interest in responding to Cone's piercing inquiry "Who is Jesus Christ for today?" and "Who is Jesus Christ for Black women?" Womanist theological queries addressing central loci of Christian theology, particularly suffering and salvation, serve as intersecting "crossways" between theology and Black women's experiences. The works of trailblazing womanist theologians Jacquelyn Grant, Delores Williams, Kelly Brown Douglas, and JoAnne Terrell represent the birth of a solid foundation in womanist Christology. These women are united by their systematic theological training at Union Theological Seminary in New York. All four women studied with the late James Cone, affectionately named the father of Black liberation theology, as either doctoral students or colleagues, while also offering poignant critiques of Cone and Black liberation theology's missing engagement with gender and sexism in its constructions of liberation for Black people. Grant (AME), Douglas (Episcopal), Williams (Presbyterian), and Terrell (formerly AME Zion, now UCC and Buddhist) provide theological insight from the perspective of three ordained clergywomen and one lay preacher. While they have similar academic and leadership backgrounds, the four scholars maintain unique Christological positions that overlap and intersect.

I name four distinctive strands of womanist Christology: reformer, radical, rejectionist, and re-visionist. Grant reforms feminist and male-dominated Black liberation theologies by addressing their pitfalls for not including the historical experiences of Black women. I identify Douglas as the radical of the group because she traces the roots of the Black Christ and the meaning of the cross within the socio-religious context of imperial power and religious exclusion. Williams follows a rejectionist approach by

---

[69]Williams, *Sisters in the Wilderness*, xiii–xiv, emphasis added.

disavowing the surrogacy of the cross for Black women. Terrell espouses a re-visionist method by rethinking traditional atonement theories that condone sacrifice for Black women and recasting the meaning of this tradition in the light of their historical antecedents. While no typology fully grasps the complexity of these thinkers, I use these categories to articulate the diversity in womanist Christological expressions. Together, these scholars have given womanist Christology a distinctive voice and identity in the religion and theology academy for the last forty years.

Near the cross is a recurring image for Black women in a contemporary age as Black women and their daughters and sons face the terrors of state-sanctioned violence at the hands of police brutality and a stand-your-ground culture. Kelly Brown Douglas makes it clear that "Trayvon and Jesus are indeed connected by the cross. . . . The cross affirms the faith of his mother [Sybrina Fulton] that his [Trayvon's] death was not in God's plan"[70] Today's Mothers of the Movement and countless Black women and men can be found standing near the site of the slain for hours,[71] witnessing and lamenting the modern-day lynching of Black people. For sure, the cross ought not to be glorified, but Black women's connection to the story and meaning of the cross cannot be ignored. In the following sections, I briefly explore womanist Christological positions on suffering and the cross.

Jacquelyn Grant the Reformer

Jacquelyn Grant provides a salient introduction to womanist Christology. The major premise of her 1988 monograph—suggested in the title *White Women's Christ, Black Women's Jesus: Feminist Christology and Womanist Response*—signifies that Black women hold a deep connection with the humanity of Jesus, who is God-incarnate or God-become-human. Grant situates Black women's linkage to Jesus within the history of the Black community. The affirmation of Jesus remains central to Black faith:

---

[70]Douglas, *Stand Your Ground*, 170.

[71]I am pointing directly to the 2014 Ferguson protests that erupted after the police left the body of eighteen-year-old Michael Brown Jr. in the sweltering summer heat for more than four hours after Brown was shot dead by twent-eight-year-old officer Darren Wilson in the middle of the Canfield neighborhood of Ferguson, Missouri. When I visited in 2015 exactly one year later along with other religious scholars, a memorial remembering Brown's life and the site of execution remained. See for a fuller treatment of this story Keeanga-Yamahtta Taylor, *From #BlackLivesMatter to Black Liberation* (Chicago: Haymarket Books, 2016).

Chief among these however, was the belief in Jesus as the "divine co-sufferer" who empowers them in situations of oppression. For Christian Black women in the past, Jesus was their central frame of reference. They identified with Jesus because they believed that Jesus identified with them. As Jesus was persecuted and made to suffer undeservedly, so were they. His suffering culminated in the crucifixion. Their crucifixion included rape, and babies being sold. But Jesus' was not the suffering of a mere human, for Jesus was understood to be God incarnate.[72]

Historically, Black women held a deep love for Jesus because Jesus loved them deeply. Jesus related to Black women as one who also endured unjust persecution, which culminated in the cross. Black women experienced crucifixion by the subjugation of slavery, which stripped their humanity, and the experience of subordination, which reduced them to a second-class status at best—or dare I say just plain bottom—in society and the Black Church.

Grant aligns with Black liberation theology's articulation of God on the side of the oppressed in their struggle for liberation. Grant locates Black women's oppression within the experience of tridimensional racism/sexism/classism.[73] "When Black women say that God is on the side of the oppressed, we mean that God is in solidarity with the struggles of those on the underside of humanity."[74] Grant argues that Jesus as God-incarnate is concerned with the "least of these," and the "least" refers to suffering Black women as those who exist at the "bottom" of the universal social ladder—the Black community, the economically poor, the community of women, and the world community.

To affirm Jesus' solidarity with the "least of the people" is not an exercise in romanticized contentment with one's oppressed status in life. For as the Resurrection signified that there is more to life than the cross for Jesus Christ, for Black women it signifies that their tridimensional oppressive existence is not the end, but it merely represents the context in which a particular people struggle to experience hope and liberation. Jesus Christ thus represents a three-fold significance:

---

[72]Grant, *White Women's Christ, Black Women's Jesus*, 212.

[73]Grant, in line with early womanist thinkers, omits sexuality, which results in a critique by Black queer women of a missing perspective of Black women's liberation. I return to this point in a later section addressing womanist Christological critiques.

[74]Grant, *White Women's Christ, Black Women's Jesus*, 209.

first he identifies with the "little people," Black women, where they are; secondly, he affirms the basic humanity of these, "the least;" and thirdly, he inspires active hope in the struggle for resurrected, liberated existence. . . . Christ among the least must also mean Christ in the community of Black women.[75]

Jesus as divine co-sufferer is concerned about Black women's suffering. Jesus restores the human dignity and worth of Black women by making them "subjects"; thus their suffering matters to his work of salvation. The cross makes real the persecution of the "least" in Jesus's story but does not represent the whole story, particularly as it relates to the Resurrection. The cross is a reminder of Black women's unjust suffering, but also a relic of the Resurrection that the liberation of Black women is possible. Through an active and empowering hope, Black women look to Jesus in their struggles against the burdens of oppression and struggle for liberation.

Grant critiques images of a white, male Jesus that illustrate Christ as only a male savior for white people. For Grant, Jesus's humanity—not his maleness—makes Christ the universal Savior for all humankind. Grant insists,

I would argue, as suggested by both [Jarena] Lee and Sojourner [Truth], that the significance of Christ is not in his maleness, but his humanity. The most significant events of Jesus Christ were the life and ministry, the crucifixion, and the resurrection. The significance of these events, in one sense, is that in them the absolute becomes concrete. God becomes concrete not only in the man Jesus, for he was crucified, but in the lives of those who will accept the challenges of the risen Savior the Christ.[76]

Jesus suffered a poor, lowly status throughout his birth, life, and ministry only to encounter the greater suffering of an unjust death on the cross. The Passion narrative reveals that God became human not only in the embodied Jesus but also in those who represent the risen Christ in the world. Grant affirms Christ as a Savior for all who recognizes the humanity of the "least."

Grant acknowledges that men have used the maleness of Jesus to justify a subordinate status for women in the church, white Christians have used a white Jesus to validate the sin of white supremacy against Black people,

[75]Grant, *White Women's Christ, Black Women's Jesus,* 217.
[76]Grant, *White Women's Christ, Black Women's Jesus,* 220.

and the bourgeoisie have used a royal Jesus to reinforce a subservient social class.[77] The tripartite assaults expose the suffering of Black women and Jesus. Grant refutes feminist Christology/ies that assume Jesus has no salvific import for women because of his male body. Grant aligns with Black liberation theology that Christ is Black in the quest to affirm the least and liberate the oppressed.[78] Grant further articulates that Christ is a Black woman because of Black women's suffering as the "least of the least." The mutual suffering shared between Jesus and Black women marks mutual liberation in Grant's view.[79] Just as the disciples were called as subjects not servants to answer the question Jesus posed—"Who do you say that I am?"—in the Gospel narratives, Black women must also respond to this question and reveal who Christ is to them. Grant confesses, "Black women say that you are the one who is with us and among us in our community struggle for survival. You are the one who is not only with us, but one of us. 'Who do you say that I am?' You are the Christ, the one who affirms us, the one who accompanies us as we move from mere survival to redemptive liberation. 'Who do you say that I am?' You are indeed the Christ."[80] For Grant, Jesus Christ is the "anointed one" who suffers with Black women and enlivens liberation for the "least" of these.

Kelly Brown Douglas the Radical

Kelly Brown Douglas in her first book, *The Black Christ*, provides clear insight as to why a white Christ has no relevance to Black people, especially Black women. Douglas turns to Christology by tracing the roots of a Black Christ from slave Christianity to the 1960s freedom struggle amid the Black Power and civil rights movements. She maintains that the theological claims of social justice in Martin Luther King Jr. and protest in Malcolm X along with the voice of the National Conference of Black Churchmen revealed that "Christ affirmed humanity, but it did not clarify whether Christ was actually Black."[81] The Blackness of Christ became more apparent in the Black theology of liberation among first-generation scholars J. Deotis Roberts,

---

[77]Jacquelyn Grant, " 'Come to My Help Lord for I'm in Trouble': Womanist Jesus and the Mutual Struggle for Liberation," *Journal of Black Theology in South Africa* 8, no. 1 (May 1994): 29.

[78]Grant, *White Women's Christ, Black Women's Jesus*, 216.

[79]Grant, " 'Come to My Help Lord for I'm in Trouble,' " 31.

[80]Jacquelyn Grant, "Subjectification as a Requirement for Christological Construction," in *Lift Every Voice: Constructing Christian Theologies from the Underside*, ed. Susan Thistlethwaite and Mary Potter Engel (Maryknoll, NY: Orbis Books, 1998), 213.

[81]Kelly Brown Douglas, *The Black Christ* (Maryknoll, NY: Orbis Books, 1994), 52.

James Cone, and Albert Cleage. While this trinity affirmed that Christ was Black, each scholar held a unique position as to what made Christ Black and how Christ's Blackness related to liberation and reconciliation. Douglas challenges Black theology's first-generation depiction of the Black Christ on four basic premises:

1. *Lack of self-critique:* How does the Black Christ respond to Black people who have bought into white culture?
2. *One-dimensional:* What does the Black Christ mean to other systems of oppression outside of racism (i.e., sexism, classism, heterosexism, etc.)?
3. *Disconnected from Black churches:* If the Black Christ emerges out of Black faith, why does Black theology fail to speak to the Black Church?
4. *Missing Black women:* So, what does the Black Christ mean for Black women?[82]

Douglas affirms that the Black Christ exists in the faces of Black women and reminds Christians of their responsibility to work toward wholeness:

A womanist Black Christ will consistently lift up the presence of Christ in the faces of the poorest Black women. These women, as an icon of Christ, are important reminders of accountability. Any theology of "survival and liberation/wholeness" that emerges from the Black community must be accountable to the least of these in that community. It is only in a commitment to ensure the life and wholeness for the "least of these" that we can grasp the radicality of who the Black Christ is for all Black people. . . . Christ is not restricted to Black women.[83]

For Grant, Christ is a Black woman, but not exclusively for Douglas. Jesus's life and ministry become central to understanding a Black Christ. "God is as Christ does" in Douglas's construction.[84] "What Jesus did becomes the basis for what it means for him to be Christ."[85] Drawing on the witness of Black women's connection to Jesus and interpretations of the Synoptic Gospels, Douglas asserts, "Womanist theology must articulate that Jesus's signifi-

---

[82]Douglas, *The Black Christ*, 84–92.
[83]Douglas, *The Black Christ*, 108–110.
[84]Kelly Delaine Brown, "God Is as Christ Does: Toward a Womanist Theology," *The Journal of Religious Thought* 46, no. 1 (1989): 7–16.
[85]Douglas, *The Black Christ*, 113.

cance as Christ is tied not to biological characteristics, but to sustaining and liberating activity on behalf of the oppressed. It must emphasize that God's incarnation as Christ does not take the exclusive physical form of the Jewish man from Nazareth. Instead, Christ can be incarnate wherever there is a movement to sustain and liberate oppressed people."[86] It is through the faith of her grandmothers that Douglas articulates a Black Christ that is present in the struggle of Black women particularly and all humanity universally.

In *What's Faith Got to Do with It? Black Bodies/Christian Souls*, Douglas probes the question "What is it about Christianity that allows it to be both a bane and blessing for black people?"[87] Douglas acknowledges that Christianity has played a paradoxical role both in fueling "white racist fury and nurturing Black faith."[88] Douglas attributes Christianity's "implicit and explicit participation in acts of human terror" to three primary assertions: a closed monotheism, a Christological paradox, and a crucifying cross.[89] Douglas interprets the "crucifying cross" at the center of Christianity. Because Jesus Christ is sacrificed on the cross, Douglas argues that a cross aligned with power "creates the possibility for Christians to persecute, indeed sacrifice, designated 'others' with religious impunity. . . . It [the cross] provides a theological anchor for sacrifice as it in fact symbolizes the sacredness of sacrifice, especially for the sexualized terror fostered by a platonized Christian tradition."[90] Douglas is critical of the cross's connection to empire and power since the rule of Constantine.[91]

> With the conversation of Constantine, Christianity moved from being a powerless, sometimes persecuted religion, in the empire, to becoming a powerful, potentially persecuting religion. Constantine's conversion essentially created an indelible link between Christianity and power. This link has not only changed Christianity's social-political status in the Western world, but most significantly it has had a theologically transformative impact on an influential Christian tradition, namely, platonized Christianity. . . . Constantine's conversion signaled to

---

[86]Douglas, "God Is as Christ Does," 16.

[87]Kelly Brown Douglas. *What's Faith Got to Do with It?: Black Bodies/Christian Souls* (Maryknoll, NY: Orbis Books, 2005), xiii.

[88]Douglas, *What's Faith Got to Do with It?*, xiii–5.

[89]Douglas, *What's Faith Got to Do with It?*, 104.

[90]Douglas, *What's Faith Got to Do with It?*, 68.

[91]Douglas and Williams agree that the cross gained increasing significance as a Christian symbol under the rule of Constantine.

Christians that their theological claims were correct: their God was the *one true* God.[92]

Constantine's conversion contributes to the centering of the cross within Christian imagination and the sanctioning of a Christianity that violently sacrifices the powerless. Contrarily for Douglas, Jesus's ministry defies the very idea of Christianity as a religion of the powerful. Christ consistently aligns his ministry with "social outsiders and challenged the very rule of power."[93] It is in the crucifixion that the powerless have "two interrelated Christian theological fundamentals: the *revelatory privilege* of the 'least regarded' and the defining integrity of divine power. . . . Divine revelation comes through those who are rendered powerless. The powerless have 'revelatory privilege' that it is through them that God chooses to make God's self known."[94] While the crucifying cross may be the epicenter of the Christian story, Douglas insists that the cross "does not set Christianity on an inexorable course of tyranny against those who are most powerless in society. Neither does it suggest that the powerless must accept the exploitation of their bodies as a form of redemptive sacrifice."[95]

Douglas argues that the cross contests platonized Christianity and its heretical tradition while simultaneously empowering a Black faith that resists any form of human terror, sacrifice, violence, or victimization. In *Stand Your Ground: Black Bodies and the Justice of God*, Douglas affirms, "The cross is at the center of Black faith."[96] Crucifixion in the first-century Roman world was the punishment for people "held in the highest contempt and with lowest regard in society."[97] Jesus's crucifixion signals a suffering solidarity between Jesus and the powerless. If the cross is the lynching tree as described by Cone,[98] then Black people are a lynched people who are denied the privileges to contest the ruling powers of this day. Contemporarily, Douglas sees the crucified Jesus in the faces of "the Trayvons, the Jordans, the Renishas, the Jonathans, and all the other victims of the stand-your-ground

---

[92]Douglas, *What's Faith Got to Do with It?*, 41.

[93]Douglas, *What's Faith Got to Do with It?*, 82, 86.

[94]Douglas, *What's Faith Got to Do with It?*, 96, 97.

[95]Douglas, *What's Faith Got to Do with It?*, 99.

[96]Douglas, *Stand Your Ground,* 172.

[97]Kelly Brown Douglas, "Crucifixion, Resurrection, and the Reversal of Power," *Feminism and Religion,* April 15, 2014, https://feminismandreligion.com/2014/04/15/crucifixion-resurrection-and-the-reversal-of-power-by-kelly-brown-douglas/.

[98]See James H. Cone, *The Cross and the Lynching Tree* (Maryknoll, NY: Orbis Books, 2011).

culture war."⁹⁹ The cross symbolizes an apparatus of evil, a crucifying power. Jesus was a threat to the powerful, so they crucified him. Here, the cross also signals Jesus's liberating power because even on the cross Jesus does not "condemn the crucifying crowd."¹⁰⁰ While the evil powers presumed that they prevailed in Jesus's death on the cross, the Resurrection reveals that neither death nor evil has the last word. Douglas contends,

> The resurrection is God's definitive victory over crucifying powers of evil. Ironically, the power that attempts to destroy Jesus on the cross is actually itself destroyed by the cross. The cross represents the power that denigrates human bodies, destroys life, and preys on the most vulnerable in society. As the cross is defeated, so too is that power. The impressive factor is how it is defeated. It is defeated by a life-giving rather than a life-negating force.¹⁰¹

For Jesus and the Trayvons, the Jordans, the Renishas, and the Jonathans, the Resurrection "will not allow the final verdict on a person's life to be a crucifying verdict."¹⁰² Douglas interprets the crucifixion-Resurrection event together as an "ultimate reversal of power" that bears witness to God's life-giving power of "the crucified being restored to life."¹⁰³

Delores Seneva Williams the Rejectionist

Delores S. Williams constructs another and perhaps more challenging perspective of the cross in relation to Black women. Williams names the social role of surrogacy as a source of oppression affecting Black women uniquely, which "raises challenging questions about the way redemption is imaged in the Christian context."¹⁰⁴ Williams understands Black women's burden of surrogacy in two ways: coerced and voluntary. The coerced surrogacy of the antebellum period "was a forced condition in which people and systems more powerful than black women and black people forced

⁹⁹Douglas, *Stand Your Ground*, 174.
¹⁰⁰Douglas, "Crucifixion, Resurrection, and the Reversal of Power," 1.
¹⁰¹Douglas, *Stand Your Ground*, 182.
¹⁰²Douglas, *Stand Your Ground*, 192.
¹⁰³Douglas, "Crucifixion, Resurrection, and the Reversal of Power," 2.
¹⁰⁴Delores S. Williams, "Black Women's Surrogacy Experience and the Christian Notions of Redemption," in *After Patriarchy: Feminist Transformations of the World's Religions*, ed. Paula Cooey, William Eakin, and Jay MacDaniel (Maryknoll, NY: Orbis Books, 1993), 1.

black women to function in roles that ordinarily would have been filled by someone else."[105] Williams traces numerous examples of coerced surrogacy ranging from Black women threatened by rape to substitute as the slaveholder's wife and satisfy slaveholders' sexual pleasures to Black women strong-armed to fulfill men's work in plantation labor and women's work in the "master's house" and slave quarters. In the antebellum period, surrogacy was legally sanctioned and Black women could not refuse the surrogacy role.[106] Au contraire, Williams describes voluntary surrogacy in a postemancipation era where Black women "could exercise choice in refusing the surrogate role."[107] Williams is clear that "social and economic realities limited Black women's power to choose full exemption from all surrogacy roles."[108] Black domestic workers in the South and North during the Great Migration provide a window into the voluntary surrogacy of women who chose to work in white homes or hotels but often because Black women had few to no employment options available to them. Choosing domestic work also meant that Black women were required to work longer hours for less pay and sustain greater injuries than poor white and immigrant women who also worked in the service industry.

Williams identifies the Mammy as an image of the oppressive role of surrogacy. Mammies represent the ultimate surrogates, as women who substituted nurturing roles for white families and reinforced patriarchy in the Black community. In line with Giddings as identified in an earlier section, the Mammy held some power but did not use this power to liberate her community. Williams makes the connection between the enslaved Mammy who fortifies slaveocracy by force and the Church Mother who accepts the surrogate role in the Black community's largest social institution, the Black Church. "Like the slave mammy, the mother of the church exerts considerable authority in the church family. But more often than not she uses her power in a way that does not challenge the power and authority of the patriarchal head of the church, usually a male preacher."[109] In Williams's view, the Church Mother assumes the tasks of nurturing the community and caring for God's children but in no way shifts the status quo.[110]

Williams invites womanist theologians to reconsider traditional redemp-

---

[105]Williams, "Black Women's Surrogacy Experience," 1.
[106]Williams, "Black Women's Surrogacy Experience," 2.
[107]Williams, "Black Women's Surrogacy Experience," 2.
[108]Williams, "Black Women's Surrogacy Experience," 6.
[109]Williams, *Sisters in the Wilderness*, 92.
[110]Williams, *Sisters in the Wilderness*, 92.

tion and atonement theories in both classical interpretations and the Black Church tradition regarding surrogacy in the Black women's experience. Williams argues,

> More often than not the theology in mainline Christian churches, including black ones, teaches believers sinful humankind has been redeemed because Jesus died on the cross in the place of humans, thereby taking human sin upon himself. In this sense, Jesus represents the ultimate surrogate figure standing in the place of someone else: sinful humankind. Surrogacy, attached to this divine personage, thus takes on an aura of the sacred. It is therefore altogether fitting and proper for black women to ask whether this image of redemption supports and reinforces the exploitation that has accompanied their experience with surrogacy. If black women accept this image of redemption, can they not also passively accept the exploitation surrogacy brings?[111]

Was Jesus forced to die? Did Jesus choose to be crucified? Was Jesus's death on the cross an act of coerced or voluntary surrogacy? Williams resists Christian atonement theories that maintain Jesus died for the sake of sinners. If Jesus is interpreted as the substitute for sin on the cross, then surrogacy becomes a divine rather than an oppressive act. In this sense, Jesus as the ultimate surrogate on the cross ordains the surrogacy of Black women. Williams calls for new images of redemption beyond the cross because of Black women's experiences of surrogacy.

Williams turns to the life and ministry of Jesus Christ to critically engage redemption rather than Jesus's crucified death. Given the accounts in the Synoptics, namely Luke 4 when Jesus announces his social vision, Williams affirms that the "Spirit of God in Jesus came to show humans life—to show redemption through a perfect ministerial vision of righting relationships."[112] Jesus's action and interaction with social outcasts, healing the sick, feeding the hungry, and unsettling the status quo says more about redemption than a single event of death in the cross. Similarly, Williams critiques male Black liberationists' framing the story of the Black community within the single exodus event of liberation. Liberation from slavery with the Emancipation Proclamation in 1863 symbolizes only the short run for Black people. The journey to freedom and continuing march for human dignity in America

---

[111] Williams, "Black Women's Surrogacy Experience," 9.
[112] Williams, "Black Women's Surrogacy Experience," 11.

locate Black people in the wilderness as they struggle to survive. Through the narrative of Hagar in Genesis 16 and 21 and female tradition of survival/quality of life, Williams raises the "wilderness" as a more accurate depiction of the severity of struggle for the Black community. Jesus overcoming the sin of temptation in the wilderness and defying the powers of coercion illustrate that "Jesus therefore conquered sin in life and not in death."[113] Moreover, the Resurrection, for Williams, "does not depend on the cross for life, for the cross only represents historical evil trying to defeat good."[114]

Williams rejects the glorification of the cross as a symbol of sanctioned violence because of Black women's surrogacy. Williams professes,

> Humankind is therefore redeemed in Jesus' life and not Jesus' death. There is nothing of God in the blood of the cross. God does not intend black women's surrogacy experience. Neither can Christian faith affirm such an idea. Jesus did not come to be a surrogate. Jesus came for life, to show humans a perfect ministerial vision that humans had forgotten long ago. However, as Christians, black women cannot forget the cross. But neither can they glorify it. To do so is to make their exploitation sacred. To do so is to glorify sin.[115]

Williams later stresses that her rejection of the cross rests in this conviction:

> Though Jesus' death is interpreted to have achieved the common good of delivering humankind from sin, it remains a violent act of murder. Every time we see a cross or crucifix, we are reminded of this murder. . . . There are no images more important to the church than the cross and the crucifix—and there are no more images more shrouded in violence.[116]

Williams belies redemption in the cross to avoid validating Black women's suffering by surrogacy and to move womanist Christology away from the death and toward the life and ministry of Jesus Christ.

---

[113]Williams, "Black Women's Surrogacy Experience," 12.

[114]Williams, "Black Women's Surrogacy Experience," 11.

[115]Williams, "Black Women's Surrogacy Experience," 12–13.

[116]Delores Williams, "A Crucifixion Double Cross?," *The Other Side* (September–October 1993): 25–26.

JoAnne Marie Terrell the Re-visionist

JoAnne Marie Terrell recenters the cross in womanist Christology as it relates to African American community in her seminal work, *Power in the Blood? The Cross in the African American Experience*. More than twenty years since the publication of her full-length volume, it is still true that Terrell has performed the most comprehensive womanist analysis of the cross, especially in comparison with the above theologians and maybe even the larger majority of Black liberation theologians. Terrell seeks to explore the profundity of the cross that makes it central to the Christian faith. She picks up the discussion of the cross in conversation with Black women's experiences by acknowledging the voices of Jacquelyn Grant, Kelly Brown Douglas, and Delores Williams that precede her. Terrell agrees with Williams that it is important to proclaim "that God did not condone the violence of the cross or black women's surrogacy; nor yet does God condone this present state of affairs. But in fairness to the story, Jesus's story, Williams should allow for its multiple impact and import in its own context, for its own day."[117] Something significant about the story of Jesus and the cross parallels the experiences of Black women.

Terrell seeks to rethink atonement as "at-one-ment" in light of what God sent Jesus to do. Whereas previous womanist thinkers turn to the Synoptic Gospels to interpret Jesus's life and ministry, Terrell turns to the Fourth Gospel and the Johannine community to counter Greek mythological beliefs that humans were created to suffer. John 3:16–17, the most celebrated passage in the Christian tradition, is a starting point for Terrell because God's intentions remain honorable to share God's love through the sending of Jesus. The Gospel writer records, "For God so *loved* the world that he gave his only Son, so that everyone who believes in him may not perish but may have eternal life. Indeed, God did not send the Son into the world to condemn the world, but in order that the world might be saved through him." Terrell claims in line with the Aaronic priesthood and the Hebrew writer that "God desires mercy and not sacrifice," thus, "Yahweh's institution of the sacrificial system and Jesus' self-sacrifice are thus construed as disclosure of God's mercy."[118] Moreover, "the belief that God, in Christ, shed God's own blood elevates the meaning of the *once for all* nature in Christ

---

[117]JoAnne Terrell. *Power in the Blood?: The Cross in the African American Experience* (Maryknoll, NY: Orbis Books, 1998), 121.

[118]Terrell, *Power in the Blood?*, 124.

Jesus' death. The divine-human dynamic in the story signifies that there is *something* of God in the blood of the cross."[119] Terrell affirms that there is significance in Jesus's death and perhaps even divine power in the blood of Jesus. In direct contrast to Williams, Terrell argues,

> Thus, the cross is about God's love for humankind in a profound sense. I believe that Christians need to ponder the implications of Christ's death continuously, because the drama testifies to the exceedingly great lengths to which God goes to advise the extent of human estrangement. It is no slight on the intelligence of black women when they confess this; rather, it reflects on what they say they need and what they say Christ's real presence, mediated through the gospel, provides—redemption and release from the self-alienation and social alienation they experience in their workaday lives.[120]

The cross is significant to Black people because they have endured unjust suffering like Jesus and the early church martyrs.[121] Jesus's death on the cross teaches about the giving of God's own self once for all to show God's undying love for a suffering humanity. There is indeed power in the blood as it reveals a life force.

The symbol of an empty cross is both a marker that Christ suffers with the suffering and a sign of Resurrection that "transfiguration happens."[122] Terrell asserts, "The crucifix is a supreme reminder of God's with-us-ness (that is, of God's decision to be at-one with us; or better said of the fact that we are already at-one). The empty cross is a symbol of God's continuous empowerment."[123] Terrell's womanist Christology is enhanced not just by Black women's experiences in general but by her own life experience—in particular, witnessing traumatic violence firsthand with the death of her mother killed by her lover. Terrell connects the blood of her mother in a violent death with the blood of Jesus on the cross. While Terrell critiques the hermeneutics of sacrifice, her mother's bloody death bears "salvific

---

[119]Terrell, *Power in the Blood?*, 124.

[120]Terrell, *Power in the Blood?*, 124–25.

[121]Joanne Marie Terrell, "Our Mothers' Gardens: Discrete Sources of Reflection on the Cross in Womanist Christology," in *I Found God in Me: A Womanist Biblical Hermeneutics Reader*, ed. Mitzi J. Smith (Eugene, OR: Cascade Books, 2015), 54.

[122]Joanne Terrell, "Transfiguration Happens," lecture presented at All Saints Church, Pasadena, CA, February 9, 2008.

[123]Terrell, *Power in the Blood?*, 125.

significance" in a "transformed, *sacramental* notion of sacrifice" that means something for the living just as Jesus's death means something for Black women.[124] For Terrell, "Jesus' own life and *sacramental* example of affirming the intrinsic worth of women enable humankind to see women's blood as sacred."[125] Terrell's dialogue about the cross is essential to engage not only Black women but the suffering of all humanity.

Womanist Christological Crosswise: Critiques and Convergences

Two primary crossways address points of both convergence and critique among the four womanist theologians addressing Black women: suffering and salvation. All four womanist theologians maintain interest in clarifying their claims in relation to Black women's experiences of oppression. In efforts to critique feminists who perpetuate a dominant experience of women through a white racialized lens, Jacquelyn Grant focuses her position on the tripartite oppression of racism, sexism, and classism to identify Black women's historical experiences. Unfortunately, Grant's articulation of such a trio leaves out Black queer women confronting the sins of homophobia and heterosexism. This remains a standing critique of Christian womanist foundational voices by womanist lesbian Renee Hill and, more recently, a growing community of womanist queer theologians. Kelly Brown Douglas corrects Grant's position by naming Black women's oppression as "multi-dimensional," which attends to the forces of oppression on multiple fronts and their intersecting identities.[126] Delores Williams takes a different path to modifying Grant and maybe even Douglas's proposals by suggesting that the unique experience of oppression of Black women—held by no other group of women to this degree—is surrogacy. Terrell grounds Black women's experience of oppression in the concrete social reality of Black women's blood traumas through HIV/AIDS and a personal account of her mother's awful death by domestic violence. These four expressions make clear that Black women's experiences are far from static, with multiple points of entry to discern the nature of their suffering.

All four women also seek to refine God-talk about Jesus Christ that interrogates and rethinks traditional atonement theories. Grant's affirmation of Christ as the "divine co-sufferer" reforms the notion that Black

---

[124]Terrell, "Our Mothers' Gardens," 53.
[125]Terrell, "Our Mothers' Gardens," 55.
[126]Douglas, "God Is as Christ Does," 8.

women's suffering is a result of their sin, but rather that the sin done to Black women resembles the sin done to Jesus. Christ is a Black woman because Jesus remains in solidarity with Black women and their suffering. Douglas radically admonishes traditional atonement theories as unfit for a womanist Christology because of their disregard for the body and the incarnation. She writes,

> Jesus as the incarnate One, both ontologically and existentially, reveals a sacred regard for the flesh. In this respect, any divine sanction of the crucifixion would contravene this central aspect of the incarnation. And so what we find is that the reality of the incarnation suggests not divine warrant but divine opposition to Jesus' crucifixion. To repeat, for God to affirm in any way the crucifixion of Jesus would set God against God's very self both in terms of God's incarnate presence in human history and ultimate reign over human history. Atonement theories that suggest that God in some way enjoined the crucifixion of Jesus for salvific purposes are therefore at best christologically misguided and at worst Christological heresies.[127]

God's power, for Douglas, refutes the crucifying power of Jesus; God does not sanction Jesus's crucifixion. Williams follows a rejectionist approach by assessing atonement through Black women's experience of surrogacy. Thus, Williams decenters the cross as an affirming symbol, but presents it as a recurrent image of death. Terrell offers a re-visionist insight to Williams's claims that rightly disavow the violence of the cross and further proposes evidence of God's love in the whole story of Jesus—incarnation, birth, life, ministry, death, and continuous intercession through the Holy Spirit—and empowerment in an empty cross. Again, these four womanist theologians exhibit a shared interest in rethinking Jesus's death and crucifixion but formulate their positions uniquely. The four models remain encouraging for the womanist theological enterprise because they showcase womanist scholars who are willing to pursue theological questions in relation to Black women from multiple angles and venture into unbounded terrain. While their positions refine each other, they converge in such a way to offer a glimpse of a steady move in a forward direction for womanist Christology.

---

[127]Douglas, *What's Faith Got to Do with It?*, 89.

Contemporary Considerations

Leading and emerging womanist theologians must return to the four womanist pioneers/pillars (Grant, Douglas, Williams, and Terrell) to articulate theologies of the cross for today's Black women.[128]

On the matter of Black women's burden of strength, which is underexplored by the four thinkers just reviewed, Chanequa Walker-Barnes aptly critiques the call to discipleship as an invitation for Black women to bear the weight of the cross as Jesus did in their quest for personal and communal salvation. In *Too Heavy a Yoke: Black Women and the Burden of Strength*, Walker-Barnes argues,

> Many StrongBlackWomen have carried their cross—and those of others—so long without support that they have crossed the fine line from discipleship to martyrdom. ... As an extension of the salvific wish, the ideology of the StrongBlackWoman imprisons women in an endless cycle in which they must continually prove their self-worth through the unholy trinity of self-denial, suffering and silence. Add to this weighty, and frequently engendered, Christian admonition to take up one's cross and the StrongBlackWoman becomes the modern sacrificial lamb with her service and suffering offered up as atonement for her gender and her race. Her martyrdom, coded in the language of "strength," is to be undertaken again and again, with only the promise of a long-distant resurrection in the hereafter.[129]

Walker-Barnes rightly criticizes as virtuous Black women's efforts to save communities and churches that lead to pathologies of self-denial. I disavow Christian discipleship that empowers Black women to "take up crosses" to follow Jesus. Black women are already burdened by suffering and do not need to choose crosses to be redeemed. God does not desire Black women's sacrifice, surrogacy, or strength to save the world. Jesus suffered the cross so that Black women do not have to. Black women can find hope in a God that says, "Come to me, all you that are weary and are carrying heavy burdens, and I will give you rest. Take my yoke upon you, and learn from me; for I am gentle and humble in heart, and you will find rest for your souls. For

---

[128]Womanist theologians Karen Baker-Fletcher and M. Shawn Copeland construct meaningful Christological positions concerning Black women that are discussed in other parts of the book.

[129]Walker-Barnes, *Too Heavy a Yoke*, 144.

my yoke is easy, and my burden is light" (Mt 11:28–29). This is a God who lifts heavy burdens and releases yokes of oppression.

No More Suffering and the Empty Cross

My interest in the symbolism of the cross and what it means for Black women to remain near the cross is illuminated by the voices of Jacquelyn Grant, Kelly Brown Douglas, Delores Williams, and JoAnne Terrell. I turn to these four theologians to support an inquiry in personal anamnesis that links my grandmother's story to the suffering of Black women through domestic service and subordination in the Black Church. With the help of this quartet and contemporary voices, womanist Christology helps me to think theologically about what the cross means in relation to the experience of my Black grandmother and rethink "at-one-ment." Hymnody provides Christians with ways, both useful and useless, for expressing faith. Though I have sung for many years with deep conviction Fanny Crosby's "Jesus Keep Me Near the Cross," it has taken the story of a Black woman whom I hold dear to articulate what "near the cross" means for the suffering.

> Jesus, keep me near the cross,
> There a precious fountain
> Free to all, a healing stream
> Flows from Calvary's mountain.[130]

Black women remaining near the cross reaffirms Grant's articulation of a divine co-sufferer. For women who were the "least of these" to be near the cross, as recorded in the Gospel writings, indicates that Jesus's most faithful followers suffered death with him in the tormenting moments on the cross and that Jesus suffers with the women on the underside in their crucifixion moments. Grant's image of a divine co-sufferer reveals that Jesus does not ordain servitude or subordination. Jesus shares in the troubles of Black women because Jesus also faced subordination in life. The call to discipleship to follow Jesus is not a duty-bound lot to suffering, but a path to salvation that seeks to release the burdens of the least. I believe that Jesus suffered with my grandmother. She lived below the poverty line, but her cupboard remained full. She raised two children alone as a single

---

[130]Frances Crosby, "Jesus, Keep Me Near the Cross" (1869).

mother, but she acknowledged that Jesus walked with her every step of the way. She suffered the loss of her firstborn, but she maintained hope in the Christian promise that she would see her child again. It was not the sins she committed that explain her suffering, but the sin done to her that caused her suffering. Her body near the cross symbolizes that Jesus is with her and she is with the Christ.

> Near the cross, a trembling soul,
> Love and mercy found me;
> There the bright and morning star
> Sheds its beams around me.[131]

Black women remaining near the cross is the recognition of Douglas's Black Christ that Christ can be seen in their faces. Though the cross symbol may be colluded with imperial and coercive power, Jesus's life and ministry prove that his crucifixion held deep regard for the flesh of the powerless. Like Douglas, I interpret the crucifixion alongside the Resurrection for Black women. My grandmother died, but the whole of the story is that she was transformed. She joins the assembly of women witnesses to the Resurrection. While she suffered many crosses, her story and her work speak in a way that denies a crucifying verdict but restores her to life. I believe Jesus cared for my grandmother's slumped-over body, which was battered and broken with pain. Though her legs were tired, she found enough courage to bend her knees in order to pray daily with divine power against her oppressive powers. Her body near the cross demonstrates Christ's everlasting care for her "black and blues-colored flesh."[132]

> Near the cross! O Lamb of God,
> Bring its scenes before me;
> Help me walk from day to day,
> With its shadows o'er me.[133]

Black women remaining near the cross is the reevaluation of Williams's dismissal of the cross in light of Black women's surrogacy oppression. Like Williams, I agree that the violent death of Jesus is made visible by the

---

[131]Crosby, "Jesus, Keep Me Near the Cross."

[132]See Kelly Brown Douglas, *Black Bodies and the Black Church: A Blues Slant* (New York: Palgrave Macmillan, 2012).

[133]Crosby, "Jesus, Keep Me Near the Cross."

cross. God does not ordain Black women's surrogacy, nor does God require surrogacy as a mark of faithfulness. In simple terms, Black women do not need to be surrogates to be faithful to God. The cross is one entry point, but more images are necessary to speak of salvation and redemption for Black women, which is why this book turns in later chapters to the story of the bent woman in Luke 13 as a vision of liberation on the journey to the cross. Yet there is something about the cross that cannot be rejected for Black women. The reminder that the cross reflects real violence has another side that remembers real liberation. I believe my grandmother suffered surrogacy oppression. Whether coerced or voluntary, she nurtured white families with domestic hospitality and attended to the rooms of elite Hyatt hotel guests. She embraced surrogate mothering, as the Church Mother, for women and men who had lost mothers or gone astray. Her redemption rested in her ability to transition from taking care of other people's homes to opening her home for all who would gather for a "soul cooked" meal. Though the image of the cross may denote violence, at the opposite end of that same cross my grandmother found a mark of redemption. Her transformed body near the cross affirms that voluntary surrogacy would not save her; only Jesus could.

> Near the cross I'll watch and wait
> Hoping, trusting ever,
> Till I reach the golden strand,
> Just beyond the river.[134]

Black women remaining near the cross is the re-visioning of Terrell's illustration of God's love as recorded in John 3:16–17. The cross remaining near Black women is an indicator that God is "with-us-ness." The cross is a marker of hope that Resurrection is awaiting and "transfiguration happens" in Christ Jesus. I align with Terrell that the cross does not sanction Black women's burden of sacrifice. There is meaning in death if it brings our theological inquiry and learning back to life. The salvific significance of Jesus's death realizes the salvific significance of Terrell's mother and my grandmother. Re-visioning the cross as a reminder of God's love is also the revivification of God's deepest intentions for humanity regardless of evil. I believe that she cherished the love of God so much that her heart grew larger by the moment. An enlarged heart was the medical diagnosis for

---

[134]Crosby, "Jesus, Keep Me Near the Cross."

her demise, similar to God's overwhelming love that shed blood in Jesus's death. Though her heart bled in her final moments of life, transfiguration was happening. I cannot imagine any other image but the cross to lift my grandmother up to Christ Jesus from all four ends of the Earth.

In conclusion, the cross is the paramount symbol of the Christian tradition. Even so, there is much to articulate about the cross and its eerie correlation with human terror and violence. The cross harbors a double-ended narrative within the Christian story as the symbol for Jesus's violent death and a scene wherein Christ's liberation manifests. The cross is not just about death; it is also about resurrected life. A certain mystical tone emerges when framing the cross in relation to Jesus's crucifixion and Black women's suffering. As I reconsider what the cross signifies on the four edges of my grandmother's grave, I am grateful that her remains lie near the cross as I sing with the heavenly chorus.

> In the cross, in the cross,
> Be my glory ever;
> Till my raptured soul shall find
> Rest beyond the river.[135]

---

[135]Crosby, "Jesus, Keep Me Near the Cross."

3

Our Saviors Are Ourselves,
Part One

The Burden to Save Democracy

You white women speak here of rights. I speak of wrongs.
—Frances Ellen Watkins Harper[1]

Nobody is free, until everybody is free.
—Fannie Lou Hamer[2]

The litmus test for America is how we treat Black women.
—Vice President Kamala Harris[3]

---

[1] This quote is a famous saying of political rhetorician Frances Ellen Watkins Harper delivered in her speech "We Are All Bound Up Together" to the suffragists at the Eleventh National Woman's Rights Convention in 1866. See Frances Ellen Watkins Harper, "We Are All Bound Up Together—May 1866," in *Proceedings of the Eleventh National Woman's Rights Convention*, ed. Robert J. Johnston (New York, 1866), 46–48.

[2] This quote is the title of a speech that Mississippi Freedom activist Fannie Lou Hamer delivered to the 1971 Women's National Caucus in Washington, DC. The speech illustrated that the country needed a greater focus for the liberation of all people. "Now, we've got to have some changes in this country. And not only changes for the black man, and not only changes for the black woman, but the changes we have to have in this country are going to be for liberation of all people—because nobody's free until everybody's free." See Fannie Lou Hamer, *The Speeches of Fannie Lou Hamer: To Tell It Like It Is*, ed. Maegan Parker Brooks and Davis W. Houck (Jackson: University Press of Mississippi, 2011), 136.

[3] A message delivered by then-senator Kamala Harris at the 2020 Democratic National Convention in a promotional video before her historic acceptance of the Democratic nomination for vice president of the United States. See Jacqueline Alemany, "Power Up: Harris Makes—and Embraces—History," *Washington Post*, August 20, 2020, https://www.washingtonpost.com/politics/2020/08/20/power-up-harris-makes-embraces-history/.

As a poor, Black, divorced domestic living on the South Side of Chicago with two growing children, Gertrude had no means to own a home in the 1960s, '70s, '80s, or '90s. She moved from apartment to apartment, looking for a place to call her own in the middle of Chicago's housing crisis.[4] Through determination, she managed to stay out of Chicago's housing projects, known to many simply as "the projects," referencing New Deal experiments[5] gone wrong that resulted in the Chicago slums for mostly poor, Black, female-headed families in the late twentieth century.[6] However, this meant that she was responsible for negotiating better living conditions on her own without the support of a tenants' group or the intervention of the Chicago Housing Authority (CHA). She paid her rent timely and expected to receive the benefits of her status as a responsible tenant with decent living conditions, adequate repairs, and proper heating, cooling, and plumbing. On several occasions, Gertrude issued requests for necessary work to be done to make the conditions of her residence livable that resulted in no movement or action by the building's superintendent or landlord. The burden of fixing a broken home was left to her. When she exhausted all her means, she stopped paying the rent, which landed her in civil court, arguing her case before a legal system that her basic housing rights had been denied. There were some small victories, but most times judges ruled against her. She was displaced, alone to survive in the wilderness, and cast out yet again in search for another place to land.

---

[4] One marker of full citizenship in America is homeownership. In "The Case for Reparations," Black journalist and essayist Ta-Nehisi Coates narrates the story of the Chicago housing crisis for Black Americans who migrated from the South to Chicago in the mid-twentieth century. Coates argues that the economic situation between Blacks and whites even in neighborhoods with close proximity were "ecologically distinct," pointing to extreme poverty, unemployment, and single-headed female households in Chicago's Black neighborhoods for decades. See Ta-Nehisi Coates, "The Case for Reparations," *The Atlantic*, May 22, 2014, https://www.theatlantic.com/magazine/archive/2014/06/the-case-for-reparations/361631/.

[5] The New Deal represented a series of social programs and industry reforms initiated by President Franklin D. Roosevelt during the Great Depression in the 1930s. The goal of the programs was to restore the economic well-being of American citizens by establishing a government-related economy. The Second New Deal, instituted in 1935, worked to establish relief and recovery for workers and urban communities. Unfortunately, many of these efforts were unsuccessful as the Great Depression worsened, leaving American industry unable to recover until the beginning of World War II in 1941. One of the challenges of the New Deal was a failure to contest structural injustices, which often resulted in greater devastation for marginalized populations. Some New Deal experiments still exist today, including Social Security, welfare, unemployment, and other governmental subsidies.

[6] See D. Bradford Hunt, *Blueprint for Disaster: The Unraveling of Chicago Public Housing*, Historical Studies of Urban America (Chicago: University of Chicago Press, 2009).

My grandmother's story illuminates the crookedness of Black women's relationship to America, "the land of the free and the home of the brave," that denies citizenship recognition while simultaneously looking to Black women to bear the burden of its moral repair. Womanist progenitor and ethicist Katie Geneva Cannon was the first to identify Black women as the "oppressed of the oppressed," representing the "most vulnerable and the most exploited members of the American society" in the struggle against white hypocrisy, and the struggle for justice, human dignity, and survival. Cannon interprets the Black woman's moral situation in this way: "The Black woman began her life of freedom with no vote, no protection, and no equity of any sort. Black women, young and old, were basically on their own."[7] It should be no surprise that early attempts to guarantee suffrage regardless of race or sex in the American Equal Rights Association (AERA) and the subsequent formations to enact women's suffrage of the National Woman Suffrage Association (NWSA) and American Woman Suffrage Association (AWSA) during the Reconstruction era left Black women out of the equation.[8] "I will cut off this right arm of mine before I will ever work or demand the ballot for the Negro and not the woman," white suffragist Susan B. Anthony confessed at an 1866 meeting of the AERA. Some white suffragists vehemently disagreed with Black men receiving the right to vote with the ratification of the Fifteenth Amendment in 1869, which split their efforts between the NWSA and AWSA in the quest for the right to vote and sidelined Black women. In a world where all the women are white and all the Blacks are men, Black women's century-long struggle to win the vote and

---

[7] Katie Geneva Cannon, *Katie's Canon: Womanism and the Soul of the Black Community* (New York: Continuum, 1995), 51.

[8] The American Equal Rights Association (AERA) was founded in 1866 at the Eleventh National Woman's Rights Convention with the goal to seek equal rights for all Americans regardless of race, color, or sex. Suffrage was at the top of the AERA's agenda gathering participation from Black men like Frederick Douglass and white women suffragists Elizabeth Cady Stanton and Susan B. Anthony. Following the passing of the Fifteenth Amendment by Congress on February 18, 1869, granting Black men the right to vote during Reconstruction, some white women suffragists incensed by the advancement of Black men split from AERA to form the National Woman's Suffrage Association (NWSA) to shift the women's vote to the top of the agenda. The question of race also divided white suffragist women, as those who were in favor of Black men voting formed the American Woman Suffrage Association (AWSA) following the dissolution of AERA in 1869, which also became the rival organization to NWSA. The NWSA focused on a constitutional amendment to win the vote for women; the AWSA pursued a state legislature approach to win the vote. While some Black women suffragists participated in the AERA, NWSA, or AWSA, the matter of Black women's vote was missing from these discussions and not at the table.

fight for fair citizenship illuminates an undying moral fervor to break significant barriers to realize equality not just for themselves but for all people.

America reawakened to the power of Black women's voice and vote in December 2017 with the Alabama Senate election to fill a vacant seat following the appointment of then-senator Jeff Sessions (R) to be the attorney general in the Trump administration. Ninety-eight percent of Black women voted for Democrat Doug Jones, a fact that shifted the political landscape and ensured that Republican Roy Moore (former chief justice accused of making sexual advances on teenage girls) was not *rewarded* with a congressional seat.[9] News reports, late-night TV shows, comedies, op-ed think pieces, and countless tweets following the election night results quickly surfaced announcing Black women "saved America."[10] The question of salvation is particularly relevant for Black women in the United States who are bound by the presumption of surrogacy and the image of their agency as domestics in this nation and repeatedly called to serve as the "cleanup crew" to save America from itself through voice and vote.

A womanist reckoning with Black women's virtues of redemption on behalf of ourselves and our communities traces such heritage through generations, as attested to in Alice Walker's exchange from mother to daughter in the second instance of the definition of "womanist": "Mama, I'm walking to Canada and taking you and a bunch of other slaves with me. Her response: 'It wouldn't be the first time.'"[11] From Harriet Tubman to Coretta Scott King to Alabama grassroots political activists DeJuana Thompson and Adrianne Shropshire to Stacey Abrams to Kamala Harris, Black women "redeeming

[9]"Alabama Exit Poll and Results for 2017 Election," NBC News, January 30, 2018, https://www.nbcnews.com/politics/2017-election/AL.

[10]See Brittney Cooper, "Stop Asking Black Women to 'Save America.' Start Organizing Your Own People," *Washington Post*, December 15, 2017, https://www.washingtonpost.com/news/posteverything/wp/2017/12/15/stop-asking-black-women-to-save-america-start-organizing-your-own-people/; Kyle Swenson, "'We Didn't Do It for You': Black Women Sound Off on 'Saving America' from Roy Moore," *Washington Post*, December 14, 2017, https://www.washingtonpost.com/news/morning-mix/wp/2017/12/14/we-didnt-do-it-for-you-black-women-sound-off-on-saving-america-from-roy-moore/; Charlene White, "In Alabama, Black Women Saved America from Itself—as They've Always Tried to Do," *The Guardian*, December 14, 2017, http://www.theguardian.com/commentisfree/2017/dec/14/alabama-black-women-saved-america-roy-moore; Blavity Team, "21 Must-Read Tweets about the Black Voters Who Helped to Elect Doug Jones," Blavity News & Politics, December 13, 2017, https://blavity.com/21-must-read-tweets-about-the-black-voters-who-helped-to-elect-doug-jones.

[11]Alice Walker, *In Search of Our Mothers' Gardens: Womanist Prose* (Orlando: Mariner Books, 2003), 4.

the soul of America" is not a new phenomenon. The relevant question in a contemporary era is, "Who or what will save Black women from oppressive tropes and traditions that mischaracterize our moral agency?"

The salvation of Black women is double-sided, forcing Black women to contend with forces of political and spiritual oppression. This chapter, part one in the consideration of the salvific role of Black women, takes up the politics of redemption for Black women in the fight for fair citizenship in America. First, it recollects the persistent and prophetic witness of Coretta Scott King, who contested voter suppression as a precursor to the 2017 suffrage activism of Black women in Alabama. Second, the chapter questions whether there is undue expectation for Black women to be the bearers of political redemption, as in the cases of the political efforts of Stacey Abrams in the Georgia elections as well as the ascension of Kamala Harris to the vice presidency, the second-highest office in the nation. Third, through the work of political scientist Melissa Harris-Perry, the chapter unveils Black women's *bendedness* in America's crooked room and their enduring quest for recognition. The next chapter, part two, engages the "divided mind of the Black Church,"[12] which replicates the political disenfranchisement of Black women in America, leaving Black women clergy and congregants to also carry the weight of its failed promise of freedom and salvation.

"Nevertheless, She Persisted": Remembering Coretta Scott King and the Bloody March to Black Suffrage in Alabama

On April 4, 1968, the assassination of a thirty-nine-year-old dreamer, Martin Luther King Jr., at the hand of white supremacist rage marked the emergence of a persistent Black widow to the national scene by the name of Coretta Scott King. A native of Alabama, an educated woman, a gifted singer and violinist, an activist born to a family committed to resistance because of the burning of their lumber mill by white neighbors,[13] Coretta Scott King's legacy of global peace and social justice began early, as she joined the National Association for the Advancement of Colored People (NAACP)[14] and the Race Relations and Civil Liberties Committees while

---

[12]See Raphael G. Warnock, *The Divided Mind of the Black Church: Theology, Piety, and Public Witness* (New York: NYU Press, 2020).

[13]See Coretta Scott King and Barbara A. Reynolds, *My Life, My Love, My Legacy* (New York: Henry Holt and Company, 2017).

[14]Founded in February 1909 as an interracial endeavor, the National Association for the

at Antioch College in Yellow Springs, Ohio, and later the New England Conservatory of Music in Boston, Massachusetts. Coretta and Martin met in Boston while students, which led to their marriage in 1953. The couple's landing in Coretta's home state, Alabama, so that King could pastor Dexter Avenue Baptist Church[15] in Montgomery placed King at the center of civil unrest and catapulted his rise to national prominence during the yearlong Montgomery Bus Boycott, as a civil rights leader at the age of twenty-six.

Coretta was not a mother just to Yolanda, Martin Luther III, Dexter, and Bernice but also to the civil rights movement, taking care of home amid bomb threats, hate mail and life-threatening pressures while King was on the road, and walking hand in hand with her husband during critical moments and marches for equal rights. Coretta's involvement in the movement is more than the tale of a dutiful housewife, as she embraced a public role in employing her musical gifts to host freedom concerts that funded the Southern Christian Leadership Conference (SCLC)[16] initiatives and making connections with political leaders that influenced the passing of the Civil Rights Act of 1964. American political scientist Jeanne Theoharis identifies Coretta Scott King as a woman of the civil rights movement whose leadership was "sidelined, hidden in plain sight." Theoharis writes in *The Atlantic*,

---

Advancement of Colored People is the largest civil rights organization, advocating for the eradication of racism in America. The mission of the NAACP is "to ensure the political, educational, social, and economic equality of rights of all persons and to eliminate racial hatred and racial discrimination." The NAACP's legacy of social justice advocacy, activism, and abolition begins with its activist founders W. E. B. Du Bois, Mary White Ovington, Moorfield Storey, and Ida B. Wells-Barnett. Today, the NAACP boasts a 112-year history, with an active commitment to dismantling racial injustices facing Black people in America and more than two million members. See NAACP, "Mission & Vision," https://naacp.org/about/mission-vision.

[15]King succeeded civil rights icon Vernon Johns as pastor of Dexter Avenue Baptist Church. Johns's sermon "Transfigured Moments" was the first Black sermon to be published in *Best Sermons of the Year* in 1926. Johns was unconventional in his approach to issues of race by helping Black women charge white rapists and attempting to dine in a whites-only cafeteria. Dexter Avenue Baptist Church saw Johns as too radical and invited a more conservative preacher, Martin Luther King Jr., after Johns's retirement. Johns's niece, Barbara Johns, led a youth protest in Virginia to resist school segregation. Barbara Johns's case was combined with four other cases to form the *Brown v. Board of Education* (1954) case in which the Supreme Court ruled racial segregation in schools as unconstitutional.

[16]Founded in 1957, the Southern Christian Leadership Conference made up a constituency of Black Church leaders who elevated Black churches as the largest social institution of the Black community to lead advocacy endeavors built on theo-ethical principles of freedom, peace, and nonviolence. Martin Luther King Jr. served as the body's first president.

A famous image from King's funeral shows her seated in a pew, dressed in black, stoic and veiled. In many ways, she has been trapped behind that veil, rendered as a sort of martyred mother figure who would redeem the nation by sacrificing her husband. "I am made to sound like an attachment to a vacuum cleaner," a friend recalled her saying, "the wife of Martin, then the widow of Martin, all of which I was proud to be. But I was never just a wife, nor a widow. I was always more than a label."[17]

Coretta picked up the movement where King left off by organizing a silent march to support the labor protests of sanitation workers[18] in Memphis, Tennessee, on April 8, 1968, just four days following her husband's death, when riots swept the nation in the wake of King's assassination. She founded the Martin Luther King Jr. Center for Nonviolent Social Change in Atlanta in 1968 to recommit the movement to global peacemaking. She spoke out against tyranny and war as early as 1965 at Madison Square Garden in New York City; spoke to Congress and world leaders while lobbying for equality and justice for "not some but of all God's children"; and spoke up for gay and lesbian communities, women's rights, youth and children, economic empowerment, and international coalitions like the campaign against apartheid in South Africa. She spearheaded the organizing of a national holiday during King's birthday, which is celebrated today in more than one hundred countries. If King was a drum major for justice, then Coretta was the pulse of the beat. The assassination of King did not stop her work or witness; in fact, it placed her on watch by the Federal Bureau of Investigation (FBI), who censored her personal letters because she posed a threat through her efforts to fortify King's legacy and further the movement.[19] Coretta worked to realize the beloved community of which King could only dream. Undeniably, the shift from King as the "most hated person" in the American psyche at the time of his death to one of the most beloved and (perhaps sanitized)

---

[17]Jeanne Theoharis, "Coretta Scott King and the Civil-Rights Movement's Hidden Women," *The Atlantic*, March 26, 2018, https://www.theatlantic.com/magazine/archive/2018/02/coretta-scott-king/552557/.

[18]King went to Memphis in April 1968 to rally the city, lead the sanitation workers strike, and advocate for hardworking Black men earning less than a livable wage (making a measly $1.80 per hour) with no benefits or days off. This rally was intended to be one of many demonstrations linking racial justice to economic justice, especially at the intersections of labor and poverty. King was assassinated before the rally, but Coretta Scott King continued the rally in honor of her husband and in support of the sanitation workers' cause.

[19]Theoharis, "Coretta Scott King and the Civil-Rights Movement's Hidden Women."

historical figures (posthumously) in American history is largely because of Coretta's legacy.[20] While the lasting image of Coretta Scott King frames her influence as nothing more than an accessory to her husband's political efforts, she defied this label through her enduring prophetic witness long after King's death.

Although she died in 2006, Coretta's memory reemerges in the political upheaval of the December 2017 special election in Alabama because of the rise of Senator Jeff Sessions (R-AL) to the position of US attorney general at the height of the Trump administration. In March 1986, her letter of dissent to the confirmation of then–US prosecutor Jeff Sessions as a federal court judge objected to Sessions's use of voter suppression in the state of Alabama. Senator Elizabeth Warren (D-MA) evoked her letter by recounting Coretta's testimony at the Senate confirmation hearing of Jeff Sessions in 2017. Coretta wrote,

> I write to express my sincere opposition to the confirmation of Jefferson B. Sessions as a federal district court judge for the Southern District of Alabama. My professional and personal roots in Alabama are deep and lasting. Anyone who has used the power of his office as United States Attorney to intimidate and chill the free exercise of the ballot by citizens should not be elevated to our courts. Mr. Sessions has used the awesome powers of his office in a shabby attempt to intimidate and frighten elderly black voters. For this reprehensible conduct, he should not be rewarded with a federal judgeship.[21]

Coretta's appeal to dismiss Sessions from one of the highest offices of the court in Alabama for denying Black elderly voters recounts the *bloody march* to suffrage for Black Americans during the height of the civil rights movement that gained national prominence in Alabama in March 1965, just twenty years before Coretta penned this letter.

Historians name the period between the Supreme Court ruling of separation of children in school based on race as unconstitutional in *Brown v. Board of Education of Topeka, Kansas* (1954) and the assassination of Martin

---

[20] The Federal Bureau of Investigation named Martin Luther King Jr. the "most dangerous Negro in America," which exposes white fury against King rattling the status quo in pursuit of racial justice.

[21] Coretta Scott King, "Letter from Coretta Scott King about Jeff Sessions," press release, February 8, 2017, https://www.warren.senate.gov/newsroom/press-releases/letter-from-coretta-scott-king-about-jeff-sessions.

Luther King Jr. (1968) as the "civil rights years," marking the efforts of Black leaders and activists addressing civil rights and liberties regarding racial segregation, educational disparity, class stratification, and voting. While the civil rights movement brought attention to the atrocities of American racism and segregation, its impact motivated a new "worldview" that spawned a series of progressive social movements around the globe.[22] The dawn of embodied protest in the mid-twentieth-century civil rights movement began with NAACP activist Rosa Parks in Montgomery, Alabama, on December 1, 1955, who confronted Alabama's segregated laws and practices by positioning her body as that which would not be moved when she refused to give up to a white male rider her seat in the colored section. While Parks was not the first Black woman to resist,[23] Parks's imprisonment sparked radical protests of more than fifty thousand Black Alabamians who joined in solidarity, exercised body capital by declining the bus as a means of travel, and disrupted the economic gains of the transit system by not cooperating until all Black bodies could take seat in all sections. Black Alabama activists continued the trail of Harriet Tubman literally "walking the miles" to freedom "in dignity rather than riding in shame,"[24] some walking five to fifteen miles a day to work, church, and school for more than a full year when no carpool was available. The Montgomery Bus Boycott yielded significant policy outcomes as the Supreme Court declared segregation on buses unconstitutional in 1957. In her autobiography, *My Life, My Love, My Legacy*, Coretta testifies that the brainchild of the movement traces back to the political strategy of Black women.

Far too much of the valuable role that women played in the Montgomery movement and other such efforts has been lost to history. It should be remembered that it was Jo Ann Gibson Robinson, an English

---

[22] At the height of the mid-twentieth century, the civil rights movement served as a powerful example to social movements around the world, many of which continue to look to King's philosophy as a source for resistance. Martin Luther King Jr. bears global and cosmic significance (i.e., to the point of near sainthood) because Coretta elevated his legacy. The significance of King and the civil rights movement is larger than the American context alone. See Kevin Gaines, "The Civil Rights Movement in World Perspective," *OAH Magazine of History* 21, no. 1 (January 1, 2007): 57–64.

[23] I am pointing here to Claudette Colvin as a young Alabama activist who refused to give up her seat nine months before Rosa Parks, but the NAACP did not select Colvin to be the face of the movement because Black respectables deemed her too young and too fiery, and she was pregnant.

[24] King and Reynolds, *My Life, My Love, My Legacy*, 121.

professor at Alabama State College and then-president of the Women's
Political Council, who put in place a plan for a citywide bus boycott
more than a year before Mrs. Parks's arrest. Robinson and Mary Fair
Burks, who was equally fervid, helped create and sustain the climate
that supported the 1955 boycott.[25]

The Montgomery Bus Boycott emerged as the first of many major demonstrations that gathered Black people in the United States to resist segregation
policies and practices by utilizing sustained nonviolent tactics that were
often designed by Black women, but Black men mostly received the praise
for them. Through the public rallies and meetings with public officials, the
Montgomery Bus Boycott also elevated Martin Luther King Jr. to national
prominence as a public figure and leading voice of the civil rights movement.

As SCLC president by 1957, King garnered support from Black Church
pastors, religious leaders, heads of community organizations, and activists who were mostly male on the frontlines engaged in "public work"
and mostly women in the background left to take care of "private work."
It should be noted that the political strategists JoAnn Gibson Robinson
and Mary Fair Burks named by Coretta were not extended a position in
the SCLC, establishing its hierarchy as a patriarchal coalition. King and
the SCLC, with the advice and support of In Friendship founders Stanley
David Levison, Bayard Rustin, and Ella Jo Baker, traveled from city to city
spreading a social gospel that rallied for Black freedom through civil dis-
obedience and nonviolent resistance. While a minority of Black churches
participated in demonstrations of the SCLC, the civil rights movement was
largely a Black Church movement, wherein social organizing and freedom
rallies took place in Black churches, and some Black religious leaders nurtured the spirit of freedom in dissenters. The civil rights movement also
mirrored the politics of gender inequality in the Black Church, sustaining
private, domestic roles for Black women and public, charismatic roles for
Black men. A direct response to this duality was the split of former SCLC
acting director Ella Jo Baker[26] and the formation of the Student Nonviolent

[25]King and Reynolds, *My Life, My Love, My Legacy,* 112.

[26]After leaving her position as a field secretary in the NAACP and gaining inspiration
from the activism of her former student Rosa Parks in the Montgomery Bus Boycott, Ella Jo
Baker left New York to work with King at the SCLC in January 1957. Baker utilized both her
resources and skills to plan events and train leaders to support the cause. Most notably, she
led the voting initiative of the SCLC called the Crusade for Citizenship. King and the SCLC
had a vision for increasing voter registration and documenting voter suppression, but they

Coordinating Committee (SNCC), which exercised a grassroots leadership approach for group action against racial violence because, in Baker's words, "strong people don't need strong leaders."[27] By the early 1960s, students felt the pulse of freedom and resisted segregation laws by organizing sit-ins and freedom rides to disrupt social normalcy and place their bodies in prohibited (whites-only) spaces throughout the South. Visual and print media reveal bodies of young activists confronting racial segregation and state-sanctioned violence as they were beat, gassed, flogged, shot, chased by dogs, hosed, jailed, and killed by white southern officials.

After the historic March on Washington in 1963 and the Civil Rights Act of 1964, which banned discrimination based on "race, color, religion, or national origin," King and the SCLC understood Black suffrage in the South as the next path toward social change. Voting established recognition of Black Americans as citizens in this nation while also making headway for other civil and human rights to be valued. For King and the SCLC, voting rights recognized the full humanity of Black Americans and equal status as stakeholders in American democracy. As a socio-religious center in the Black belt of the South, King chose Selma, Alabama, to execute demonstrations for voting rights in 1965 because of its strong activist base already established by Black woman suffragist Amelia Pratt Boynton, who requested King's leadership and the grassroots efforts of the SNCC. According to Coretta, "For blacks, Selma was rock bottom, a place where words such as *democracy, representative government,* and *citizenship* had no meaning."[28] In January 1965, the SCLC and SNCC instituted a voting rights campaign in Selma wherein protestors pursued voter registration offices to retrieve ballots in peaceful protest. Arbitrary literacy testing of resisters' knowledge of Alabama governance and violent attacks by police soon halted these local efforts. The death of activist Jimmie Lee Johnson—killed by a white state trooper in Marion, Alabama—sparked national attention and moved

---

needed Baker and her connections to execute it. The relationship between King and Baker spiraled downward as King resented Baker's independent and well-networked leadership, and Baker despised King's charismatic leadership. After the 1960 sit-ins of North Carolina A&T students at Woolworth's lunch counter in Greensboro, North Carolina, Baker left the SCLC to help young activists organize the Student Nonviolent Coordinating Committee (SNCC) at her alma mater, Shaw University. Baker's nickname was "Fundi," a Swahili term identifying one who teaches a skill to the next generation. This name was captured in the title of the 1981 film *Fundi: The Story of Ella Baker* about her life and legacy.

[27] Barbara Ransby, *Ella Baker and the Black Freedom Movement: A Radical Democratic Vision* (Chapel Hill: University of North Carolina Press, 2003), 188.

[28] King and Reynolds, *My Life, My Love, My Legacy,* 237.

the campaign to undertake a public march from Selma to Montgomery.[29]

"Securing the right to vote was a blood covenant," in the words of Coretta Scott King.[30] On March 7, 1965, named Bloody Sunday, roughly six hundred protestors led by the SCLC's Hosea Williams and SNCC's John Lewis proceeded to the Edmund Pettus Bridge where county sheriff Jim Clark and state troopers lined the highways wearing gas masks and helmets while holding billy clubs and electric cattle prods. A national televised audience watched Clark and troopers attack marchers viciously by chasing and flanking them with bullwhips and rubber hoses, firing tear gas, and injuring marchers' limbs, skulls, ribs, and other body parts. On March 9, 1965, King called clergypersons and religious leaders to join the efforts and march a second time but retreated to avoid another violent confrontation by troops. King's retreat could not stop mob rule that night as three Klansmen attacked a group of clergy after leaving a restaurant that ended in the death of James Reeb, a white Unitarian Universalist minister from Boston. From March 21 to 25, 1965, with court protection, approximately three hundred marchers set foot in their "Sunday's best" to walk fifty-seven miles over a four-day span from Selma to Montgomery to defy Alabama voting practices and protest state-sanctioned violence. More than fifty thousand activists descended on the Alabama state capitol in Montgomery with Coretta and Martin leading the way, casting a vision (or maybe an illusion) of Black Americans as no longer "enemies of the state" but as full, free citizens.[31] The Selma marches fostered the thirty-sixth US president, Lyndon B. Johnson, to sign into federal law the Voting Rights Act of 1965 (effective August 6 of that year) that rejected any state or local tactics to keep citizens from exercising the right to vote on the basis of race as described in the Fifteenth Amendment. Though the act was signed into law at the federal level, states were slow to employ its mandates, especially in the Jim Crow South.

The history of the Selma-to-Montgomery march and its pervasive whitelash[32] locates Alabama at the center of voter suppression and voter

---

[29]The assassination of Malcolm X on February 21, 1965, in the Audubon Ballroom in Harlem, New York City, happened just a few days after Jimmie Lee Johnson's funeral. Malcolm X's death is significant to the Selma events because he visited Selma while King was in jail and met with Coretta Scott King to show his newly enlightened affirmation of the voting campaign and the efforts of King's movement.

[30]King and Reynolds, *My Life, My Love, My Legacy,* 236.

[31]King and Reynolds, *My Life, My Love, My Legacy,* 252.

[32]Popularized by CNN commentator and analyst Van Jones, the term "whitelash" connotes white backlash or the response of white Americans to curb or hinder racial progress after a significant or dramatic shift. Historians point to Jim Crow during the Reconstruction

disenfranchisement. In Coretta's view, any attempts to restrict voting rights represent direct assaults against American democracy. Coretta argues,

> Free exercise of voting rights is so fundamental to American democracy that we can not tolerate any form of infringement of those rights. Of all the groups who have been disenfranchised in our nation's history, none has struggled longer or suffered more in the attempt to win the vote than Black citizens. No group has had access to the ballot box denied so persistently and intently.[33]

Coretta's 1986 letter spoke of tactics used by Jeff Sessions as a US Attorney in the 1984 election to repress, investigate, and incriminate elderly Black voters like Albert Turner of the Harris-Perry County Civic League while not pursuing similar legal action against white counterparts known for wrongdoing at the ballot box. Coretta testified that Sessions's "politically-motivated voting fraud prosecutions to his indifference toward criminal violations of civil rights laws, indicates that he lacks the temperament, fairness and judgment to be a federal judge."[34] The dissent against Sessions concerning his racist rhetoric and discriminatory practices to the US Senate Judiciary Committee including Coretta's letter encouraged the committee to deny his nomination by President Ronald Reagan for a federal judgeship in 1986 (10-8 split vote),[35] but Sessions was later elected as attorney general of Alabama in 1994 and to the US Senate in 1996, 2002, 2008, and 2014. The US Senate accepted and filed Coretta's testimony in 1986, but it was mostly forgotten until Senator Elizabeth Warren read Coretta's nine-page letter aloud to verbalize her dissent to the confirmation of Alabama senator Jeff Sessions as the US attorney general in February 2017.

"Nevertheless, she persisted." This phrase was applied to Senator Warren by then–Senate Majority Leader Mitch McConnell (R-KY) for her undisciplined and unruly plea against confirming Sessions in 2017. When she broke the rules of social decorum at a congressional hearing and was

---

era following the Civil War, the social decline following the civil rights movement, and more recently the election of Donald Trump following the presidency of Barack Obama as instances of whitelash.

[33] King, "Letter from Coretta Scott King about Jeff Sessions."

[34] King, "Letter from Coretta Scott King about Jeff Sessions."

[35] The Senate's rejection of Sessions's nomination in 1986 was more like a slap on the wrist since he sought and won even higher offices in subsequent election years both in Alabama and on the national scene.

removed, Senator Mitch McConnell tweeted, "Sen. Warren was giving a lengthy speech. She had appeared to violate the rule. She was warned. She was given an explanation. Nevertheless, she persisted."[36] Senator Warren was silenced by McConnell and reprimanded for breaking Rule 19, a standing rule for Senate decorum. The underside to herstory or the missing story behind the now-popular feminist mantra "Nevertheless, she persisted" is that the lengthy speech Senator Warren read aloud was Coretta's 1986 letter.

While Senator Warren received the public commendation, the persistence to confront a corrupt democracy evidenced in Coretta's letter represents a canonical virtue for Black women. Persistence is what womanist ethicist Katie Cannon calls *unshouted courage*:

> the quality of steadfastness, akin to fortitude, in the face of formidable oppression . . . it involves the ability to "hold on to life" against major oppositions. It is the incentive to facilitate change, to chip away at the oppressive structures, bit by bit, to celebrate and rename their experiences in empowering ways. "Unshouted courage" as a virtue is the often unacknowledged inner conviction that keeps one's appetite whet for freedom.[37]

Coretta exercised persistence before such rhetoric was "feminist" or popular by waging her power and influence during the civil rights years and long after to confront a crooked American political system. Three Black queer women—Alicia Garza, Opal Temeti, and Patrisse Cullors—embody the succession of such persistence whose unrelenting pursuit of freedom and justice as architects of the Black social movement in a contemporary era calls America to recognize the human dignity of Black people and affirm #BlackLivesMatter.[38] Senator Warren's reading of Coretta's letter from the

---

[36] Amy B. Wang, "'Nevertheless, She Persisted' Becomes New Battle Cry after McConnell Silences Elizabeth Warren," *Washington Post*, February 8, 2017, https://www.washingtonpost.com/news/the-fix/wp/2017/02/08/nevertheless-she-persisted-becomes-new-battle-cry-after-mcconnell-silences-elizabeth-warren/.

[37] Cannon, *Black Womanist Ethics*, 144.

[38] #BlackLivesMatter emerged first in 2012 as a protest hashtag developed by three Black queer millennial women, Alicia Garza, Opal Tameti, and Patrisse Cullors, initially as a knee-jerk response to the killing of seventeen-year-old Trayvon Martin in Florida and the troubling acquittal of George Zimmerman. The deaths of Trayvon Martin, Michael Brown, Eric Garner, Renisha McBride, Sandra Bland, Tamir Rice, and countless other fallen Black bodies to police brutality and their contested grand jury decisions for almost a decade has reignited a radical Black resistance movement with a blending of innovative cyber and

hallway brings into closer view Black women's struggle for recognition as trustworthy moral agents who continue to save America from itself.

Bound Up with All of Humanity:
The Fight for Citizenship and Political Power

The year 2020 marked the one hundredth anniversary of women's suffrage in America, which is largely the story of a white women's movement and white women's right to vote. The women's movement that began in Seneca Falls in 1848 and continued with the ratification of the Nineteenth Amendment in 1920 guaranteed that the right to vote would not be denied based on sex but did not secure voting rights for Black women. Black women's participation in this fight for voting rights in the nineteenth and early twentieth centuries is a complicated herstory. Most notably, white suffragists Alice Paul, Lucy Burns, and the NWSA—who organized the national suffrage march in Washington, DC, on March 3, 1913, one day before the inauguration of President Woodrow Wilson—encouraged Black women who registered and joined to march in the back. Such a missive indicates the issue of Black women's vote on the backburner at best or of no concern to white suffragists at all. The activism of Black suffragists Sojourner Truth, Mary Ann Shad Cary, Ida B. Wells, Mary Church Terrell, Nannie Helen Burroughs, and Nellie Quander, to name a few, is often missing from the narrative of women's suffrage.

In *Vanguard: How Black Women Broke Barriers, Won the Vote, and Insisted*

---

concrete demonstrations employing the body as a means of protest to make Black lives matter in America. Thousands of local and global protestors and activists, under the banner of #BlackLivesMatter across numerous grassroots coalitions, have organized, galvanized, and radicalized against the ugly, terrorizing, and dehumanizing realities facing Black folx— men, women, trans, gender-nonconforming—in life and death. The August 2014 scene of Ferguson, Missouri, in the wake of the death of Michael Brown Jr. recalled the Edmund Pettis Bridge on Bloody Sunday in March 1965 when police and the National Guard lined the highways wearing gas masks and carrying billy clubs and machine guns. If not apparent before, Brown's death made clear that Black bodies were under siege in America, and public protest tactics beyond a hashtag were necessary to confront the terror of Black social death. See Leah Gunning Francis, *Ferguson & Faith: Sparking Leadership & Awakening Community* (St. Louis: Chalice Press, 2015); Patrisse Khan-Cullors and Asha Bandele, *When They Call You a Terrorist: A Black Lives Matter Memoir* (New York: St. Martin's Press, 2018); Alicia Garza, *The Purpose of Power: How to Build Movements for the 21st Century* (New York: One World, 2020); Keeanga-Yamahtta Taylor, *From #BlackLivesMatter to Black Liberation* (Chicago: Haymarket Books, 2016).

on Equality for All, historian Martha S. Jones argues that nineteenth- and twentieth-century Black women understood voting as a pathway to full citizenship in America, but they also learned from the racist exclusion of white women that to forge this path they had to form their own movement.

> Black women laid the groundwork for their movement in the rocky soil of women's antislavery conventions, Black Methodist conferences, and the heart of Black politics: the colored convention movement. Their counterparts among white middle-class women were at the start of their own movement, one that insisted upon building power within discrete women's spaces. These differences, though not stark or all-defining, suggest how American women charted divergent routes to power and political rights going forward. These differences were not only structural or strategic. And they cannot be reduced to the effects of racism. Black women would never sever their political power from the movements and organizations that set at the heart of their communities. At times, their drive to power led them to convene as women. But all roads brought them back to the needs of the African American public culture in which they had been formed.[39]

Black women leaned into the vision of Black abolitionist and suffragist Frances Ellen Watkins Harper, who asserted in an 1866 speech to white women and Black male suffragists, "We are all bound up together in one great bundle of humanity, and society cannot trample on the weakest and feeblest of its members without receiving the curse in its own soul."[40] The matter of suffrage revealed that Black women could not look to the solidarity of white women or the protection of Black men, but needed to form their own movement to save a nation with a sin-sick soul. Harper's declaration—like Black sociologist and suffragist Anna Julia Cooper's "When and where I enter, in the quiet, undisputed dignity of my womanhood, without violence and without suing or special patronage, then and there the whole Negro race enters with me"[41]—illuminates the communal and universal impulse of the political and social movement of Black women that would never be

---

[39]Martha S. Jones, *Vanguard: How Black Women Broke Barriers, Won the Vote, and Insisted on Equality for All* (New York: Basic Books, 2020), 68.

[40]Frances Ellen Watkins Harper, "We Are All Bound Up Together—May 1866," in *Proceedings of the Eleventh National Woman's Rights Convention*, ed. Robert J. Johnston (New York, 1866), 46–48.

[41]Anna J. Cooper, *A Voice from the South* (New York: Oxford University Press, 1988), 81.

to save Black women alone. Jones writes, "Black women knew the power of the vote and what it meant to use it. How to get there was the question. . . . And suffrage alone was too narrow a goal for Black women. They went on to seek the vote but on their own terms and to reach cures for what ailed all humanity."[42] In this sense, Black women's political and social movement may be defined by an enduring quest for human dignity.

The fight to secure the vote placed Black women and their bodies on the frontlines of civil rights and women's rights in America. The narrative of Fannie Lou Hamer recounts another bloody battle for citizenship that levied brutal and intimate assaults on the bodies and lives of Black women in America. When Hamer went to the ballot box in Indianola, Mississippi (the hometown of my paternal family), "to register to become a first-class citizen"[43] in 1962, she encountered more than rejection, but also bodily terror through intimidation, imprisonment, and sexual violation by white southern officials and coerced Black prisoners. Hamer's lament of being "sick and tired of being sick and tired" illuminates her struggles: sterilization without her consent in 1961, and the multiple consequences she endured for pursuing voter registration in Mississippi, including the loss of her share-cropping job, loss of her home to bombing, and significant bodily injuries such as the loss of eyesight in one eye, kidney damage, and a worsened limp because of racially charged beatings. Jones contends, "Fannie Lou Hamer had been rebuffed, harassed, beaten, and sexually assaulted at the hands of local officials. Her experiences as an activist in the early 1960s were a testament to why Black women need the vote and needed it immediately. . . . If the ballot box was a battleground, so too was Hamer's body."[44] As a leading figure of the Mississippi Freedom Democratic Party desiring to receive a seat among liberals, Fannie Lou Hamer's historic televised speech at the 1964 Democratic National Convention (DNC) confronted so-called white northern progressives and some Black political leaders about their failure to uphold democracy by dismissing the numerous attacks against the freedom of the most vulnerable. Hamer indicted a nation as she declared her dissent to the DNC: "And if the Freedom Democratic Party is not seated now, I question America. Is this America, the land of the free and the home of the brave, where we have to sleep with our telephones off of the hooks because our lives be threatened daily, because we want to live as decent human beings,

---

[42]Jones, *Vanguard*, 122.

[43]Hamer, *The Speeches of Fannie Lou Hamer*, 107.

[44]Jones, *Vanguard*, 256–57.

in America?"[45] Coming from Mississippi, or what Hamer called "the land of
the tree and the home of the grave,"[46] Hamer understood that the absence of
political power in America coupled with terrorizing assaults against Black
life exposes a nation that condemns the humanity of the disenfranchised.
In Hamer's view, "America is a sick place and man [*sic*] is on the critical
list. But we are determined to bring a change not only for ourselves, but I
believe we are God's chosen people."[47] Black women could not wait for a
white savior or even a male savior to change the course of history, even in
progressive spaces; they needed to step into the work of social change and
salvation to realize democracy in a crumbling America for the liberation
of all, because as Hamer confessed at the 1971 National Women's Political
Caucus, "Nobody is free until everybody is free."[48]

The Abrams Playbook: Fair Vote and the New American Majority

Stacey Abrams, the first Black woman to win a major nomination for
governor—the highest office of the state—in the United States, stands at
the height of the contemporary Black women's political movement in her
efforts to organize a fair vote and a fair fight for citizenship for all Americans,
especially the powerless. As a student of the Obama presidential elections in
2008 and 2012, which yielded the largest minority voter turnout in history,
the Abrams playbook is simple. Rather than competing with the opposing
party for swing voters (a failed strategy for Hillary Clinton's presidential
campaign in 2016), Abrams registers and targets the "New American Majority," representing "that coalition of people of color, young people, and
moderate to progressive whites."[49] Millennials and GenZers lead this pack
as the largest generational cohorts in America. Abrams's strategy is to enlist
this voting population deemed undesirable by both parties. In 2018, this
led to her apparent victory, with 1.9 million votes—the highest number
of Democratic votes in Georgia history.[50] Despite voter interposition and

---

[45]Hamer, *The Speeches of Fannie Lou Hamer*, 45.

[46]Hamer, *The Speeches of Fannie Lou Hamer*, 126. See also Cone, *The Cross and the Lynching Tree*.

[47]Hamer, *The Speeches of Fannie Lou Hamer*, 115.

[48]Hamer, *The Speeches of Fannie Lou Hamer*, 136.

[49]Stacey Abrams, *Our Time Is Now: Power, Purpose, and the Fight for a Fair America* (New
York: Henry Holt and Company, 2020), 12.

[50]Stacey Abrams, "I Know Voting Feels Inadequate Right Now," *New York Times*, June 4,
2020, https://www.nytimes.com/2020/06/04/opinion/stacey-abrams-voting-floyd-protests.
html.

nullification, Abrams declared she "won" the 2018 election by tripling the voter turnout of Latino and Asian American Pacific Islander voters, elevating youth voter participation by 139 percent, shifting Black voters closer to the peak of 2008 with 1.2 million votes, and earning the highest percentage of white votes for the Democratic ticket in Georgia—all of which placed her historic gubernatorial campaign in the limelight of the nation.[51] Abrams won the election in this regard because she "transformed" the electorate in Georgia, but her opponent, Brian Kemp (R-GA), as the secretary of state exercised his power to close polls, redline voting districts, block new Georgia voter registrations for typographical errors, and implement technologies of "exact match" to reject more than 53,000 Georgia voter registrations of mostly poor people of color. In other words, Brian Kemp stole the Georgia gubernatorial election, by a mere 54,723 votes.

On November 16, 2018, Abrams did not concede, but she served notice in her speech ending the election that the fight for a fair vote was on. Abrams admitted to *Vogue* that she "sat shiva for ten days and then began plotting."[52] Abrams did what Black women do in the face of unrelenting odds; she exercised persistence by organizing Fair Fight Action to "expose, mitigate, and reverse voter suppression."[53] This fight was not simply to win another election but to repair a faulty system that undermined equality for all citizens. In her response to Congressman John Lewis (D-GA) identifying voting as "almost sacred," Abrams argues, "Voting is an act of faith. It is profound. In a democracy, it is the ultimate power. Through the vote, the poor can access financial means, the infirm can find health support, and the burdened and heavy laden can receive a measure of relief from a social safety net that serves all. And we are willing to go to war to defend the sacred."[54] When the right to vote is not guaranteed to all citizens, American democracy fails to live up to its promise of life, liberty, and justice for all. Black women's persistent fight for the vote aims to "repair the breach"

---

[51] Abrams, *Our Time Is Now*, 18.

[52] The expression "sitting shiva" represents a Jewish mourning ritual for immediate family relatives that lasts for seven days following the burial. It draws from the book of Job when Job sits on the ground with his friends in mourning for seven days and nights in Job 2:13. Abram references this experience of mourning following the loss of her gubernatorial election in 2018. Alexis Okeowo, "Can Stacey Abrams Save American Democracy?," *Vogue*, August 12, 2019, https://www.vogue.com/article/stacey-abrams-american-democracy-vogue-september-2019-issue.

[53] Fair Fight, "About Fair Fight Action," accessed May 1, 2024, https://fairfight.com/about-fair-fight/.

[54] Abrams, "I Know Voting Feels Inadequate Right Now."

of a broken democratic system. According to Abrams, "The contours and tactics of voter suppression have changed since the days of Jim Crow, Black Codes, or suffragettes, but the mission remains steady and immovable: keep power concentrated in the hands of the few by disenfranchising the votes of the undesirable."[55] In Abrams's view, the recurring strategies to "deny and delay" voters that are rampant in the United States illustrate that the "fight for voting rights has never ended."[56]

Abrams's persistent fight against voter suppression shifted the 2020 battleground at the ballot box in Georgia. The close poll margins of the November 2020 election placed the Georgia Senate race in the hot seat because a 2021 runoff would determine the majority party in the US Senate for the next four years. Flipping Georgia blue would be no easy challenge because both Democratic Senate candidates faced Republican incumbents in a historically "red" state. The transformation of the Georgia electorate by Abrams ushered in a new way of doing politics, which motivated the Democratic Party to tap Abrams's playbook and the political strategy of Black women activists like LaTosha Brown of the Black Voters Matter Fund (who played a pivotal role in the 2017 Alabama Senate election) to secure a win in the 2020 Georgia Senate elections. The election of Rev. Raphael Warnock (D-GA) as the first Black senator in Georgia and Jon Ossoff (D-GA) as the first Jewish senator in Georgia and first millennial senator in American history are a direct result of Abrams's hard-fought efforts to redeem the New American Majority. Abrams's strategy recovered registrations of rejected voters, enlisted roughly 800,000 new voters, and motivated Black voters to turn out to the polls in record numbers—thus saving democracy.[57] Abrams captured it best in her op-ed in the *New York Times*: "Voting will not save us from harm, but silence will surely damn us all."[58] In the case of the Georgia elections, Abrams's fight secured a political seat for a Black man and a white man under the progressive "blue wave," but Abrams was left to "lead from the outside"[59] with public commendation and no political

---

[55] Abrams, *Our Time Is Now*, 21.

[56] Abrams, *Our Time Is Now*, 23.

[57] To be clear, saving democracy is not simply Abrams's alignment with leftist or progressive politics. Abrams's efforts widened the playing field for new voters to be counted and new communities to gain voice in the democratic project. It should be no surprise that Abrams's fair vote initiatives were followed by a fight for a fair count in the 2020 Census to emphasize the power of the New American Majority and to ensure that these communities remain visible to political leaders and policymakers.

[58] Abrams, "I Know Voting Feels Inadequate Right Now."

[59] See Stacey Abrams, *Lead from the Outside: How to Build Your Future and Make Real*

seat at the table. Like Hamer, Black women saving the nation signals more burden than promise as Abrams's fight on the front lines for citizenship and power did not guarantee personal reward. In another vein, Abrams did not forsake public scrutiny as critics attacked her moral character when running for office because of her debt ratio, which is a prime example of America punishing Black women for the wealth gaps that it created by slavery, Jim Crow, segregation, and unequal economic opportunities for those on the underside. Abrams is depicted as morally unfit as a Black woman to lead a state government because of high debt, but otherwise highly capable in the Georgia Senate election to elevate Black and white men to political prominence. The personal is political as the burdens of sacrifice, surrogacy, and strength taunt the humanity of Black women in a nation that craves Black women's moral discernment and simultaneously denies Black women's labor and leadership.

Stacey Abrams stands within a long lineage of Black political women like Shirley Chisolm, Barbara Jordan, Carol Mosley Braun, and so many others who understood that social change involves power at the polls and a seat at the political table. According to the Higher Heights for America PAC, the only political action committee devoted to electing progressive Black women to all levels of American governance, "Black women are a powerful electorate with the proven ability to decide elections. But our political capital has yet to translate into a representative number of Black women holding office or robust, long-term policies that effectively address our concerns."[60] The numbers tell the story with more than "16 million Black women eligible to vote and 67% registered."[61] If it wasn't for Black women, no Black president would have been elected in America. It is Black women's political movement historically and contemporary power as a voting bloc (96 percent) that helped Barack Obama to secure a victory in the 2008 and 2012 presidential elections. Though Clinton did not win the electoral college bid for the presidency in 2016, 94 percent of Black women supported her to become the first woman nominated for president by a major political party and to win the popular vote. In simple terms, progressive candidates like Democrat Doug Jones in the 2017 Alabama Senate election rely on Black women (98 percent for Jones) to secure office, but this does not translate into short- or long-term policy outcomes that address

---

Change (New York: Henry Holt and Company, 2019).

[60] Higher Heights for America PAC, "By the Numbers," accessed May 1, 2024, https://www.higherheightsforamericapac.org/by-the-numbers/.

[61] Higher Heights for America PAC, "By the Numbers."

Black women's political issues and concerns in America. The 2020 election required new terms of political engagement for Black women that placed all political parties on notice.

A Fighting Chance: The Ascension of Vice President Kamala Harris

No one could predict that another white man in the form of former vice president Joe Biden would become the face of "progressive politics" and win the 2020 presidential election. The whitelash against a mixed Black man with eight years in power motivated the 2016 election of Republican Donald Trump, a conservative extremist who played the race card and initiated birther attacks against President Obama to discredit his American citizenship. To remove the Republican incumbent in 2020, the Democratic Party had to play its A-game, with diverse candidates from multiple political perspectives and social locations including six women (two women of color), twenty-two men (six men of color), and the first openly gay male to run in the presidential primary. Senator Kamala Harris (D-CA) launched her "For the People" campaign for presidency on January 21, 2019 (the MLK holiday), at the home of her nascent political career and mecca of Black culture, her alma mater, Howard University. Harris gave a speech later that week in her hometown of Oakland, California, about the failures of the Trump administration. White conservatives, liberals, and Black progressives were quick to single out Harris's early political career as a prosecuting attorney and attorney general of California, the largest state in the United States, as evidence that Harris was morally unfit to lead the nation. In her memoir *The Truths We Hold: An American Journey*, Harris confesses,

> My vision of a progressive prosecutor was someone who used the power of the office with a sense of fairness, perspective, and experience, someone who was clear about the need to hold serious criminals accountable and who understood that the best way to create safe communities was to prevent crime in the first place. To do those things effectively, you also need to run a professional operation.[62]

Perhaps less to Harris and more to the danger of a Black women upholding often unjust laws of a failed criminal justice system, Harris was punished

---

[62]Kamala Harris, *The Truths We Hold: An American Journey* (New York: Penguin Press, 2019), 72.

by activists and progressive critics for doing her job well, with too many convictions on her record in the age of mass incarceration. As a Black woman in the American political sandbox, Harris did not escape anti-Black and misogynoir stereotyping that policed her sexuality and criticized her 2014 marriage to a white man along with her a new title as "Momala" in a modern blended family.[63] While Harris became the leading Black candidate in the 2020 presidential race, she ended her campaign in December 2019 in what could be argued as just the right time. The lackluster Biden campaign appeared to flop until the endorsement of Black congressman Jim Clybourn (D-SC) in the South Carolina primary and what journalists deemed "salvation in South Carolina"[64] through the support of 64 percent of Black voters on February 24, 2020, which shifted Biden's trajectory toward a surprising upward turn just days before a global pandemic.

Historians will mark 2020 as the year of a global pandemic, public protest, and progressive politics.[65] Though the early occurrence of the novel coronavirus (COVID-19) traces back to winter 2019, the White House declared the outbreak a national emergency on March 13, 2020. For many, March 13 was a day of reckoning that a national shutdown could no longer be evaded as stay-at-home orders loomed, and federal, state, and local governments moved swiftly to close schools, institutions, retail stores, restaurants, physical plants, and places of worship to contain the virus. For Breonna Taylor, a 26-year-old Black millennial woman, March 13 marked a fatal ending as Louisville police barged into her home under a no-knock warrant and fired

---

[63]"Momala" is the name given to Kamala by her stepchildren through her marriage with attorney Doug Emhoff. While it is unclear why Ella and Cole Emhoff selected the name, "mamelah" is a Yiddish term of endearment meaning "little mama." Harris celebrated the name on the 2020 presidential campaign trail declaring that the title "Momala" is the one that means the most to her. Harris demonstrates unconventional mothering that defies socially accepted roles for Black women.

[64]See Josh Boak, "Anatomy of a Comeback: How Biden Won the Democratic Presidential Nomination," *Detroit News*, June 6, 2020, https://www.detroitnews.com/story/news/politics/2020/06/06/biden-comeback-nomination-democratic/111915566/; Meg Kinnard, "Clyburn: Bush Called Him a 'Savior' for Boosting Biden," Associated Press, January 20, 2021, https://apnews.com/article/election-2020-joe-biden-donald-trump-elections-south-carolina-5aa4825cdd42d638b52cfb633b66352b.

[65]My exploration of the racial, generational, and religious markers of COVID-19 began in an earlier article. See Melanie C. Jones, "Who's Saving Whom?: Black Millennials and the Revivification of Religious Communities," in *Religion, Race, and COVID-19: Confronting White Supremacy in the Pandemic*, Stacey M. Floyd-Thomas, ed. (New York: NYU Press, 2021), 54–77. I build upon ideas presented in this article to give context to the year of 2020 and in the history of Black social movements and American politics in this chapter.

several rounds that resulted in her untimely death. Seemingly, Americans were caught in the crosshairs of multiple pandemics, or an unholy trinity of COVID-19, COVID-1619, and what womanist ethicist Stacey Floyd-Thomas names as "COVID-45,"[66] that revealed devastating consequences for Black lives in America in the face of disease, racial injustice, and poor governance that has been four hundred years in the making. Following the state-sanctioned killings of George Floyd by a law enforcer's knee on his neck and Breonna Taylor in her home, thousands of protesters in the summer of 2020 flooded the streets of major cities across the nation, risking their health to contest police brutality and elevating a decade-old millennial-led #BlackLivesMatter movement to become one of the largest social movements in history. With a nation battling crisis, the political stakes were higher than ever, motivating more than 150 million Americans to take the chance for social change and power the polls in one of the largest voter turnouts in American history.

As the presumptive Democratic nominee by August 2020, former vice president Biden understood he needed to take a cue from Abrams's playbook and identify a running mate who represented both in identity and perspective the New American Majority to win against a sitting president. The 2017 December Senate win in Alabama proved the voting power of Black women and signaled that a Black woman should at least make the short list for a running mate. Biden chose one of his fiercest contenders and fellow senator Kamala Harris, whom he named as a "fearless fighter for the little guy" and "one of the country's finest public servants," to help him build America back better.[67]

Senator Kamala Harris (D-CA) delivered her 2020 Democratic National Convention speech to accept the nomination for vice president of United States on the week of the one hundredth anniversary of the Nineteenth

---

[66]COVID-45 is a direct critique against the failed leadership of President Donald J. Trump, the forty-fifth president of the United States. During the early onset of COVID-19, the Trump administration did not act on safety protocols to protect American citizens, which elevated the impact of the virus on American soil. President Trump's naming of the virus as the "Chinese virus" heightened violence against Asian American and Pacific Islanders (AAPI). Failure to contain the virus because of poor governance contributed to disproportionate effects in the Black and brown populations.

[67]Joe Biden (@joebiden), "Joe Biden on Instagram: 'I Have the Great Honor to Announce That I've Picked @KamalaHarris—a Fearless Fighter for the Little Guy, and One of the Country's Finest . . . ,'" Instagram, August 11, 2020, https://www.instagram.com/p/CDwyziWhWrW/?hl=en.

Amendment. Harris did not miss the moment to recognize Black women, the true patriots of America, who worked persistently to secure voting rights and realize democracy long after the 1920 ratification. Harris asserts, "Without fanfare or recognition, they [Black women] organized, testified, rallied, marched, and fought—not just for their vote, but for a seat at the table. These women and the generations that followed worked to make democracy and opportunity real in the lives of all of us who followed."[68] Harris named Black suffragists Mary Church Terrell, Mary Mcleod Bethune, Fannie Lou Hamer, Diane Nash, Constance Baker Motley, Shirley Chisholm, and her Indian mother Shyamala Gopalan Harris as women whose shoulders she stands upon and whose values and vision she shares of a nation committed to the theory and practice of freedom.

Herstory was made in 2020. The Biden-Harris presidential ticket won more than seventy-four million votes, earning the highest total in American history. In a voting margin that exceeded projections, Harris was elected— among many firsts, the first woman, first Black woman, first Asian American, first HBCU-educated, and first Black Greek–lettered sorority member to become vice president of the United States. To be clear, Black women made this reality possible. It was the Black Women's PAC led by the persistent political powerhouses Donna Brazile, Minyon Moore, Leah Daughtry, and Yolanda Caraway that pushed Biden, once he was named the Democratic frontrunner, to select a Black woman as his running mate. Harris knew that Black women would save the day at the polls, as shown in her *Essence* article published a day before Election Day, expressing gratitude to Black women for having her back. Harris affirms, "Generations of Black women marched and organized and fought to give us this right . . . knowing that, one day, Black women would be a force in our democracy."[69] Biden repeated this sentiment in his November 2020 victory speech: "And especially for those moments when this campaign was at its lowest—the African American community stood up again for me. They always have my back, and I'll have yours."[70] Biden's first act toward this promise was selecting Harris,

[68]Kamala Harris, "Transcript: Kamala Harris' DNC Speech," CNN, August 20, 2020, https://www.cnn.com/2020/08/19/politics/kamala-harris-speech-transcript/index.html.

[69]Kamala Harris, "Kamala Harris: I'm Grateful That Black Women Have Had My Back," *Essence,* November 2, 2020, https://www.essence.com/feature/kamala-harris-election-2020-black-women/.

[70]Joe Biden, "Transcript of President-Elect Joe Biden's Victory Speech," Associated Press, November 7, 2020, https://apnews.com/article/election-2020-joe-biden-religion-technology-race-and-ethnicity-2b961c70bc72c2516046bffd378e95de.

energizing Black voters and signaling to them that more would be done during his time in office.

Like Abrams, Harris represents a vision forward for Black women's movement for human dignity. While the ascension of Vice President Kamala Harris casts a glimmer of hope or even a shining star in the vanguard of Black women's political movement, her rise is not the symbol of the height of progress. Black women as the domestic default to clean up filthy politics in the wake of a national crisis echoes a recurring narrative and undue burden for Black women to save America, often for more risk than reward. Harris ran for president first and was more qualified at the time of her running in 2020 than Senator Barack Obama in 2008. Like Senator Hillary Clinton, Harris is both twice as good and still second best or "runner-up" to her male counterparts. Vice President Kamala Harris in the White House does not mean Black women's political movement has ended. Harris will not escape the public scrutiny of her commitment to the "least of these" through her political decision-making in the ways that President Obama evaded during his eight years in office. Moreover, the nonpartisan Brennan Center for Justice reveals that the whitelash against this Biden-Harris win sparked more than seventeen states in 2021 alone to enact new voting laws (twenty-eight and counting), including more aggressive strategies of voter suppression at the polls.[71] The symbolic significance of Kamala Harris donned in the white suffragist suit on November 2020 victory night was a nod to more than fashion: a timely reminder that the "time is now" and Black women's fight for full citizenship and struggle for recognition has only just begun.

I, Too, Am America: Melissa Harris-Perry's *Sister Citizen,* the Crooked Room, and the Problem of Recognition

Black political scientist Melissa Harris-Perry, in her groundbreaking text *Sister Citizen: Shame, Stereotypes and Black Women in America [For Colored Girls Who've Considered Politics When Being Strong Wasn't Enough]*, argues that Black women in America "fully embody" the struggle for recognition, which is the "nexus of human identity and national identity."[72] The "internal,

[71]Brennan Center for Justice, "Voting Laws Roundup: May 2021," May 28, 2021, https://www.brennancenter.org/our-work/research-reports/voting-laws-roundup-may-2021.

[72]Melissa V. Harris-Perry, *Sister Citizen: Shame, Stereotypes, and Black Women in America [For Colored Girls Who've Considered Politics When Being Strong Isn't Enough]* (New Haven, CT: Yale University Press, 2011), 4.

psychological, emotional, and personal experiences of black women are inherently political . . . because black women in America have always had to wrestle with derogatory assumptions about their character and identity. These assumptions shape the social world that black women must accommodate or resist in an effort to preserve their authentic selves and to secure recognition as citizens."[73] Drawing on cognitive psychology and political philosophy, agents in any given context determine what is upright by their perception of their surroundings and the social world. Harris-Perry traces the mischaracterizations of Black women's moral virtue through prevailing myths and stereotypes that situate Black women in America in a crooked room. Harris-Perry argues, "When they confront race and gender stereotypes, black women are standing in a crooked room, and they have to figure out which way is up. Bombarded with warped images of their humanity, some black women tilt and bend themselves to fit the distortion. . . . It can be hard to stand up straight in a crooked room."[74] Harris-Perry names the "slanted images of the crooked room as the problem of recognition."[75]

Harris-Perry defines recognition through the Hegelian philosophy of *Anerkennung*, which points to the interconnections of knowing and acting subjects. The relationship between citizen and state provides a solid framework for understanding the politics of recognition. Citizens are defined by their belonging to the state, while the state must demonstrate recognition of its citizens to affirm such belonging. According to Harris-Perry, "Citizens want and need more than a fair distribution of resources: they also desire meaningful recognition of their humanity and uniqueness, and they are willing to make sacrifices to get it."[76] Black women's suffrage is a prime example of the fight for citizenship as a quest for recognition in America. Black women in America face the Du Boisian double consciousness of navigating a nation of which they are both native and outcast. The right to vote in a democracy represents one way that citizens are recognized and their voices are valued. The absence of basic democratic rights like voting denies citizenship and signals a rejection of Black women's human dignity. Citizens in the context of democracy rely on what Harris-Perry identifies as the social contract wherein "individuals subject themselves to rules, constraints and collective burdens imposed by the state (such as taxes and military service) in exchange for safety and services provided by the state

---

[73]Harris-Perry, *Sister Citizen*, 5.
[74]Harris-Perry, *Sister Citizen*, 29.
[75]Harris-Perry, *Sister Citizen*, 25.
[76]Harris-Perry, *Sister Citizen*, 36.

(such as security and social programs)."[77] The American social contract promises "life, liberty, and the pursuit of happiness" as collective rights for its citizens. Unfortunately, these rights are not always freely given to citizens and require the political organizing of collective groups to gain necessary public recognition.

Recognition is not simply about rights but also about wrongs in the relationship between the American state and Black women. Harris-Perry asserts, "Citizenship is more than an individual exchange of freedoms for rights; it is also membership in a body politic, a nation, and a community. To be deemed fair, a system must offer its citizens equal opportunities for public recognition, and groups cannot systematically suffer from misrecognition in the form of stereotype and stigma."[78] While oppressed populations have sacrificed their bodies and selves both by coercion and voluntary means to advance the American state, citizenship recognition has often been denied to these groups, especially when considering rights like voting or delayed government intervention in cases of disaster. To take it further, Black women face detrimental consequences when policymakers use mischaracterizations and stereotypes to make decisions that negatively impact Black women's lives. Black women in America face a broken social contract that historically denies the promise of freedom and equality while misrecognizing Black women's bodies and character.

In the white supremacist capitalist heteropatriarchal system that constitutes American society, *the gaze*[79] frames one aspect of the mechanics of America's power relations through multiple infiltrating surveillances on subjugated bodies. Black feminists and womanists have long argued that the gaze penetrates and ensnares the Black female body historically. From the narrative of Saartije Baartman exhibited for European audiences, to enslaved African women facing bodily overexposure on the auction

---

[77]Harris-Perry, *Sister Citizen*, 36.

[78]Harris-Perry, *Sister Citizen*, 36–37.

[79]Critical social and postcolonial theorists identify "the gaze" as a philosophical and figurative term that connotes a psychological and social relation of power as it relates to social perception. The gazed are subject to the gazer in this power dynamic, which often normalizes ways of being that misrecognize the gazed while hiding the gazer's power. In the work of philosopher Michel Foucault, the gaze functions as a mechanism of discipline or establishing social control over groups. See Michel Foucault, *Discipline & Punish: The Birth of the Prison*, trans. Alan Sheridan (New York: Vintage Books, 1995). Black feminist bell hooks writes exclusively about Black traditions of "looking back" as an oppositional stance of resistance to contest these forces of social control. See bell hooks, *Black Looks: Race and Representation* (New York: Routledge, 2015).

blocks during the antebellum period, surveillance remains a primary tool of Western culture to control Black women. Such visibility is a trap. Black women's hypervisibility in today's media does not diminish stigmatization. Harris-Perry highlights a contemporary example of the hypervisibility of Black women during Hurricane Katrina: "Black women were at the eye of the rhetorical storm of Hurricane Katrina. It is on the bodies, minds, and lives of black women that the story of Katrina was written."[80] Images of a Black mother and child (somewhat of a Katrina Black Madonna) scurrying the streets of New Orleans in ruin emerged as the storm's most visible narrative in the media. These images blasted across every major media network, making visible Black women's suffering and marking misrecognition by the American state when Katrina victims (mostly Black) struggled to fend for themselves for three days before sustained government intervention arrived. In the case of Katrina, the hypervisibility of Black women did not render citizenship recognition, safety, or celebration of their moral fortitude against death-dealing odds, but reinforced entrapment.

Through the work of Hannah Arendt, Harris-Perry links recognition to human self-actualization and striving. Recognition builds a sense of self as humans receive affirmation of their worth and value. Misrecognition distorts identity and diminishes self-esteem and self-worth, especially in oppressed groups. Harris-Perry argues, "As members of a stigmatized group, African American women lack opportunities for accurate, affirming recognition of the self and yet must contend with hypervisibility imposed by their lower social status. As a group, they have neither the hiding place of private property nor a reasonable expectation of being properly recognized in the public sphere."[81] Instead, Black women struggle to navigate a crooked world, often on their own, while being overexposed and underprotected. The problem of recognition for Black women, in Harris-Perry's estimation, points to voting rights but moreover to the political damages Black women endure by myth and stereotype that result in "shame, suffering, and unequal policy outcomes"[82] in America's crooked room.

Stereotypes represent controlling images that stabilize the social perception of a person or group into oversimplified categories that characterize and confine their agency. According to Black feminist philosopher Patricia Hill Collins, controlling images are used in America to "justify Black

---

[80]Harris-Perry, *Sister Citizen*, 15.

[81]Harris-Perry, *Sister Citizen*, 39.

[82]Harris-Perry, *Sister Citizen*, 251.

women's oppression."[83] Womanist ethicist Emilie Townes, in her classic volume *Womanist Ethics and the Cultural Production of Evil*, argues that controlling images precede history and memory. Through analyzing these images, social ethicists interpret and analyze deeper, interior histories and re-member counternarratives in the cultural production of evil, which is the "ways in which a society can produce misery and suffering in relentlessly systematic ways and sublimely structural ways."[84] Controlling images and stereotypes operate within what Townes names as a fantastic hegemonic imagination that secures "systematic, structural evil in place" and "uses a politicized sense of history and memory to create and shape *its* worldview."[85] For Townes, the fantastic hegemonic imagination exposes not just "supernatural events and phantasms" but the "ordinariness of evil" or the ways that controlling images operate as normative, popular, and commonplace.[86] Three prevailing stereotypes defining Black women in America—such as angry Sapphires, magical Mammies, and lascivious Jezebels—work to fixate and overdetermine Black women's agency as morally deviant. While this chapter interprets Black political women through empowering images of Black women's political agency, these figures do not escape misrecognition, especially in the public eye. In fact, America's crooked room bends the lives of Black political women, making their character susceptible to public scrutiny through demeaning stereotypes.

Sapphire and Baby Mama Drama

The campaign and election to president of Barack Obama resurfaced the controlling image of the "Angry Black Woman" through political caricatures of Michelle Obama in 2008. Harris-Perry recalls the characterization of Michelle as "angry about something" by Fox News contributor Cal Thomas on June 18, 2008, comparing Michelle to Congresswoman Maxine Waters, Congresswoman Cynthia McKinney, and Black mothers who are "angry" about their sons killed in drive-by shootings.[87] Thomas lumps all Black

---

[83]Patricia Hill Collins, *Black Feminist Thought: Knowledge, Consciousness, and the Politics of Empowerment*, 2nd ed., Routledge Classics (New York: Routledge, 2009), 76.

[84]Emilie Maureen Townes, *Womanist Ethics and the Cultural Production of Evil* (New York: Palgrave Macmillan, 2006), 12.

[85]Townes, *Womanist Ethics and the Cultural Production of Evil*, 21.

[86]Townes, *Womanist Ethics and the Cultural Production of Evil*, 21.

[87]Harris-Perry, *Sister Citizen*, 86–87.

women into an angry archetype, including Michelle, to illustrate that there is no profile of a Black woman other than angry "except for Oprah."[88] The Angry Black Woman evokes the Sapphire stereotype to define Black women as "shrill, loud, argumentative, irrationally angry and verbally abusive."[89] Sapphire further identifies a "bad black woman, the black 'bitch,' and the emasculating matriarch."[90]

Michelle faced castigation on the campaign trail for her round butt, her exposed arms, her decision to care for her children, and her demeanor. Perry notes, "Michelle Obama most forcefully encountered the myths about black women in three areas: conversations about her body, discussions about her role as mother, and speculations about her marriage."[91] Fox News displayed a headline during an interview with Michelle Malkin—"Outraged Liberals: Stop Picking on Obama's Baby Mama"[92]—which worked to demean Michelle's sexuality even within the confines of a respectable marriage and signal Michelle as a dominating matriarch. Harris-Perry notes, "Baby mama is a derogatory term for the mother of children born outside of marriage; it usually implies that the woman is difficult and bothersome to the children's father—thus the slang phrase 'baby mama drama.'"[93] Michelle's unwillingness to take on traditional First Lady roles situated her as an overpowering woman and emasculating figure to her husband in the eyes of many of her early critics. Though Michelle did not desire or seek a political title initially, she was characterized as an Angry Black Woman for disavowing proximity to white power. In America's crooked room, Michelle was supposed to be happy (at least visually and vocally) to receive acceptance from white power structures while on the rise to becoming America's political elite in 2008. Michelle's reluctance to smile on demand during the campaign and public speeches that Obama's campaign was the return to or beginning of hope for America, labeled her as perpetually "angry about something." The problem of the Angry Black Woman stereotype is misrecognition because, as Morgan and Bennett make clear, "it holds Black women responsible for power they do not possess, power that is, in fact, being utilized in very

---

[88]Harris-Perry, *Sister Citizen*, 87.

[89]Harris-Perry, *Sister Citizen*, 87.

[90]Harris-Perry, *Sister Citizen*, 88.

[91]Harris-Perry, *Sister Citizen*, 277.

[92]Angela Onwuachi-Willig and Osamudia James, "The Declining Significance of Presidential Races," *Law and Contemporary Problems* 72, no. 4 (2009): 89–108.

[93]Harris-Perry, *Sister Citizen*, 273.

real ways by members of other social groups who can claim emotional innocence as they hide behind, and persecute, the 'Black Bitches' of our cultural imaginations."[94]

Mammy and Scandal

The recurring image of Black political women as domestic servants to white hegemony who are responsible for taking care of America's dirty political laundry evokes the Mammy stereotype. Harris-Perry describes the Mammy image this way:

> Mammy is a symbol of black women as competent, strong, and sassy, yet she is beloved among white people because she uses all of her skills and talents to serve white domestic interests. Mammy makes sure that white children are well fed, that white women are protected from the difficulties of household labor, and that white men have a safe and comfortable home to return to at the end of the day. She ensures order in the white world by ignoring her own family and community. Her devotion and attention are for others, not for herself or her family.[95]

One popular example of a contemporary image of Mammy is Shonda Rhimes's *Scandal* (2012–2017), a television series that dramatizes the story of Oliva Pope, Washington's fixer who is expected to clean up the political messes of America's powerful, resulting in compromising and fatal realities for her job, family, and personal health and well-being. The TV drama is loosely based on the story of Judy Smith, a former press aide in the George H. W. Bush administration who identifies as a crisis management expert with high-profile political and celebrity clients. Black feminist cultural critics have sought to narrate the "paradox" of *Scandal* with empowering and disempowering images that replicate both Mammy and Jezebel stereotypes for Black women. As outlined in Pope's character biography on ABC, "What makes Olivia Pope the best is that she doesn't fix problems. She fixes clients. She fixes people. They come to her at their lowest moment. On the worst day of their lives. Covered in blood, on the verge of conviction when rock bottom is in sight and there's nowhere left to turn they come to Olivia Pope

---

[94]Marcyliena Morgan and Dionne Bennett, "Getting Off of Black Women's Backs: Love Her or Leave Her Alone," *Du Bois Review: Social Science Research on Race* 3, no. 2 (September 2006): 485–502, https://doi.org/10.1017/S1742058X06060334, 499.

[95]Harris-Perry, *Sister Citizen*, 284.

for salvation."[96] Black feminist cultural critic Rachel Allen Griffin retorts, "Read critically, ABC's framing of Olivia as a fixer who delivers 'salvation' clearly aligns her with the societal expectation for Black women to serve as caretakers, which has been and remains a definitive feature of the mammy archetype."[97] Though Pope starring Kerry Washington is elegantly clad, donning white suits and white hats with an eye for justice, the character evokes the myth of the "Magical Negro" or Mammy who sustains the moral depravity of whiteness with voter fraud, election rigging, torture, and intimate violence.

Jezebel the Hoe

Womanist theologian Kelly Brown Douglas names Jezebel as "the paramount image for Black womanhood in White culture."[98] Misrecognizing the Black woman's sexuality and character as an "evil, scheming, seductive woman" with an "insatiable sexual appetite, being extraordinarily passionate, and being sexually aggressive and cunning" framed her as the lascivious other to pious white women (and pious Mammys) and the moral deviant whose body must be tamed by white power.[99] Black feminist cultural critic Tamura Lomax writes extensively about the Jezebelian discourse in *Jezebel Unhinged: Loosing the Black Female Body in Religion and Culture*. Lomax contends,

> Though jezebel may sometimes traverse race and ethnicity in America, her primary and most cogent home is among black women and girls. This was established in at least four ways: (1) the force of a pornotropic gaze that projected previous Africanisms on black enslaved bodies, merging a cultural reading of biblical Jezebel, jezebel the racial trope, and black women and girls; (2) the construction of a capitalist society, which distinguished between white and black women through interpretations of race, gender, and labor; (3) the institution of white femininity as Victorian, natural, and standard; and (4) plantation sexual politics.[100]

[96]Rachel Alicia Griffin, "Olivia Pope as Problematic and Paradoxical," *Feminist Theory & Pop Culture*, January 2015, 38.

[97]Griffin, "Olivia Pope," 38.

[98]Kelly B. Douglas, *Sexuality and the Black Church: A Womanist Perspective* (Maryknoll, NY: Orbis Books, 1999), 36.

[99]Douglas, *Sexuality and the Black Church*, 36.

[100]Tamura A. Lomax, *Jezebel Unhinged: Loosing the Black Female Body in Religion and*

Jezebel the Queen Mother in the biblical text faces castigation because she maintains her commitments to her gods, stays loyal to her husband, and wields the power of the monarch with the same influence as her contemporary the prophet Elijah. Second Kings presents a long, detailed narrative including four scenes of Jezebel's death to illustrate a fallen queen being thrown out of the window and her body eaten by dogs. Even to her death, Jezebel adorns her body with makeup, dresses in the finest clothing of royal splendor, and waits for her perpetrators as an act of agency to die on her own terms. Lomax asserts, "Unlike Ahab, Jezebel does not dissolve into oblivion. She thrives appearing again and again, responding to and triggering fear and fantasy and desire and distaste over and over, dying a violent death each time, reminding women what happens when they stand outside of cultural scripts."[101] While the biblical narrative does not describe a sexually promiscuous woman, Jezebel is maligned because of her self-possession and power. Black women who exercise ambition and wield power are often portrayed and reduced to sexual, seductress prowess.

The salacious rumors to malign Vice President Kamala Harris's political influence were evident during the Biden-Harris 2020 presidential campaign. Though present in her previous political run, Harris's misrecognition as Jezebel intensified upon Biden's announcement that Harris would be his running mate. The conservative ads and memorabilia developed by a seller named the Oxygen Bandit appeared on Amazon and other websites to encourage voters to "Just Say No to Joe and the Hoe" and affirm cultural myths that Harris could only be eligible for this level of political responsibility if she slept her way to the top.[102] Just two days after the Biden-Harris inauguration on January 22, 2021, white Southern Baptist pastor Tom Buck of First Baptist Church of Lindale, Texas, tweeted, "I can't imagine any truly God-fearing Israelite who would've wanted their daughters to view Jezebel as an inspirational role model because she was a woman in power."[103] Buck's tweet links Harris to the Jezebel stereotype because of her political agency and power. Buck revokes both Harris's gender and race in the Jezebelian image. Buck clarifies, "To be clear, if Trump had been the first white man

---

Culture (Durham, NC: Duke University Press, 2018), 23.

[101]Lomax, *Jezebel Unhinged*, 43.

[102]Stephanie Guerilus, "Amazon Takes Down 'Joe and the Hoe' Shirts Belittling Kamala Harris," TheGrio, August 19, 2020, https://thegrio.com/2020/08/19/amazon-joe-the-hoe-shirts-kamala-harris/.

[103]Tom Buck (@TomBuck), "I can't imagine any truly God-fearing Israelite . . . ," Twitter, January 22, 2021, https://twitter.com/TomBuck/status/1352610389914214400.

to hold the office of President, I wouldn't have wanted my sons to look up to him as a role model . . . certainly not because of the color of his skin."[104] After harsh criticism, Buck further explained his attacks against Harris the following day: "For those torn up over my tweet, I stand by it 100%. My problem is her godless character. She not only is the most radical pro-abortion VP ever, but also most radical LGBT advocate. She performed one of the first Lesbian 'marriages.' Pray for her, but don't praise her!"[105] Buck makes the case that Harris's progressive politics renders a "godless character." Though missing from Buck's language, the underlying cause of Harris's morally bereft actions is her identity as a Black woman. Harris becomes a Jezebel whose body and power need to be tamed and brought down, certainly not celebrated.

A Bent Condition

The prevailing stereotypes often overlap in America's crooked room while also hindering public perceptions about Black women's bodies and character. Harris-Perry argues that Michelle Obama faced demeaning assaults based on all three of the controlling images—Jezebel, Mammy, and Sapphire. However, just as former first lady Michelle Obama is stereotyped by these images, she consistently claps back by subverting the misrecognition imposed upon her body and character. Black feminist cultural critic Brittney Cooper illuminates Michelle's embodied opposition with the example of the "ponytail politics" Michelle uses to clap back or showcase public dissent at Trump's election.[106] Michelle's subversion is double-sided, with positive and negative consequences for Black women who exercise a similar self-possession against these pervasive images. At one end, Michelle represents most Black women who resist these stereotypes through a subversive sass in the public sphere. Contrarily, Michelle may expose a political privilege of which not every Black woman can fight back successfully. In line with Harris-Perry, the political consequences of these stereotypes are significant. Legal scholars Angela Onwuachi-Willig and Osamudia James confirm, "The legal implications of such images of black women in our society are serious, in both a historical and a contemporary context. Stereotypical images of

---

[104]Buck, "I can't imagine."

[105]Tom Buck (@TomBuck), "For those torn up over my tweet, I stand by it 100%," Twitter, January 23, 2021, https://twitter.com/TomBuck/status/1352974668832112640.

[106]Brittney Cooper, "Ponytail Politics: Decoding Michelle Obama's Hairstyle at Trump's Inauguration," *Christian Century*, February 28, 2018.

black women, especially if unmarried, have worked to reinforce policies and rhetoric that have attacked the existence, survival, and continuation of black families, especially those in lower socioeconomic brackets."[107] Legal theorist Dorothy Roberts, in *Killing the Black Body: Race, Reproduction, and the Meaning of Liberty*, describes one of the most tragic political and legal consequences for Black women: involuntary sterilization as referenced in Hamer's story.[108]

For Douglas, misrecognizing Black women's sexuality justifies white hegemonic control in the Western imagination. Douglas writes,

> The significance of Jezebel and Mammy to the institution of slavery, and more especially to White patriarchal power, shows why these images are so central to White culture and thus so persistent and abiding. By distorting the sexuality of Black women, White culture effectively dehumanized them. Such dehumanization made them most vulnerable to rape by White men. The weapon of rape provided an effective means of control. In essence, the Jezebel and Mammy images crafted in White culture allowed White people to cruelly exploit Black female bodies with relative impunity. Such exploitation is a linchpin to the survival of White hegemony.[109]

Building on Harris-Perry, Black queer activist Charlene Carruthers takes it further to suggest, "Black women are quarantined to the crooked room" in the larger structure of Black oppression.[110] Misrecognition of Black women's bodies and character justify and validate white hegemonic control of Black lives. In Townes's view, the fantastic hegemonic imagination reveals that neither the privileged nor the oppressed can break away from its influence. Townes writes, "the fantastic hegemonic imagination is in all of us. It is found in the privileged and the oppressed. It is no respecter of race, ethnicity, nationality, or color. It is not bound by gender or sexual orientation. It can be found in the old and the young. None of us naturally escape it, for it is found in the deep cultural codings we live with and through in U.S. society."[111] Both

---

[107]Onwuachi-Willig and James, "The Declining Significance of Presidential Races," 103.

[108]Dorothy E. Roberts, *Killing the Black Body: Race, Reproduction, and the Meaning of Liberty*, 2nd Vintage Books ed. (New York: Vintage Books, 2017), 90.

[109]Douglas, *Sexuality and the Black Church*, 44–45.

[110]Charlene A. Carruthers, *Unapologetic: A Black, Queer, and Feminist Mandate for Radical Movement* (Boston: Beacon Press, 2018), 42.

[111]Townes, *Womanist Ethics and the Cultural Production of Evil*, 21.

by strategies of resistance and accommodation, Black women continue to tilt their lives and actions to confront these controlling images that result in devastating political consequences for their bodies and lives.

My womanist articulation of Black women's bendedness by multidimensional oppressions at the crossways of race, gender, sexuality, and class that are intersecting and interlocking in a white supremacist capitalist heteropatriarchal America and the Black Church aligns with Harris-Perry's description of the sociopolitical attacks levied against the character of Black women in America's crooked room. The problem of recognition in America is directly linked to Black women's quest for political liberation. Multidimensional systems of oppression are not just vicious, but they function, to borrow from womanist theologian Delores Williams, as *demonarchy* tormenting the humanity of Black women. Williams contends, "Demonarchy can be understood as the demonic governance of black women's lives by white male and white female ruled systems using racism, violence, violation, retardation, and death as instruments of social control . . . a traditional and collective oppression of white government in relation to black women."[112] Attention to Black women's agency and misrecognition is essential for womanist theology and ethics to redeem Black women's humanity, but also to reveal the embodied power that Black women possess to unbend our lives, institutions, and world.

The Lives We Save May Be Our Own

Senator Jeff Sessions's 2017 promotion to attorney general opened a seat in the Senate and demanded a special election in Alabama to fill the slot between two candidates: Republican Roy Moore (a candidate alleged for sexual violation of teenage girls, but also known for racist, homophobic, and transphobic remarks) and Democrat Doug Jones (though he was known for his prosecution of the Ku Klux Klan bombers of the Sixteenth Street Baptist Church containing four little girls in 1963, Jones also advertised his Senate campaign with racially insensitive ads). With the appointment of Trump's presidential cabinet amid the developing of policies to repeal Deferred Action for Childhood Arrivals (DACA), and Sessions himself in

---

[112]Delores S. Williams, "The Color of Feminism: Or Speaking the Black Woman's Tongue," in *Feminist Theological Ethics: A Reader*, ed. Lois K. Daly (Louisville, KY: Westminster John Knox Press, 1994), 51.

2018 quoting Romans 13 as a move to justify anti-immigration and building a wall of exclusion, it may be argued that Trump's presidential campaign to Make America Great Again was synonymous with "Make America Hate Again."[113] If America has ever exercised moral virtue, which points to the historical moments when its citizens have lived up to the democratic virtues of liberty, justice, and equality, then such greatness can only be marked upon the backs of oppressed people, particularly the labor and political movement of Black women. The 2017 Alabama Senate election marked a turning point in America that could no longer deny that "Black women are a voting powerhouse."[114] According to Higher Heights PAC, "Black women made up 17% of voters who cast ballots in the 2017 recent U.S. Senate election in Alabama, but they account for less than 14% of the state's population."[115] The 98 percent changemaking vote that led to Jones's victory in the 2017 Alabama election was not a result of Jones's campaign but Black women leading "grassroots organizations like Woke Vote led by DeJuana Thompson and Black Political Action Committee (BlackPAC) led by Adrianne Shropshire knocking on doors and registering voters."[116] December 2017 revealed Black women in Alabama recognizing, "The lives we save may be our own," and in the process, we may save America too."

In the middle of a global pandemic, conservative extremists inspired by President Trump led an attempted Capitol coup on January 6, 2021, to wage war against democracy because of the shifting political landscape and the ratification of a new Democratic regime. CNN quickly identified the Capitol attacks as a "day that shook America" when homegrown terror struck the nation again.[117] It is no mystery that the Georgia Senate win of January 5,

---

[113]Sessions warned Americans to "obey the laws of the government because God has ordained them for the purpose of order" in Romans 13:1. This passage was formerly used by slaveholders to ordain slavery as also purposed by God. Julie Zauzmer and Keith McMillan, "Jeff Sessions Cites Romans 13, a Bible Passage Used to Defend Slavery, in Defense of Family Separations," *Washington Post*, June 15, 2018, https://www.washingtonpost.com/news/acts-of-faith/wp/2018/06/14/jeff-sessions-points-to-the-bible-in-defense-of-separating-immigrant-families/?arc404=true.

[114]Higher Heights for America PAC, "By the Numbers."

[115]Higher Heights for America PAC, "By the Numbers."

[116]Marie Solis, "Black Women 'Saved America' from Roy Moore—Now Vote Them into Office, Political Activists Say," *Newsweek*, December 15, 2017, https://www.newsweek.com/thank-black-women-vote-office-political-activists-748619.

[117]CNN's phrasing regarding the insurrection as the "day that shook America" traces back to September 11, 2001, when America endured the attacks by Islamic terrorist group al-Qaeda. The suicide missions enabled four moving planes to crash into US-designated targets

2021, made possible by the political agency of Stacey Abrams and grassroots activism of Black women, and the election of President Joe Biden and Vice President Kamala Harris, escalated the Capitol siege. Seemingly, the bloody insurrection in the aftermath of a "transformed electorate" and "changing faces of leadership" with Black women behind the scenes and at the helm revealed greater challenges ahead.

At the inauguration of the forty-sixth president of the United States, Joe Biden, and Vice President Harris on January 20, 2021, the first Youth Poet Laureate Amanda Gorman delivered a timely public address, "The Hill We Climb," reminding America that this is an inflection point in the American story. In the aftermath of the coup that illuminated a historically divided nation, Gorman's poetic battle cry declaring, "This is the era of just redemption,"[118] echoes Black suffragist women. Media firestorms following Gorman's call for social change quickly crowned Gorman as the voice of the New American Majority.[119] American editorial cartoonist Andy Marlette of the *Pensacola News Journal* published an image titled "Amanda Gorman to the Rescue," of a fearless Gorman clad in the golden cape and scarlet mantle of a superhero carrying a weak and fragile Uncle Sam as a depiction of Gorman as America's savior.[120] The problem of this image is that the salvation of America and democracy cannot be the burden of only Black women. In fact, to place such a mantle on Black women is to divinize the burdens of sacrifice, surrogacy, and strength. It is not enough to #thankBlackwomen and not to #payBlackwomen through adequate compensation for their labor. Black women need more than appeals to #trustBlackwomen because of their keen discernment motivated by a moral imperative for justice for all, but Black women need people of all colors, persons of all races and genders, and the whole of America to recognize Black women by rejecting

---

in New York, Washington, DC, and Pennsylvania, killing three thousand people and injuring countless others. Almost twenty years later, the Capitol coup attempt exposed terror within the United States as alt-right extremists descended on the Capitol in efforts to take back the country and revoke America's formative ideal of democracy.

[118]Amanda Gorman, "Read: Youth Poet Laureate Amanda Gorman's Inaugural Poem," CNN, January 20, 2021, https://www.cnn.com/2021/01/20/politics/amanda-gorman-inaugural-poem-transcript/index.html.

[119]Liesl Schillinger, "How Amanda Gorman Became the Voice of a New American Era," *The Guardian*, January 22, 2021, http://www.theguardian.com/books/2021/jan/22/how-amanda-gorman-became-the-voice-of-a-new-american-era.

[120]Andy Marlette (@AndyMarlette), "New Cartoon: Poet and American Super Hero, @TheAmandaGorman," Twitter, January 21, 2021, https://twitter.com/AndyMarlette/status/1352273352661069825.

the oppressive stereotypes, stigmas, and tropes that entrap Black women's bodies and devalue their moral agency.

The 98 percent of Black women who went to the polls in December 2017 in Alabama did not go because Doug Jones was the least racist candidate; they went to save themselves. Black women have always known that our saviors are ourselves and that the salvation of Black women is never just for Black women alone. This is why Harriet Tubman "walked to Canada" for herself and for her people on numerous occasions without a map or a trail, but with the Spirit as a divine compass. Perhaps the lesson is #followBlackwomen, or at least make way for Black women as they work with God to struggle for wholeness, advocate for suffering communities, transform selves and this world as it is known not in the "sweet by and by," but in the here and now, and by extension, do the work of saving America, again and again.

4

Our Saviors Are Ourselves, Part Two

Redeeming the Soul of the Black Church

Women, if the soul of this nation is to be saved, I believe you must become its soul.

—Coretta Scott King[1]

*This **hope** we have as an anchor of the soul, both sure and steadfast, and which enters the **Presence** behind the **veil**, where the forerunner has entered for us, **even** Jesus, having become High Priest forever according to the order of Melchizedek.*

—Hebrews 6:19–20 (NKJV, emphasis added)

Salvation is a central locus in Christian theology and a moral crisis for oppressed populations. As an anti-oppression paradigm that takes seriously the survival and liberation of Black women, while advocating for the well-being of all, womanist theology embodies God-talk for the least of these. While survival represents the means, liberation—the freedom and flourishing of Black women—is the ultimate telos. Womanist theology as an approach in liberation theology grapples with four central questions: (1) Who are the

---

[1] This is a popular quote attributed to Coretta Scott King. NPR journalist Debbie Elliot reported that King spoke these words to a group gathered at a Poor People's Campaign rally in Washington, DC days after the assassination of her husband Martin Luther King Jr. in 1968. Debbie Elliott, "After MLK's Death, Coretta Scott King Went to Memphis to Finish His Work," NPR, April 8, 2018, sec. 1968: How We Got Here, https://www.npr.org/2018/04/08/597703360/after-mlks-death-coretta-scott-king-went-to-memphis-to-finish-his-work.

oppressed? (2) From what and from whom must the oppressed be saved? (3) Who are the liberators? (4) What is the liberation for, or to what end?

Religious historian Sheila Briggs, in her classic article "Can an Enslaved God Liberate? Hermeneutical Reflections on Philippians 2:6–11," argues that the oppressed bear "an indirect hermeneutical privilege" that proffers an analogical reconstruction of the past to discern the basis of the social relationships that rendered the condition of oppression.[2] Briggs contends, "The oppressed—and not the oppressor—have an interest in recognizing the true nature of the social relationships, in which they are, so they can alter it."[3] The economic and political history of Black women from slavery to freedom begs the question of whether a liberating God has concern for Black women. Celie, the protagonist in Alice Walker's *The Color Purple*, laments, "If he [God] ever listened to poor colored women, the world would be a different place, I can tell you."[4] In Celie's imagination, the Western archetype of God as "big and old and tall and graybearded and white" inhibits Black women from finding themselves in God's image and care. Adapting Walker's theological suspicion in the 1980s, womanist scholars interrogating geopolitical realities as well as theological categories with Black women at the epistemological center soon developed a progressive interest in articulating what Jesus Christ Liberator means to and for Black women. Womanist inquiries analyzing key tenets of the Christian tradition such as sin, suffering, and salvation serve as intersecting crossways between theology and Black women's moral agency.

What must Black women do to be saved? Womanist soteriology emerges at the crossroads of valuations of the body and soul. In a world that seeks to deny Black women's human dignity, the salvation of Black women is the reclamation of our identity, redemption of our personhood, remembering of our stories, restoration of our bodies, and recognition of our moral character. It is not the wrongdoing of Black women from which we must be saved, but the wrong done to Black women from oppressive systems and powers in the society as traced in the labor force in chapter 2, the American political scene in chapter 3, and most notably the Black Church, as discussed in this chapter. Black women's salvation is both material and immaterial, pointing to liberation from the sociopolitical, biophysical, and psychospiritual forces that stifle Black women's freedom and flourishing.

---

[2] Sheila Briggs, "Can an Enslaved God Liberate?: Hermeneutical Reflections on Philippians 2:6–11," *Semeia* 47 (1989): 142.

[3] Briggs, "Can an Enslaved God Liberate?," 142.

[4] Alice Walker, *The Color Purple* (Orlando: Harcourt, 2003), 193.

Such forces expose both the white supremacist capitalist heteropatriarchal American society and the Black Church as systemic and institutional perpetrators that condemn and ultimately suck the life out of Black women in their struggle for wholeness.

First, this chapter implicates the Black Church and early movements in Black theology for ignoring and discrediting Black women's participation in shaping the soul of Black liberation. In efforts to lift the veil to reveal the hidden figures of Black social changemaking, this section offers womanist theology as a corrective to the Black Church and Black theology in its quest to expand the Black liberative imagination to value every body. Second, I return to Melissa Harris-Perry's notion of the crooked room to unmask the Black Church's obsession with saving Black women as a distortion of the Christian mission and the gospel of liberation. While Harris-Perry rightly names womanist theology as a prophetic response to the separate and unequal status of Black women in the Black Church, I critique Harris-Perry for misinterpreting the womanist theo-ethical vision as an undue burden for Black women to save ourselves and ultimately *become* God. In contradistinction to Harris-Perry, the third move of this chapter takes up the promise of womanist theologies of salvation and ethics of redemption for Black women in the United States living in a death-dealing society that locates Black women in the crosshairs of political and theological assaults. In efforts to address the ethical problems and discern the necessary moral action, womanist ethicist Emilie Townes argues in *Breaking the Fine Rain of Death: African American Health Issues and a Womanist Ethic of Care*, social ethicists must return to the question of salvation "again and again."[5] Womanist perspectives on sin, suffering, and salvation inform pathways toward a womanist theo-ethical model of mutual liberation and co-partnership between Black women and God to liberate Black women, and in so doing, redeem the soul of the Black Church.

Lifting the Veil: Black Women and the Soul of Black Liberation

While the starting point of Black women's political agency is the Black Church, Black women are often missing from the narratives of the spiritual

---

[5]Emilie Maureen Townes, *Breaking the Fine Rain of Death: African American Health Issues and a Womanist Ethic of Care* (Eugene, OR: Wipf & Stock, 2006), 26.

and prophetic witness of that institution. The Black Church's race to freedom depicted as the public proclamation of solely Black men ignores Black
women's contributions and distorts its vision of freedom and liberation for
the Black community. Black women redeeming the soul of America *and* the
Black Church points to reclaiming a vision of Black liberation that includes
every body and the perquisites of *somebodiness* for everybody.[6]

Behind the Veil: The Souls of Black Folk *and the Negro Church*

At the turn of the twentieth century, Black sociologist W. E. B. Du
Bois—in his timeless 1903 classic, *The Souls of Black Folk*—analyzed the
spiritual and philosophical dimensions of Black life in America. Du Bois
names the enduring problem of the twentieth century as the "color line" and
situates his analysis not within the construct of race like his philosophical
contemporaries, but within spiritual language (e.g., songs, sermons, etc.)
and theological symbolism (e.g., the Veil).[7] The title alone negates the
construction of Blackness by whiteness as a soulless other and avows the
human dignity of Black people as "folk" or the commonsense people who
represent the carriers of culture in American society.

In the opening of the volume, Du Bois situates the social and moral
predicament of Black people within two probing theo-ethical questions
from the shadows of his childhood encounters (facing the looks of a white
girl): "How does it feel to be a problem?"[8] and "Why does God make me
an outcast and a stranger in my own house?"[9] Du Bois narrates the psy-
chosocial awareness, dubbed "double-consciousness," that Black Americans
endure while navigating a society in which they are both native and outcast.
Double-consciousness points to the duality of "two souls, two thoughts, two
unreconciled strivings, two warring ideals in one dark body" that frame
African American identity and experience.[10] Most significantly, Du Bois
characterizes "the Veil" as a metaphor to describe the spiritual strivings and
social stance of the Black community trapped by the penetrating white gaze.

---

[6]The term *somebodiness*, coined by Black liberation theologian James Cone, speaks to the
self-affirmation that Black people developed to counter a white supremacist world that
denied their humanity. See James H. Cone, *The Spirituals and the Blues: An Interpretation*
(Maryknoll, NY: Orbis Books, 1999), 5.

[7]W. E. B. Du Bois and Brent Hayes Edwards, *The Souls of Black Folk* (Oxford: Oxford
University Press, 2007), 15.

[8]Du Bois and Edwards, *The Souls of Black Folk*, 7.

[9]Du Bois and Edwards, *The Souls of Black Folk*, 8.

[10]Du Bois and Edwards, *The Souls of Black Folk*, 8.

Du Bois articulates the Black experience as "this sense of always looking at one's self through the eyes of others, of measuring one's soul by the tape of a world that looks on in amused contempt and pity."[11] On one end, the Veil symbolizes a guise that inhibits one's ability to both see and be seen fully. The Veil casts a shadow that covers the true identity of the concealed. Such a shadow produces contempt and shame for the looked-upon in efforts to be both understood and recognized, which marks the condition of African Americans as between two worlds "within the Veil" and living in the valley of the shadow of death. On the other end, children "born with a Veil" (en caul or encased in a thin membrane from the amniotic sac usually over their face or eyes) bear witness to the gift of "second-sight" or prophetic and psychic insight in Black folklore that marked a sign of a special destiny.[12] Such a gift endows Black consciousness with the ability to not "pass" easily into the chasm of whiteness but to turn away from the white gaze and create counterworlds of being and becoming that move from the shadow of death to new life.

Du Bois analyzed the Negro Church of the Reconstruction period by identifying its shortcomings "behind the Veil" wrestling with its twoness. The Negro Church, described by Du Bois, existed as the "social centre of Negro life . . . the most characteristic expression of African character"[13] and "a real conserver of morals, a strengthener of family life, and the final authority on what is Good and Right."[14] However, the social forces of the "Negro Problem"[15] or the double life fostered a "peculiar wrenching of the soul"[16] that corrupted Black religious life and shifted the Negro Church from loving communities of shared faith to "groups of cold, fashionable devotees, in no way distinguishable from similar white groups save in color of skin"—and "into large social and business institutions catering to the desire for information and amusement of their members, warily avoiding unpleasant questions both within and without the black world."[17] For Du Bois, intracommunal strife, gender conflict, religious escapism, and white imitation stood at the center of the corruption of the turn-of-the-century Negro Church. Du Bois framed the Negro Church as missing the "guiding

---

[11]Du Bois and Edwards, *The Souls of Black Folk*, 8.
[12]Du Bois and Edwards, *The Souls of Black Folk*, 8.
[13]Du Bois and Edwards, *The Souls of Black Folk*, 130.
[14]Du Bois and Edwards, *The Souls of Black Folk*, 131.
[15]Du Bois and Edwards, *The Souls of Black Folk*, 136.
[16]Du Bois and Edwards, *The Souls of Black Folk*, 136.
[17]Du Bois and Edwards, *The Souls of Black Folk*, 139.

star of the past" (which Du Bois located in the soulful Sorrow Songs of the enslaved) and searching "in the great night [for] a new religious ideal."[18]

Somebodiness: Black Theology, Black Power, and Distorted Visions of Black Liberation

Black theology traces its roots to the bodies and souls of African people and culture that carried a cosmological and teleological sense of interconnectedness between humanity, the Divine, and the material world from the shores of Africa through the Middle Passage to the New World. In *Slave Religion: The "Invisible Institution" in the Antebellum South*, religious historian Albert Raboteau traces the influences of African traditional religions and new religious ideas that formed a multivocal religiosity of the enslaved. Raboteau asserts,

> One of the most durable and adaptable constituents of the slave's culture, linking African past with American present, was his [*sic*] religion. It is important to realize, however, that in the Americas the religions of Africa have not been merely preserved as static "Africanisms" or as archaic "retentions." The fact is that they have continued to develop as living traditions putting down new roots in new soil, bearing new fruit as unique hybrids of American origin. African styles of worship, forms of ritual, systems of belief, and fundamental perspectives have remained vital on this side of the Atlantic, not because they were preserved in a "pure" orthodoxy but because they were transformed.[19]

Black theology developed in the resistance and struggle for freedom by enslaved Africans who escaped to find God in the invisible, sacred dwellings in the South away from the encroachment of white oppression and later outside white churches in the formation of visible, autonomous institutions in the North. A Black theological consciousness was nurtured in the civil rights and Black Power movements as Black people resisted white segregation and Black theologians systematized theological perspectives that affirmed the humanity of Black people.

Historians Daina Ramey Berry and Kali Nicole Gross, in *A Black Women's History of the United States*, chronicle the untold and undertold stories of

---

[18]Du Bois and Edwards, *The Souls of Black Folk*, 139.

[19]Albert J. Raboteau, *Slave Religion: The "Invisible Institution" in the Antebellum South* (Oxford: Oxford University Press, 2004), 4.

Black women's roles and significant contributions in shaping the American story. Berry and Gross maintain, "African American women played crucial roles in the civil rights movement at every level."[20] While my grandmother migrated to Chicago in the early 1960s, a few years before her arrival, another Chicago single mother, Mamie Till-Mobley, catapulted to national prominence following the brutal murder of her fourteen-year-old son, Emmett Till. Like most Black migrant families in the Midwest, Till-Mobley sent her son to spend his summer vacation with cousins in Money, Mississippi, in the Mississippi Delta. Till's glance and disputed interaction with a twenty-one-year-old white woman, Carolyn Bryant, in a convenience store broke the social codes of proper exchanges between Black men and white women in the Jim Crow South, which resulted in a fateful end. Bryant's husband, Roy, along with his half-brother, J. W. Milam, armed with guns and white vitriol, seized Till from the house of his great uncle. The men beat, flogged, battered, shot, lynched, and tied Till's body to a cotton gin fan to drown in the Tallahatchie River. Local Mississippi officials recovered Till's mutilated body three days later and sought to bury the body quickly to cover up the story. Till-Mobley advocated that Till's remains be shipped to Chicago and insisted the casket remain open for public viewing to expose "the monstrous face of white supremacy" and gut-wrenching smell of tortured flesh.[21] More than fifty thousand Chicagoans witnessed and millions of Black Americans saw what was done to Till's body through photographs captured by David Jackson and published by *Jet* magazine. The kidnapping and drowning of Emmett Till in the sweltering summer heat of 1955 (like the murder of Trayvon Martin in Sanford, Florida, during Black history month of 2012 or the shooting of Michael Brown in the belly of the summer of 2014 in Ferguson, Missouri, or the killing of George Floyd in Minneapolis, Minnesota, amid multiple pandemics of 2020) marked the ongoing struggle of Black bodies for physical protection from the brutality of whiteness.[22] While

---

[20] Daina Ramey Berry and Kali N. Gross, *A Black Women's History of the United States*, Revisioning American History (Boston: Beacon Press, 2020), 164.

[21] Berry and Gross, *A Black Women's History of the United States*, 167.

[22] In the trial later that year, an all-white petit jury found Bryant and Milam not guilty. The assailants later confessed to the murder of Emmett Till and sold their story to *Look* magazine. In 2017, Duke researcher Timothy Tyson published *The Blood of Emmett Till*, confirming Carolyn Bryant's admission that Emmett Till did not make verbal and sexual advances toward her in their less-than-a-minute exchange in the store on that August day. See Timothy B. Tyson, *The Blood of Emmett Till* (New York: Simon & Schuster, 2017). President Joe Biden signed the Emmett Till Antilynching Act, establishing lynching as a hate crime, on March 29, 2022.

Till's ravished body provoked national awareness of the urgency of Black liberation, an everyday Black single mother—Mamie Till-Mobley—gave rise to a new dawn of Black resistance. With one fearless decision and a subsequent lifelong commitment to activism, Till-Mobley became a mother of the civil rights movement who demonstrated Black women as champions of righteous discontent bent on looking back and reclaiming the disfigured Black body from the bottom of the Western imagination.[23]

Till-Mobley's courageous resistance stirred souls and sparked outrage by Black activists, including Rosa Parks and the Black women architects of the Montgomery Bus Boycott in December 1955 (the same year of the killing of Emmett Till), who organized a sustained protest to place their bodies on the line and confront the exploitation and commodification of Black bodies. From the perspective of "The Spiritual Body Politic," Sheila Briggs describes the civil rights movement as "the body liberating the soul." Briggs asserts,

> In the marches, blacks experienced their bodies as their own; irrespective of how little property or education they possessed they had their bodies, and because they had their bodies they had rights. In the civil rights movement, blacks made *Habeas Corpus* apply to them. In a racist society, black bodies have been despised, they have been exposed to aesthetic and moral censure: they have been seen as ugly and promiscuous, the bodies of menials and prostitutes. The involvement of blacks in physical protest challenged these cultural stereotypes when black bodies expressed dignity, solidarity, forbearance, resolution, courage, hope. This was less a case of the body mirroring the soul than of the body reshaping the soul.[24]

Briggs recasts Martin Luther King Jr.'s story in *Strength to Love* of Black freedom fighter Mother Pollard. When asked whether she was tired dur-

---

[23]I am drawing from bell hooks's notion of the "oppositional gaze" that resists constructs that sustain Black people as only being looked upon, but there is power in turning the gaze and "looking back" that demonstrates resistance, but also agency. For hooks, "There is power in looking." Till-Mobley reclaimed the power of her story and son's life by lifting the veil of her son's maimed body, but also forcing the world to look upon him. See bell hooks, "Oppositional Gaze: Black Female Spectators," in *Black Looks: Race and Representation* (New York: Routledge, 2015), 115–31.

[24]Sheila Briggs, "The Spiritual Body Politic," paper presented at the For the Trumpet Shall Sound: Protest, Prayer, and Prophecy Conference, Emory University, Atlanta, October 1988, http://www.domcentral.org/library/spir2day/884054briggs.html.

ing the yearlong Montgomery Bus Boycott, she declared emphatically, "My feets is tired, but my soul is rested."[25] The broader herstory of the civil rights movement reveals numerous Black women as movers, shakers, and shapers of a Black consciousness and spiritual witness that fashioned the soul of Black liberation.

The civil rights and Black Power movements awakened the resurgence of the Black Christian radical tradition. The 1966 statement on "Black Power" published in the *New York Times* by the National Council of Negro Churchmen (which later became the National Council of Black Church-men—NCBC) demonstrated Black clergy confronting the "gross imbalance of power and conscience between Negroes and white Americans" while indicting white Christianity as hypocritical and antithetical to the gospel of liberation.[26] Black systematic theologian James Cone, affectionately known as the father of Black liberation theology, began his theological quest in the late 1960s with the central question of Black liberation theology: "What does it mean to be unashamedly Black and unapologetically Christian?" Cone positioned the starting point of Black liberation theology with life itself and within the condition of Black people in America at the height of twentieth-century movements toward Black liberation. As early as his first publication, *Black Theology and Black Power,* in 1969, Cone defined Black theology as a discourse committed to reclaiming self-worth in Black people through the lens of the Christian faith.

> The task of Black Theology, then, is to analyze the black man's [*sic*] condition in the light of God's revelation in Jesus Christ with the purpose of creating a new understanding of black dignity among black people, and providing the necessary *soul* [my emphasis] in that people, to destroy white racism. Black Theology is primarily a theol-ogy of and for black people who share the common belief that racism

---

[25]Briggs, "The Spiritual Body Politic." See also Martin Luther King and Coretta Scott King, *Strength to Love* (Minneapolis: Fortress Press, 2010), 132–33.

[26]The Black clergymen writers and signers of this statement represented mostly northern Black clergy who valued Martin Luther King Jr.'s efforts toward integration in the South, but they believed integration was not a solution and inadequate if reduced to a "false kind of 'integration' in which all power was in the hands of white people." These Black clergymen affirmed Black power as "already present" in Black churches and Black institutions that needed to be awakened and affirmed to work with God for racial justice. "Black Power: Statement by the National Council of Negro Churchmen, July 31, 1966," in James H. Cone and Gayraud S. Wilmore, eds., *Black Theology: A Documentary History,* 2nd ed. (Maryknoll, NY: Orbis Books, 1993), 19–26.

will be destroyed only when black people decide to say in word and deed to the white racist: 'We ain't gonna stand any more of this.' The purpose of Black Theology is to analyze the nature of the Christian faith in such a way that black people can say Yes to blackness and No to whiteness and mean it.[27]

American chattel slavery steeped in whiteness coupled with racial, economic, and sexual exploitation functioned to denigrate the bodies and souls of Black people. For Cone, "The essence of ante-bellum black religion was the emphasis on the *somebodiness* of black slaves."[28] Cone identified the preacher and the sermonic moment as central to revaluing the human worth and dignity of the enslaved by announcing, "You are created in God's image. You are not slaves, you are not 'niggers'; you are God's children."[29] The enslaved also utilized spirituals and the blues as early sources to reject theological beliefs that God desired their bondage and to reclaim their very existence that had been denied by white oppression as worthy of God's care and freedom. In *The Spiritual and the Blues: An Interpretation*, Cone writes,

> The basic idea of the spirituals is that slavery contradicts God; it is a denial of God's will. To be enslaved is to be declared nobody, and that form of existence contradicts God's creation of people to be God's children. Because black people believed that they were God's children, they affirmed their *somebodiness*, refusing to reconcile their servitude with divine revelation. They rejected white distortions of the gospel, which emphasized the obedience of slaves to their masters. They contended that God willed their freedom and not their slavery.[30]

The struggle for recognition of Black human dignity persisted beyond enslavement as Black people continued to resist an unjust American culture and white anti-Christianity that maintained Black inferiority.

The primary threat against the somebodiness of Black people in Cone's schema is American racism. Racism in any form that renders Black people

---

[27]James H. Cone, *Black Theology and Black Power*, 50th anniversary ed. (Maryknoll, NY: Orbis Books, 2018), 132.

[28]James H. Cone, *The Spirituals and the Blues* (Maryknoll, NY: Orbis Books, 1992), 16.

[29]Cone, *The Spirtuals and the Blues*, 17. Cone quotes this sermon from Howard Thurman. See Howard Thurman, *Deep River and the Negro Spiritual Speaks of Life and Death* (Richmond, IN: Friends United Press, 1999).

[30]Cone, *The Spirtuals and the Blues*, 33.

powerlessness is anti-Christian—in direct opposition to the gospel of Jesus Christ. The racist participation and silence of the white church from slavery to segregation bore witness to its rejection of Christ. Cone writes in an essay titled "The White Church and Black Power," "If there is any contemporary meaning of the Antichrist (or 'the principalities and powers'), the white church seems to be a manifestation of it. It is the enemy of Christ. It was the white 'Christian' church which took the lead in establishing slavery as an institution and segregation as a pattern in society by sanctioning all-white congregations."[31] In efforts to reconcile the Christian nonviolence of Martin Luther King Jr. and the radical Black nationalism of Malcolm X,[32] Cone's resolve was concrete that Black Power is Christ's message to the church of the twentieth century to deny white oppression at every turn:

> Black Power, even in its most radical expression, is not the antithesis of Christianity, nor is it a heretical idea to be tolerated with painful forbearance. It is, rather, Christ's central message to twentieth-century America. And unless the empirical denominational church makes a determined effort to recapture the man Jesus through a total identification with the suffering poor as expressed in Black Power, that church will become exactly what Christ is not.[33]

Black Power refuted any articulation of Christianity that sustained the oppression of Black people. It further disavowed "any concept of God that makes black suffering the will of God."[34] Cone's reclamation of Black human dignity or *somebodiness* in Black theological constructions confronted the duplicity of white Christianity and articulated the need for the Church to be converted to the God of liberation who identifies through the Jesus of history and the Christ of faith with the conditions of oppressed peoples. In Cone's estimation, the white church that has perpetuated the denigration of Black humanity throughout history must answer to the question "What must I do to be saved?"[35]

In its "second stage," Black liberation theology further advocated for

---

[31]James H. Cone, "The White Church and Black Power," in *Black Theology: A Documentary History*, ed. James H. Cone and Gayraud S. Wilmore, 2nd ed. (Maryknoll, NY: Orbis Books, 1993), 73.

[32]Cone, *Black Theology and Black Power*, xxvi.

[33]Cone, *Black Theology and Black Power*, 1.

[34]Cone, *Black Theology and Black Power*, 140.

[35]Cone, *Black Theology and Black Power*, 92.

transformation in the Black Church concerning its theological witness. [36] Since liberation is God's ultimate response to the oppressed as narrated in scriptural accounts of the exodus story and articulated in the Gospel writings about Jesus Christ, Christ *is* Black in Cone's theology through identification with the oppressed. The Church must *become* Black to identify with Christ and stand on the side of the suffering. Building upon Du Bois's critique of the Negro Church for losing its way, Cone posited that the twentieth-century Black Church also needed to undergo conversion from white control and beliefs that disempowered Black people. Cone argued, "If the black church organizations want to remain faithful to the New Testament gospel and to the great tradition of the pre–Civil War black church, they must relinquish their stake in the status quo and the values in white society by identifying exclusively with Black Power. Black Power is the only hope of the black church in America."[37] The Black Church held greater responsibility beyond a place of gathering to affirm Black existence, but to *be* Christian the Black Church needed to interrogate the white social structures oppressing Black people. The Black Church could not be absolved from political responsibility to resist the dominant powers in its elevation of the somebodiness in Black identity. Moreover, Cone recognized that the dissension between denominational and local Black churches on the question of political liberation signaled that few Black churches held an "institutional commitment to organize church life and work for the creation of freedom."[38]

Though Cone was not alone in his stance (i.e., members of the NCBC), Cone rattled early Black theologians and Black Church pastors who understood Black Power as a militant, secular ideology—first initiated by young radical activist Stokely Carmichael—that was unaffiliated with the Christian evangelistic mission of salvation and opposed to King's integrationist vision. By the same token, Black Power, as both a political concept against white control and a movement paradigm, posed challenges for Cone's vision (and that of other Black theological contemporaries) of Black liberation because of its patriarchal, sexist, and misogynist leanings that privileged only Black male voices and leadership. The absence of Black women writers or signatories on the 1966 NCNC "Black Power" statement illustrates the missing perspectives of Black women in the early Black liberative theological imagi-

---

[36]James H. Cone and Gayraud S. Wilmore, eds., *Black Theology: A Documentary History*, 2nd ed. (Maryknoll, NY: Orbis Books, 1993), 5.

[37]Cone, *Black Theology and Black Power*, 123.

[38]James H. Cone, "Black Ecumenism and the Liberation Struggle," *The Journal of the Interdenominational Theological Center* 7, no. 1 (1979): 6.

nation and discounts the numerous ways Black women shaped the Black freedom movements. Similarly, Cone's early works exhibit a patriarchal willfulness and sexist blind spot by failing to even mention Black women and children in his first volume. Cone reformed the notion of Black Power in later works to articulate a wider ecumenical scope of Black liberation for all oppressed peoples consistent with the gospel of liberation (articulated in Luke 4:8–19) at the crux of the Christian faith, but Cone's conversion came only after sustained critiques by Cone's Black women students about the missing perspectives of Black women and children in his Black theological constructions and the Black Church.

There is no question that James Cone and Black liberation theology fostered one of the most significant theological movements of the twentieth century in both the United States and abroad. Cone's articulation of God on the side of the oppressed held universal impetus influencing domestic and global theologies of liberation, including Native American theology, African liberation theologies, Latin American liberation theologies, and minjung theologies. While the formation of the Ecumenical Association of Third World Theologians (EATWOT) in 1976 marked an intentional effort of mostly male theologians throughout Africa, Asia, and Latin America to turn theologically away from the West and toward the Global South, Cone's writings influenced many of these voices by insisting that interrogation of their political struggles was a theological task.[39] The 1993 EATWOT conference centered Cone's work and the question of the globalization of Black theology. However, Cone was far from perfect. Early US Black theologians and Black religious scholars critiqued Cone for constructing Black liberation theology with an overuse of white sources and dialogue with white theologians (Cecil Cone), overdetermining Black liberation and reconciliation (J. Deotis Roberts), and overdefining Black liberation in purely Christian

---

[39]The first EATWOT conference in Tanzania gathered twenty-two participants, including the United States and nations across the Caribbean, Latin America, Asia, and Africa. Though several may have been invited, only one woman participated in the first gathering. Two-thirds-world women theologians faced an uphill battle for inclusion and the rise to leadership in EATWOT. African feminist theologian Mercy Amba Oduyoye identified the sexism and exclusion of women in EATWOT as an "irruption within an eruption." Oduyoye founded the Circle of Concerned African Women Theologians (1989) in response to this maltreatment and later became the first woman president of EATWOT (1996–2001). See Oluwatomisin Oredein, "Interview with Mercy Amba Oduyoye: Mercy Amba Oduyoye in Her Own Words," *Journal of Feminist Studies in Religion* 32, no. 2 (2016): 153–64, https://doi.org/10.2979/jfemistudreli.32.2.26.

terms (Gayraud Wilmore and Charles Long).[40] Nonetheless, Cone's fiercest critics were his Black women students, who addressed the invisibilization of Black women in early Black theological constructions. Though several Black women, namely Frances Beale, Theressa Hoover, and Pauli Murray,[41] addressed the need for the liberation of Black women in Black churches and feminist theology, Jacquelyn Grant was first to publish an early critique of her mentor Cone and the Black theological project.

In her 1979 article "Black Theology and the Black Woman," Grant invites Black liberation theology, especially Black theology, to turn to itself and reckon with the experiences of Black women, "the most oppressed of all oppressed," in its development.[42] Grant asks a piercing question: "Where are the black women in black theology?" She contends that the invisibility of Black women in Black theology is directly related to the failure of the Black Church to situate the liberation of Black women within its conception of the gospel of liberation. Grant argues,

> If the liberation of women is not proclaimed, the church's proclamation cannot be about divine liberation. If the church does not share in the liberation struggle of black women, its liberation struggle is not authentic. . . . The failure of the black church and black theology to proclaim explicitly the liberation of black women indicates that they cannot claim to be agents of divine liberation. If the theology, like the

---

[40]Black theologian and student of Cone Dwight Hopkins writes extensively about the distinctions between first-generation Black theologians related to politics and culture. Hopkins identifies James Cone and J. Deotis Roberts as Black political theologians and Gayraud Wilmore and Charles Long as Black cultural theologians. Building upon each other, Black political theologians sought to utilize theology as a means to confront the white political structures impacting Black people's daily lives. Black cultural theologians resisted, to borrow from Audre Lorde, using the "master's tools to dismantle the master's house." They sought to draw on the wealth of Black sources within and beyond Black Christianity to construct a new language toward Black liberation. See Dwight N. Hopkins, *Introducing Black Theology of Liberation* (Maryknoll, NY: Orbis Books, 1999). Cecil Cone, the brother of James Cone, made the case against Cone that the starting point of theology was not politics, but God and God's revelation in the community. See Cecil Wayne Cone, *The Identity Crisis in Black Theology* (Nashville: AMEC, 1975). Cone's critics influenced Cone's return to the theological sources of the Black community and the Black Church in later works. See James H. Cone, *For My People: Black Theology and the Black Church* (Maryknoll, NY: Orbis Books, 2024).

[41]See Cone and Wilmore, *Black Theology,* 279–338.

[42]Jacquelyn Grant, "Black Theology and the Black Woman," in *Words of Fire: An Anthology of African-American Feminist Thought*, ed. Beverly Guy-Sheftall (New York: New Press, 1995), 320.

church, have no word for Black women, its conception of liberation is inauthentic.[43]

Grant articulates that any vision of Black liberation that does not include Black women is indeed crooked. Grant parallels Black theology with the civil rights and Black Power movements of the 1960s with its exploitation of Black women's work and denial of Black women's leadership and voice. For Grant, the exclusion of Black women in Black theology reduces Black women to "invisible creatures who are on the outside looking into the black experience, the black church, and the black theological enterprise."[44] Grant critiques early Black theologians (including Cone) for imitating the failure of white theology on the matter of racism if sexism remains unaddressed. Grant asserts,

> It is my contention that if black theology speaks of the black community as if the special problems of black women do not exist, it is no different from the white theology it claims to reject precisely because of its inability to take account of the existence of black people in its theological formulations.[45]

Grant's early writings illuminate Black women theologians seeking to deconstruct the crookedness in Black theology and the Black Church to level the playing field for Black women's voices and find a moral ground of equity and inclusion. Grant, alongside other Black women students of James Cone at Union Theological Seminary of New York—namely Christian social ethicist Katie Geneva Cannon and systematic theologian Delores Williams—refined Cone's vision of Black liberation and birthed the womanist theological enterprise to elevate the somebodiness of Black women.

Cone acknowledges that the significant strengths of nascent Black theology cannot be weighed without addressing its weaknesses, including a "negative overreaction to white racism," "lack of social analysis," "lack of economic analysis," and "lack of sexual analysis."[46] Cone admits that the missing analysis of sexism in Black theology denied the intersectional na-

---

[43]Jacquelyn Grant, "Black Theology and the Black Woman," in *Words of Fire: An Anthology of African-American Feminist Thought*, ed. Beverly Guy-Sheftall (New York: New Press, 1995), 325, 330.

[44]Grant, "Black Theology and the Black Woman," 331.

[45]Grant, "Black Theology and the Black Woman," 330.

[46]Cone, *For My People*, 132–37.

ture of oppression facing Black people that ultimately narrowed the scope of Black liberation. Cone writes, "Our failure to deal with this problem [sexism] weakened our struggle for liberation. If black theologians do not acknowledge this problem with the intentions of overcoming it, I see no way that the problem of racism can be eliminated. Sexism, racism, and classism though not identical are interconnected, and thus none can be adequately dealt with without also dealing with the others."[47] Cone accepted the critique of his Black women students and called the Black Church to draw the circle wider in its efforts toward Black liberation by confronting its sexism. Cone addresses Black male pastors in his lecture and essay "Black Ecumenism and the Liberation Struggle":

> The difficulty that black male ministers have in supporting the equal- ity of women in the church and society stems partly from the lack of a clear liberation-criterion rooted in the gospel and the present struggles of oppressed peoples. In many contexts the black church is as backward and obscene on the issue of sexism as the white church. It is truly amazing that many black male ministers, young and old, can hear the message of liberation in the gospel when related to rac- ism but remain deaf to a similar message in the context of sexism.[48]

Black power in the Black Church that functions solely as male power over women is no Black power at all. Like Grant, Cone labeled sexism as a vestige of the lingering imprint of the white church on the Black Church. Cone ap- pealed to Black male theologians and church leaders: "I firmly believe that the black church cannot regain its Christian integrity unless it is willing to face head-on the evil of patriarchy and seek to eliminate it."[49] The failure of the Black Church to confront its sexism and patriarchy undermines any Christian claim to the gospel of liberation and participation in the full liberation of the Black community.

The Divided Mind of the Black Church and the Problem of Incarnation

A student of James Cone trained in Black liberation theology, the senior pastor of Atlanta's historic Ebenezer Baptist Church (the spiritual home of

[47]Cone, *For My People*, 136–37.

[48]James H. Cone, "Black Ecumenism and the Liberation Struggle," *The Journal of the Interdenominational Theological Center* 7, no. 1 (1979): 7.

[49]Cone, *For My People*, 199.

King), and the first Black senator of the state of Georgia (D-GA), Raphael Warnock furthers the notion of the duality of the mission of the Black Church as an internal debate between Black Church pastors and Black theologians in his 2014 volume, *The Divided Mind of the Black Church: Theology, Piety, and Public Witness*. Warnock exposes the mission of the Black Church as torn between two ideals: piety and protest, otherworldly and this-worldly, evangelical and prophetic. Warnock asserts,

> The double-consciousness of black Christianity—that is, a faith profoundly shaped by white evangelicalism's focus on individual salvation (piety) yet conscious of the contradictions of slavery and therefore focused also on sociopolitical freedom (protest)—provides a meaningful angle and a conceptual framework through which to inquire into the black church's sense of vocation and a basis for teasing out the nuances of a meaningful theology of the church.[50]

Born out of the freedom struggle, Warnock locates the Black Church as the institution within the Black community that has "offered the most sustained response to racism."[51] Though committed to resisting racial segregation, the visible Black Church in its early formation carried over Western orthodoxy that offered no new doctrines or Christian beliefs apart from white churches. As a result, Warnock draws from Black Christian ethicist Peter Paris that "black church leadership has conflated Western Christian doctrine with its own sensibilities about freedom."[52] The problem as identified by Black theologians like Cone is that white Christian doctrines perpetuate white power structures that offer second-class citizenship to Black people and subvert the very freedom that Black churches cultivated in the first place. Womanist theology further critiques the adoption of Western Christian doctrines by the Black Church that perpetuate oppressive practices such as sexism that pervert any understanding of Black liberation altogether.

Womanism as a theological approach and prophetic social movement advocates for the survival and liberation of Black women and the Black community. Early students of Cone (Jacquelyn Grant, Katie Geneva Cannon, Delores S. Williams), alongside other Black women theologians, ethicists (Emilie Maureen Townes), sociologists (Cheryl Townsend Gilkes), and biblical scholars (Renita Jean Weems and Clarice Martin), critiqued

---

[50]Warnock, *The Divided Mind of the Black Church*, 3.
[51]Warnock, *The Divided Mind of the Black Church*, 14.
[52]Warnock, *The Divided Mind of the Black Church*, 16.

Black liberation theology and white feminist theology in the 1980s for their failure to address the experiences of Black women in any significant way. Adapting novelist Alice Walker's definition and the southern folk expression that emerged from the Black community, the term "womanist" provided the essential language to name their efforts and situate Black women at the starting point of doing theology and ethics.

Katie Cannon, in her 1985 essay "The Emergence of Black Feminist Consciousness," provides a historical backdrop for Black women's significance and experiences of oppression from the antebellum period through the twentieth century. Cannon depicts the moral situation of Black women facing triple threats in "the struggle for human dignity, the struggle against white hypocrisy, and the struggle for justice."[53] Since the Middle Passage and throughout chattel slavery, Black women faced bodily attacks of objectification that denied their humanity and reduced their roles to production, reproduction, and sexual satisfaction. Cannon uncovers ways the "rightness of whiteness" prevailed through the "de facto social segregation and the disenfranchisement of Blacks" that persisted during the Reconstruction and Great Migration eras to establish the inferiority of Black people and "severely restrict Black women to the most unskilled, poorly paid, menial work."[54] Despite these odds, Black women understood they could not rely on the gentility afforded to white women and "became crusaders for justice" by confronting the terrors of their time (e.g., Ida B. Wells-Barnett and the Anti-lynching Crusade).[55] Cannon outlines the victimization of Black women by the triple jeopardy of racism, sexism, and classism as the impetus for a Black feminist consciousness, which she recasts as a Black womanist consciousness, that bears a prophetic calling to "break away from the oppressive ideologies and belief systems that presume to define their reality."[56] Cannon affirms the spirituality of the Black Church and the prophetic tradition of the Bible, particularly the Jesus stories of the New Testament accounts, as sustaining Black women in their unrelenting pursuit of justice. Cannon draws on a central theme in Black liberation theology to assert that "Jesus provides the necessary soul for liberation."[57] Thus, Black women look to Jesus as the source of their faith and the strength of their life

---

[53]Katie Geneva Cannon, *Katie's Canon: Womanism and the Soul of the Black Community*, rev. 25th anniversary ed. (Minneapolis: Fortress Press, 2021), 19–30.

[54]Cannon, *Katie's Canon*, 23–24.

[55]Cannon, *Katie's Canon*, 27.

[56]Cannon, *Katie's Canon*, 29.

[57]Cannon, *Katie's Canon*, 29.

who affirms their humanity and aids their moral discernment in the face of manifold evil. Later, Cannon defines the womanist theo-ethical task as both (1) interpretive—to unmask the "intrusive markers" that hinder Black women's agency and freedom, and (2) liberative—to unearth the moral acts that Black women have used to unbend oppressive forces and redeem themselves and the Black community.[58]

Utilizing Black and womanist theologies, Warnock pursues a sustained theological self-inquiry of the mission of the Black Church in relation to the "meaning of the gospel."[59] Warnock raises King as pastor and public theologian whose quest to "redeem the soul of America" through his public ministry "embodied the clearest American version of a gospel emphasizing social transformation and a vision of a church surrendered to that work."[60] King's theology of the beloved community denounced segregation as fundamentally unchristian because it rejected the revelation of the kingdom of God that is unity in Christ.[61] From a womanist standpoint, King as the recurring archetype of Black radical resistance at the center of the Christian faith for Black theologians eclipses the role of Black women, like Coretta Scott King and Ella Baker, who were motivated by deep Christian convictions and an unrelenting moral fervor to bring King's vision to prominence as articulated in previous sections. The Black Church patriarchy at the core of the civil rights and Black Power movements diminished the labor and leadership of Black women while ensuring that a King alone could rise to the top.

Warnock addresses critical questions posed by womanist theologians to Black theology and the Black Church about the meaning of the mission of the Black Church, given that the stories and lineage of Black women's piety and prophetic activism are missing from Black Church historiography. While Warnock rightly captures the duplexity of the Black Church mission between saving souls (piety) and liberating bodies (protest) between Black Church pastors and Black theologians, womanist theologians have long argued ways that both sides of the aisle participate in ignoring Black women. Womanist theological articulations of the mission of the Black Church attend to the dual tension of liberation and survival, which Warnock describes as "the steady rekindling of a spiritual militancy and deep piety

---

[58]Cannon, *Katie's Canon*, 197.
[59]Warnock, *The Divided Mind of the Black Church*, 5.
[60]Warnock, *The Divided Mind of the Black Church*, 21.
[61]Warnock, *The Divided Mind of the Black Church*, 60.

that manifests itself in political action."[62] Much like the suffrage movement with white women, Black women remain sidelined from the overarching narrative of the spiritual and prophetic movement of the Black Church.

In *Witnessing and Testifying: Black Women, Religion, and Civil Rights*, womanist ethicist Rosetta Ross traces the important role of religion in Black women's political activism during the civil rights movement. According to Ross, Black suffragist Fannie Lou Hamer, a daughter of a preacher reared in the Black Baptist Church, named the dual nature of the Black Church as both blessing and burden for the Black community's political advancement. On the one end, Hamer found her political-preaching voice while speaking in Black churches and "credited churches with giving African Americans the strength to survive."[63] On the other end, Hamer "criticized churches (and clergy) for failure to respond sufficiently to the needs of communities, for missing opportunities of the Civil Rights Era, and for betraying African Americans to the Movement's opposition and collaborating with the opposition."[64] Ross recounts Hamer's lament,

> "Sometimes I get so disgusted I feel like getting my gun after some of these chicken eatin' preachers," she once said. "I know these Baptist ministers. . . . I'm not anti-church and I'm not anti-religious, but if you go down Highway 49 all the way to Jackson, going through Drew, Ruleville, Blaine, Indianola, Moorhead, all over you'll see just how many churches are selling out to white power structures."[65]

Hamer rightly convicts the visible Black Church for adopting patterns of white power structures that negate Black freedom and harm Black lives. Black churches not only in the South as Hamer reports but also in the North, like segregated Chicago, sabotaged the political efforts of the civil rights movement. Some Black male religious leaders halted investment in economic advancement because of fear of whitelash, such as Rev. Clay Evans endured in 1966 when he opened Fellowship Missionary Baptist Church of Chicago to King and the SCLC for Operation Breadbasket,[66] an SCLC

---

[62] Warnock, *The Divided Mind of the Black Church,* 171.

[63] Rosetta E. Ross, *Witnessing and Testifying: Black Women, Religion, and Civil Rights* (Minneapolis: Fortress Press, 2003), 111.

[64] Ross, *Witnessing and Testifying,* 111.

[65] Ross, *Witnessing and Testifying,* 111.

[66] The Southern Christian Leadership Conference (SCLC) launched Operation Breadbasket in 1962. Modeled after a patronage program developed by Leon Sullivan of Philadelphia, the

economic justice program designed to negotiate equitable employment for Blacks and other minorities. Political and economic power brokers in Chicago denied loans and building permits to Clay Evans and Fellowship for more than seven years as an act of retaliation against Evans's support of King. Other Black male pastors feared that King and the SCLC would take over the city and succeed in prominence among Black communities and white authorities, so they pushed King and the movement out of the city in 1967. Yet King's removal did not halt Black political movement in Chicago, because of Black women like ordained minister Addie T. Wyatt, who founded Vernon Street Church of God alongside her husband, Claude Wyatt, and helped to organize the National Organization of Women (NOW) and the Coalition of Labor Union Women (CLUW) to fight for better labor conditions for women.

By 1966, Operation Breadbasket expanded its efforts in Chicago under the leadership of Chicago Theological Seminary (CTS) seminarian and Baptist minister Jesse L. Jackson. Driven by the motto "Your Ministers Fight for Jobs and Rights," the Chicago operation sought to bring bread to Black communities through jobs and justice.[67] The ministers first targeted the dairy industry, then Pepsi-Cola and Coca-Cola brands, and later supermarket chains, resulting in wide early success generating thousands of new jobs and revenue to the Black community. Motivated by Jackson's theological education at CTS connecting Jesus and justice, Chicago's Breadbasket efforts held theo-cultural significance as Chicagoans gathered weekly for Saturday morning forums to discuss the economic agendas of the community and witness Jackson's sermons. Following King's assassination in 1968, tensions between Ralph Abernathy and Jesse Jackson concerning different models for leading social change prompted Jackson's split from the SCLC. Jackson held on to the vision of Operation Breadbasket and re-launched his efforts under the banner of Operation PUSH (People United to Save [later Serve] Humanity), which later merged with the Rainbow Coalition to become

---

program was designed to create economic opportunities for economically disadvantaged Black communities. SCLC surveyed the employment practices of corporations and industries with consumer products supported by Black communities. If companies dismissed SCLC petitions for fair and equitable employment, participating clergy encouraged parishioners to protest and withdraw their business.

[67] In each city, Operation Breadbasket initiatives exercised different interests and approaches that catered to the needs of the local community. Operation Breadbasket Chicago focused its efforts on labor, jobs, and employment practices. See Martin L. Deppe, *Operation Breadbasket: An Untold Story of Civil Rights in Chicago, 1966–1971* (Athens: University of Georgia Press, 2017).

what is known today as the Rainbow PUSH Coalition (RPC). The mission of RPC is "to protect, defend, and gain civil rights by leveling the economic and educational playing fields, and to promote peace and justice around the world."[68] Though RPC encourages strengthening bonds between races and blending a kaleidoscope of colors, ethnicities, and nationalities for the work of social change in the image of the rainbow, unequal distribution of power concerning gender remains. As the largest civil rights organization still active today, RPC envisions a multiracial, multi-issue, progressive coalition for saving humanity and serving the community by maintaining the archaic Black Church leadership paradigm of the 1960s with one Black charismatic male preacher at the helm since its inception. Even within the Black prophetic church tradition, Black women face misrecognition that undermines the significant contributions of Black women to the political witness of the Black Church.

The divided mind of the Black Church perpetuates devastating consequences for Black women both within and outside the church. Black women's political organizing bears its roots in the Black Church as Black women continue to fight to receive full rights as members within an institution they helped to birth and sustain. Historian Martha Jones highlights 1848 as significant to Black churchwomen in Black Methodist circles; in that year, Black women won the vote to receive licenses to preach (though it was later rescinded) at the AME General Conference months before the Seneca Falls Convention, known to many as the first women's rights convention (but no Black women were present) in Seneca Falls, New York. The win of Black churchwomen in 1848 recalls the devastating blow of 1844 when the petition incensed the conference but did not pass.[69] Since the days of Jarena Lee in the AME Church and Julia Foote in the AME Zion Church, Black women learned how to maneuver the second-class citizenship of the American political landscape because of their experience contesting Black Church polity that left Black women out of decision-making. Du Bois identified the Negro Church as the "governments of men."[70] The subordination of Black women in the Black Church remains congruent with white evangelical beliefs that fortify what feminist biblical scholar Elisabeth Schüssler Fiorenza names as

---

[68]Rainbow PUSH Coalition, "Organization and Mission," accessed May 1, 2024, https://www.rainbowpush.org/organization-and-mission.

[69]Jones, *Vanguard*, 60–63.

[70]Du Bois and Edwards, *The Souls of Black Folk*, 131.

the institutional, structural power of "kyriarchy,"[71] despite being antitheti-cal to the gospel of Jesus Christ, which is the liberation of the oppressed.

In *Toward a Womanist Ethic of Incarnation*, former student of Cone and womanist theological ethicist Eboni Marshall Turman theorizes Du Bois's Veil to uncover the American "problem of incarnation," which marred Blackness and etched the Black body as less than human in the Western imagination, and the Veil's rupture in the Black Church. Du Bois's double consciousness and construction of the Veil emphasized the psychic frag-mentation and "precarious predicament" of Black life.[72] There is no question that the Veil illuminates deep theological meaning as a symbol of separa-tion between the "holy place" and the "holy of holies" in the tabernacle of Hebrew Scriptures (Ex 26:33) and a boundary that Jesus transgresses between divinity and humanity on the cross with the sign of the splitting of the Veil into two (Mt 27:50–51), thus breaking down any barrier of access to the Divine. For Turman, the Veil, in Du Bois's writings, exposes the "color line"—a boundary between the white and Black worlds—and the potential for radical transformation.[73] Turman argues,

> DuBois's *The Souls* further suggested that the Negro who is "born with a veil" on the dark side of racial injustice is "gifted with second-sight" that grants her the prophetic ability to see, interpret, and transform the world in distinct ways. Thus, DuBois's dialectic does not only intend to normalize black people's experience of the *Veil*, but in radical fashion it also seeks to assert the *Veil* as a mechanism of empowerment for the oppressed. In other words, DuBois's dialectic situates the *Veil* that had formerly functioned as the protagonist of Negro fragmentation as a primary tool for racial uplift. What had heretofore been perceived as boundary, DuBois radically reconceived as bridge.[74]

---

[71]To avoid the gender binary of patriarchy, Fiorenza draws on the Greek word "kyrios" to name a system of domination that links to empire and "domination by the emperor, lord, master, father, husband, elite propertied male." Fiorenza describes kyriarchy as "a more comprehensive systematic analysis of empire, in order to underscore the complex inter-structing of dominations, and to locate sexism and misogyny in the political matrix—or better, 'patrix'—of a broader range of domination." Elisabeth Schüssler Fiorenza, *The Power of the Word: Scripture and the Rhetoric of Empire* (Minneapolis: Fortress Press, 2007), 14.

[72]Eboni Marshall Turman, *Toward a Womanist Ethic of Incarnation: Black Bodies, the Black Church, and the Council of Chalcedon* (New York: Palgrave Macmillan, 2013), 77.

[73]Turman, *Toward a Womanist Ethic of Incarnation*, 78.

[74]Turman, *Toward a Womanist Ethic of Incarnation*, 79.

Even while born as a movement of resistance to confront bodily injustice and nurture the souls of Black people, the Black Church's problem is incarnational, Turman contends, which points to soul-snatching and body-denying practices that divinely ordain mostly men to lead and govern behind the Veil. In efforts to "make men" and "save bodies" motivated by the impulse of the social gospel, Turman critiques the mostly male "moral managers of the Black Church" who uphold the very oppression that the Black Church seeks to resist toward Black churchwomen (in particular) and other differentiated bodies.[75] In other words, the intracommunal oppression within the Black Church and voyeurism of Black churchwomen's bodies and souls harbor similar characteristics of the white supremacist gaze that frames Blackness as non/subhuman and places the Black community in contempt. Turman constructs a womanist ethic of incarnation that calls the Black Church to lift the Veil and move beyond the guise of liberation that leaves some bodies out of the scope of transformation. Turman turns to Black women "as the incarnate image of God in the world—the 'same substance' of God as to his humanity, and thus posits black women as the primary resource for resisting injustice and reconstituting the body and soul of the black church."[76] The contemporary #BlackLivesMatter movement signals a Black Church reckoning of a failed mission on all fronts as queer Black millennial women, the oppressed of the oppressed, lead the Black liberation movement of the twenty-first century, a successor to the civil rights and Black Power movements, out of dependency on the Black Church politic to cast a womanist theo-ethical vision of Black liberation that includes *all* of us.

I, Too, Am the Black Church: Black Women, a Crooked Gospel, and the Theopolitics of Redemption

Theressa Hoover, the first African American woman mission executive in the United Methodist Church, wrote, "To be a woman, black, and active in religious institutions in the American scene is to labor under triple jeopardy."[77] Drawing from cognitive psychology studies and political philosophy, Melissa Harris-Perry adopts the metaphor of the "crooked room"

---

[75]Turman, *Toward a Womanist Ethic of Incarnation*, 127.

[76]Turman, *Toward a Womanist Ethic of Incarnation*, 161.

[77]Theressa Hoover, "Black Women and the Churches: Triple Jeopardy," in *Black Theology: A Documentary History*, vol. 1, ed. James H. Cone and Gayraud S. Wilmore, 2nd ed. (Maryknoll, NY: Orbis Books, 1993), 293.

to illustrate Black women constrained increasingly by the structural forces of oppression that restrict and contort Black women's decision-making.[78] In a crooked room, stereotypes and distorted images of Black women misrecognize Black women's moral agency and incite political damages that deny Black women's full humanity and full citizenship status as Americans. Though Harris-Perry earned degrees in English (Wake Forest University) and political science (Duke University), she also studied theology at Union Theological Seminary in New York with significant introductions to the Black liberationist and womanist theological traditions. Both Harris-Perry's academic pursuits and the larger reality of Black women as the most religious group in America substantiate her turn to theology in the latter half of *Sister Citizen*. According to a 2012 study by the *Washington Post* and the Kaiser Family Foundation, "Nine out of ten African American women" rely on their faith in God in moments of distress.[79] Harris-Perry shifts to Black women's faith as a portal to unpack the role of God-talk and the crooked room.

In her chapter titled "God" in *Sister Citizen*, Harris-Perry recognizes that many Black women hold fast to "faith in a benevolent and loving God" to "straighten out the crooked room of race and gender stereotypes."[80] On one end, faith is the source of Black women's resilience against devastating odds. At the other, faith unlocks another pathway to address the peril facing Black women. Harris-Perry calls out the Black Church as an institution that participates in reinforcing damaging assaults toward Black women through "institutionalized gender inequity."[81] While the Black Church formed as an institution of resistance against racial injustice, the Black Church upholds a culture of oppression against Black women, the very subjects who sustain its presence and witness, by denying their labor, voice, activism, and leadership. Harris-Perry attests, "One way to think about how black women experience the black church is as a metaphor with the American state: they are citizens of it, but because of their identities, they are still struggling for full recognition within it."[82] The misrecognition Black women encounter from pervasive sexism, gender discrimination, and misogynoir in Black Church

---

[78]Melissa V. Harris-Perry, *Sister Citizen: Shame, Stereotypes, and Black Women in America; [for Colored Girls Who've Considered Politics When Being Strong Isn't Enough]* (New Haven, CT: Yale University Press, 2011), 5.

[79]Theola Labbé-DeBose, "Black Women Are among Country's Most Religious Groups," *Washington Post*, July 6, 2012, sec. Local, https://www.washingtonpost.com/local/black-women-are-among-countrys-most-religious-groups/2012/07/06/gJQA0BksSW_story.html.

[80]Harris-Perry, *Sister Citizen*, 222.

[81]Harris-Perry, *Sister Citizen*, 223.

[82]Harris-Perry, *Sister Citizen*, 223.

culture disavows the full humanity of Black women as made in the image of God and worthy of dignity, affirmation, and access.

T. D. Jakes, Woman, Thou Art Loosed!, and the Business of Saving Black Women

The Black Church's adoption of white power structures and white evangelical interpretive traditions that reinforce the subordination of women as a revelation of the Christian faith has distorted its central mission to the business of *saving* Black women. Black women occupying majority status in Black churches does not equate to shared leadership or full recognition as primary stakeholders in decision-making or power brokers in the development of the institutions they sustain. Most Black male clergy understand that one of the most essential ministries of the Black Church is to Black women because of the population size. However, some Black male clergy invest in ministering to Black churchwomen only to magnify their platforms, popularity, sociopolitical influence, and spiritual capital. The hyperobsessive occupation of Black churches to turn its gaze toward Black women functions as misrecognition that witnesses the struggles and pain of Black women (sometimes ordained by the Black Church) as entry points to not minister to, but to manipulate, monopolize, and monetize Black women's suffering. In this sense, Black women are perhaps the biggest consumer and commodity of the Black Church, even to their detriment. Though there are numerous examples in priestly and prophetic circles of Black churches, one popular example of the commodification of Black women's pain is Bishop T. D. Jakes and the Woman, Thou Art Loosed! (WTAL) movement.

What began as a Sunday school study of Luke 13:10–17 by Pentecostal revivalist T. D. Jakes in a storefront church in West Virginia in 1992 morphed into a mega women's movement attracting thousands of Black churchwomen across denominational lines and religious backgrounds to the Georgia World Congress Center in Atlanta in 1996 under the T. D. Jakes Ministries and WTAL brand. For twenty-five years before its grand finale and "evolution" in September 2022,[83] the number of Black churchwomen

---

[83] At the 2022 Finale WTAL, Bishop Jakes announced and crowned his daughter Pastor Sarah Jakes Roberts as the new leader of WTAL who would lead the movement to its next level of destiny through her budding platform, Woman Evolve, developed from her reading of the Genesis account of Eve in the Bible. In many ways, Jakes Roberts continues the legacy of her father by seeking to minister to the pain of Black women, but she also departs from her father in reclaiming the virtue of "troubled" Black women through her reading of Eve

attending the WTAL conference ranged from ten thousand to twenty-five thousand at its height and thousands more through mass distributed recordings and livestreaming. Jakes admits that WTAL catapulted his influence and televangelist ministry to national prominence, moving his ministry from small beginnings in West Virginia to megachurch massive in Dallas, Texas, because of monumental support from Black churchwomen across the nation. The brand name "Woman, Thou Art Loosed!" resonates with many Black women as verbatim from the popular King James Version of Luke 13:12, which illustrates the narrative of the bent woman redeemed by Jesus.

In his million-copy bestseller *Woman, Thou Art Loosed!*, first published in 1993, Jakes characterizes Luke 13 and his reading of the "infirmed woman" into three categories: "the person, the problem, and the prescription."[84] Jakes frames this Lukan woman as the problem with a moral infirmity, a physical or mental weakness, that needs "loosening" or "saving" by Jesus with little to no attention addressing the forces that cause her condition. Jakes writes, "This woman's dilemma is her own, but perhaps you will find some point of relativity between her case history and your own. She could be like someone you know or have known; she could even be like you."[85] Jakes acknowledges the infirmed woman as unable to stand up straight but never addresses her bendedness. In fact, Jakes does not use the word "bent" in his analysis at all, but only "infirmity" and "crippling condition." Jakes parallels this woman with the experiences of contemporary women (who are largely Black women consuming his works) to form the central thesis of the WTAL movement, which inscribes Black women as bound by *their* wrongdoing, not the wrong done to Black women by oppressive systems revealed through their bendedness. Seemingly, Black women are blamed and shamed for the oppression they endure while being charged to act as agents to save themselves through faithfulness to Jesus. Jakes scripts Black women in a perpetual state of contempt bent by their moral and spiritual failures. Jakes's reading of the Lukan account is incomplete because he fails

---

and the call to evolve. Moreover, Jakes Roberts makes pathways that Jakes cannot make with Black women because she embodies the story of moving from shame to virtue as an unwed teenage mother struggling to find identity during the same period of the launch, growth, and expansion of WTAL. The best person to continue what Jakes started and redeem what Jakes got wrong is Jakes Roberts. Black millennial women, in particular, await this liberative possibility. See *Loosed to Evolve | Bishop T. D. Jakes Passes the WTAL Torch to Pastor Sarah Jakes Roberts*, 2022, https://www.youtube.com/watch?v=5loxNl7CgO4.

[84] T. D. Jakes, *Woman Thou Art Loosed! 20th Anniversary Expanded Edition: Healing the Wounds of the Past* (Shippensburg, PA: Destiny Image, 2012), 15.

[85] Jakes, *Woman Thou Art Loosed!*, 15.

to finish the passage in Luke 13:14–17 of Jesus confronting the hypocrisy of the very society and religious community that bent the women double; thus, Jakes misses the true Christian mission and Jesus's charge to speak against the oppressive conditions that seize the most vulnerable. The WTAL brand successfully sustains a crooked ideology that Black women are the problem while simultaneously casting a vision for women's empowerment that eclipses the call to the Black Church and its leaders to follow Jesus and confront the powers that wound. Unfortunately, Black churchwomen have internalized Jakes's misguided interpretation and bought into the WTAL brand by the masses.[86] The popularity and profitability of the WTAL empire prompted Jakes to later produce a stage play, two films—*Woman Thou Art Loosed* (2004) and *Woman Thou Art Loosed: On the 7th Day* (2012)—countless devotionals, Bible series, and educational curriculum under this banner. Additionally, Jakes expanded the WTAL platform to launch the global preaching ministries of several notable women preachers (Prophetess Juanita Bynum, Paula White, and Dr. Jazmin Sculark, to name a few) whom Black feminist and womanist scholars also critique for reinforcing such theologies of contempt for Black women.[87]

Black feminist religious and cultural critic Tamura Lomax, in *Jezebel Unhinged*, provides one the most sustained critiques of Jakes and WTAL

---

[86]On its "Homecoming" finale 2022 website for the final conference, WTAL boasts, "More than two decades ago, Woman, Thou Art Loosed! became the center of women's empowerment. Its valuable insights have given women the platform to elevate their influence through the magnitude of its momentum—abounding in conversations powerful enough to shift society, and creating strong, sisterly bonds." See "Woman Thou Art Loosed—The Online Community for Woman Thou Art Loosed," accessed March 31, 2023, https://wtal.org/.

[87]See Brittney Cooper, "How Sarah Got Her Groove Back, or Notes toward a Black Feminist Theology of Pleasure," *Black Theology* 16, no. 3 (September 2, 2018): 195–206, https://doi.org/10.1080/14769948.2018.1492299; Keri Day, " 'I Am Dark and Lovely': Let the Shulammite Woman Speak," *Black Theology* 16, no. 3 (September 2, 2018): 207–17, https://doi.org/10.1080/14769948.2018.1492300; Melanie C. Jones, "The Will to Adorn: Beyond Self-Surveillance, toward a Womanist Ethic of Redemptive Self-Love," *Black Theology* 16, no. 3 (September 2, 2018): 218–30, https://doi.org/10.1080/14769948.2018.1492303; Tamura Lomax, "Black Bodies in Ecstasy: Black Women, the Black Church, and the Politics of Pleasure: An Introduction," *Black Theology* 16, no. 3 (September 2, 2018): 189–94, https://doi.org/10.1080/14769948.2018.1492298; Monique Nicole Moultrie, *Passionate and Pious: Religious Media and Black Women's Sexuality* (Durham, NC: Duke University Press, 2017); Monique Nicole Moultrie, "Putting a Ring on It: Black Women, Black Churches, and Coerced Monogamy," *Black Theology* 16, no. 3 (2018): 231–47, https://doi.org/10.1080/14769948.2018.1492304; Kimberly D. Russaw, "Veils and Lap Cloths: The Great Cover-Up of Bynum and the Bible in Black Churches," *Black Theology* 16, no. 3 (September 2, 2018): 248–62, https://doi.org/10.1080/14769948.2018.1492302.

that maps ways Black women are compelled and condemned by Jakes's "woman" as interpreted through Luke 13. Lomax contends,

> For many, Jakes was possibly the first man to ever acknowledge their trauma, and, moreover, to prophesy their triumph. He encouraged women and girls to exercise individual agency to "loose" themselves from the stresses of their pasts and problems, and to live more abundantly in the present. "Woman, Thou Art Loosed" became a marketplace of optimism to women across the globe investing thousands of dollars annually in Jakes's products. Yet Jakes produced an important context for uniting women and talking about their problems that simultaneously humanized and further problematized them. "Woman, Thou Art Loosed" undeniably appeals to certain personal and collective yearnings, sensibilities, tribulations, cadences, motivations, and experiences. Concomitantly, it produces feminine theology and technology that on the surface empowers women to heal from previous injuries caused by the memorialization of unresolved emotional, physical, sexual, and psychological trauma; embrace self-sufficiency through creativity and industry; and prepare themselves for their knight in shining armor. Underneath the surface it remixes the discourse on black womanhood, producing new and old talking points on proper and improper womanly ways of being.[88]

On one hand, Jakes sees the struggles of Black women and humanizes their experiences. On the other, Jakes misrecognizes their moral virtue and relegates their redemption to hyper-proper sexuality and confining respectability. Lomax questions "Whose Woman Is This?" and queries whether Jakes as the "master salesman" and "compassionate preacher" constructs both the "problem" and the "solution."[89] Lomax argues, "Jakes's discourse on loosing stands as solution. However, it reveals double meaning, drawing our attention to how women need healing from the emotional and psychological scarring from the trauma of violence on one end, and underlining previous notions of black womanhood as a site of deviance, hypersexuality, and crisis on the other."[90] Lomax rightly analyzes the linkage between Jakes's woman in Luke 13 and the ideal woman Jakes uses to convert Black women to hyper-

---

[88]Tamura A. Lomax, *Jezebel Unhinged: Loosing the Black Female Body in Religion and Culture* (Durham, NC: Duke University Press, 2018), 131.

[89]Lomax, *Jezebel Unhinged*, 132–33.

[90]Lomax, *Jezebel Unhinged*, 133.

feminine sexuality and patriarchal submission in their intimate relationships with men and God as depicted in his subsequent bestseller and sacred love songs soundtrack, *The Lady, Her Lover, and Her Lord.*[91] Jakes's central aim to "heal the wounds of the past" and to "forge ahead into the future" does not result in setting the woman free but instead fortifies her bendedness.[92] I think it is important to locate Jakes not as an anomaly but at the height of a Black Church tradition wherein Black pastors and leaders prescribe jaded Christian doctrine to Black churchwomen Sunday after Sunday. Jakes rises to the top of Black Church culture as what Lomax describes as the "ne plus ultra of Black preaching," but does so undeniably on the backs of Black women. According to womanist scholar Paula McGee in *Brand New Theology: The Wal-Martization of T. D. Jakes and the New Black Church*, Jakes blends the sacred and secular dimensions of pastor and entrepreneur. "Bishop T. D. Jakes, in the last forty years, has successfully branded himself as a *liberator of women*. Women believe that Jakes is just like Jesus—when, according to the Gospel of Luke, he healed the infirmed woman with the words: 'Woman thou art loosed.' Jakes has successfully convinced women all over the world that they need *to be loosed*, and they need to be *loosed by him*."[93] However, Jakes the archetype is paradigmatic of the larger corruption within the moral fabric of the contemporary Black Church.

Lomax traces a similar phenomenon in Black producer, screenwriter, and entertainer Tyler Perry's mass media writings, plays, TV shows, and films that target Black churchwomen with a Christian ethical undercurrent that takes up central themes of the Christian faith.[94] Lomax continues her argument from her coedited volume, *Womanist and Feminist Responses to Tyler Perry's Productions* (2014), to suggest connections between the Protestant work ethic, neoliberalism, and Perry's productions. Lomax asserts,

> most of his films use the following template: familiar Christian themes, such as forgiveness, faith, and redemption; American ideals, such as cis-gender heterosexual marriage and/or patriarchal fairy tale endings; an overuse of black female stereotypes, for example, the black-

---

[91]See T. D. Jakes, *The Lady, Her Lover, and Her Lord* (New York: Berkeley, 2000).

[92]Jakes, *The Lady, Her Lover, and Her Lord*, back cover.

[93]Paula L. McGee, *Brand* New Theology: The Wal-Martization of T. D. Jakes and the New Black Church* (Maryknoll, NY: Orbis Books, 2017), 12.

[94]See LeRhonda S. Manigault-Bryant, Tamura A. Lomax, and Carol B. Duncan, eds., *Womanist and Black Feminist Responses to Tyler Perry's Productions* (New York: Palgrave Macmillan, 2014).

woman-as-bitch or the black-woman-as-w(ho)re; storylines about basic human needs, wants, and expressions, such as love, safety, family, laughter, protection, companionship, success, romance, revenge, lust, and anger; and everyday tales of despair (e.g., adultery, violent abuse, betrayal, and abandonment) and triumph in which Perry's ideas of justice eventually prevail. Perry's weaving together of various forms of non-Christian inclinations, violence, and familiar Christian dogma enable black women to simultaneously affirm their complex humanity, experiences, and Christian character. That is, one can view a Perry film and witness the messiness, contradictions, temptations, and trials of life while still holding firm to one's faith. And though faithfulness and good behavior ultimately prevail in his productions, viewers can identify with the ebbs and flows of the character's journey. Additionally, the idea that good works eventually pay off provides hope and clearly aligns with the Christian message.[95]

It should be no surprise that Perry's claim to fame emerged in 2004 when he turned Jakes's *Woman, Thou Art Loosed!* bestseller into a mass-produced film. Jakes's problematic reading of the Luke 13 woman in the book is nowhere near as odious toward Black women as presented in the film. The protagonist Michelle Jordan (played by Kimberly Elise) tells her story of the downward spiral of abuse, addiction, and prostitution to Bishop Jakes from the jail cell after killing her sexually abusive perpetrator and mother's boyfriend at a T. D. Jakes revival. The character Michelle pays the hard penalty of her actions in a confined cell with no accountability of the traumatic forces that limit her choices. Whereas the movie juxtaposes the forgiveness Michelle "owed" her abuser by not seeking revenge, there is no forgiveness for Michelle but only confinement. Jakes and Perry see Michelle's humanity but misrecognize her character as the vicious perpetrator and not the complex victim. As mass media moguls and business partners, Jakes and Perry capitalize on Black churchwomen as one of the largest consumers of Black entertainment with Black women as the subjects of their works while also making, multiplying, and magnifying stereotypical images and tropes of Black women that uphold and reinforce Black women's oppression. Lomax extends her critical reading of Jakes and Perry to address the next generation of popular charismatic preachers like Pastor Jamal H. Bryant—"These

---

[95]Lomax, *Jezebel Unhinged,* 173.

Hoes Ain't Loyal"[96]—and former Potter's House of Denver pastor Chris Hill, who once used the flippant analogy "You can't turn a hoe into a housewife" in the sermonic moment to highlight Black Church investment in the pain of Black women for selfish gain. Bryant and Hill move beyond "playing the victim" to outright hypocrisy and manipulation by disciplining women's "un-ladylike" sexualities, given their own public scandals of salacious affairs televised on Bravo's *Real Housewives of Potomac*[97] and blasted on countless networks.[98] These examples and countless more uncover a pervasive moral dilemma within the Black Church that twists the gospel to maintain its relevance at the expense of sacrificing Black women.

From the popular to the prophetic, Black feminist and womanist ethicist Keri Day's work exposes ways that even socially conscious Black churches participate in the misrecognition of poor Black women. In *Unfinished Business: Black Women, the Black Church and the Struggle to Thrive in America*, Keri Day uses the critique of Jakes "as a black capitalist who uses theatrical multimedia strategies to exploit black women" to ask the question "Is the 'Black Church' home for poor Black women?"[99] Day points to the "unfinished business" of the Poor People's Campaign that halted the civil rights and Black Church movements for economic justice from impacting the lives of poor Black women. To be evenhanded, Day acknowledges that some Black churches have attempted to respond to the needs of poor Black women through "charity-based ministries—food banks, clothing

---

[96]Pastor Jamal Harrison Bryant, former senior pastor of Empowerment Temple AME Church in Baltimore, Maryland, and current senior pastor of New Birth Baptist Church in Lithonia, Georgia, preached a controversial sermon in June 2014 about the plight of Black women and concluded with the lyric "These hoes ain't loyal" from Chris Brown's song "Loyal." See here: *I'm My Enemies Worst Nightmare PT1*, 2014, https://www.youtube.com/watch?v=6DcT_0H2EnQ; *I'm My Enemies Worst Nightmare PT2*, 2014, https://www.youtube.com/watch?v=HL0ajTAPZzw; #teamEBONY, "These Pastors Ain't Loyal," *Ebony*, June 5, 2014, https://www.ebony.com/jamal-h-bryant-aint-loyal-sermon-043/; Wesley Case, "Rev. Jamal Bryant Quotes Chris Brown's 'Loyal' in Sermon," *Baltimore Sun*, June 4, 2014, https://www.baltimoresun.com/features/bs-xpm-2014-06-04-bal-jamal-bryant-pastor-quotes-chris-brown-loyal-story.html.

[97]"RHOP Reunion: Monique Samuels Reads 'Receipts,' Calls Gizelle Bryant's Relationship with Ex 'Fake,'" *Peoplemag*, December 13, 2020, https://people.com/tv/rhop-reunion-monique-samuels-reads-receipts-calls-gizelle-bryants-relationship-with-ex-fake/.

[98]Leonardo Blair, "Potter's House Denver Pastor Chris Hill Accused of Affair with Married Member," *Christian Post*, April 4, 2017, https://www.christianpost.com/news/potters-house-denver-pastor-chris-hill-accused-of-affair-with-married-member.html.

[99]Keri Day, *Unfinished Business: Black Women, the Black Church, and the Struggle to Thrive in America* (Maryknoll, NY: Orbis Books, 2012), 15.

drives, career services, etc." and "faith-based entrepreneurship that fosters community development projects, giving rise to more entrepreneurial and employment opportunities within poor black communities," but these efforts "fail to address larger structural injustices that perpetuate poverty"[100] and to "consider how issues of the American economy exacerbate Black women's deprivation."[101] The linkage of oppressive systems—like poverty, which Black women did not create but must survive—to an "individual moral failure," or perhaps even a "spiritual failure"[102] of Black women in the mind and hearts of some Black churches perpetuates the mischaracterization of Black women's moral agency and situates Black women not only in a crooked room, as noted by Harris-Perry, but up against what I name as a *Crooked Gospel*.

The Gospel according to Black Women and Straightening the Crooked Room

Since the true mission of the church is to preach the good news of the revelation of Jesus Christ, what, then, is the gospel according to Black women? Harris-Perry acknowledges Black liberation and womanist theologies as academic, theological enterprises committed to the work of re-inscribing the somebodiness and human dignity that America has failed to extend to Black people for more than four hundred years. The notion that "God exists on the side of the oppressed" popularized by Cone and consistent with contemporary Black and womanist theologians reveals God's identification with and preferential concern for those on the underside. Harris-Perry interprets the meaning of a God of liberation to further assert that "black people will receive from God what they fail to receive from American social and political structures: recognition."[103] Early Black liberation theologies that overlooked the contributions of Black women, who represent the Black Church majority, give a first glimpse of Black women's misrecognition in theological constructions of liberative God-talk. It further revealed the need for Black women to see themselves and name their unique relationship with God.

The term "womanist" comes from the Black idiomatic expression "you actin' womanish" that is derived from the Black southern folk culture of a

---

[100]Day, *Unfinished Business*, 31.
[101]Day, *Unfinished Business*, 32.
[102]Day, *Unfinished Business*, 42–46.
[103]Harris-Perry, *Sister Citizen*, 226.

mother relating to her girlchild. Motivated by her editor to define "womanist" in the title of her 1983 collection, *In Search of Our Mother's Gardens: Womanist Prose*, Alice Walker sought to name the distinctive political aims of Black women beyond the white feminist scope in the 1980s, culminating in the notable adage "Womanist is to feminist as purple is to lavender."[104] In Walker's definition, a womanist reckoning with the liberation of self and community traces back through generations in the exchange from mother to daughter. As quoted by Harris-Perry at the top of her "God" chapter, Walker describes a womanist as "traditionally capable, as in 'Mama, I'm walking to Canada and taking you and a bunch of other slaves with me.' Her response: 'It wouldn't be the first time.'"[105] In efforts to continue the quest toward freedom and "walk to Canada," Black women in the religious academy sourcing Walker's conception of womanism spawned a forty-year-old tradition utilizing womanist approaches to situate Black women at the center of theological construction and ethical analysis. Katie Cannon explains the womanist project in religion this way:

> The chief function of womanism is not merely to replace one set of elitist, hegemonic texts that have traditionally ignored, dismissed, or flat out misunderstood the existential realities of women of the African diaspora with another set of Afrocentric texts that had gotten short shrift and pushed to the margins of the learned societies. Rather, our objective is to use Walker's four-part definition as a critical, methodological framework for challenging inherited traditions for their collusion with androcentric patriarchy as well as a catalyst in overcoming oppressive situations through revolutionary acts of rebellion. [My] overall goal in this project is to recast the very terms and terrain of religious scholarship.[106]

I write in the Part One framing of the twenty-fifth anniversary edition of *Katie's Canon*, "Cannon adopts Alice Walker's four-part definition of womanist as a critical, intersectional, methodological framework to confront inherited traditions and hegemonic ideologies that ordain Black women's oppression while simultaneously redeeming their experiences and cul-

[104]Alice Walker, *In Search of Our Mothers' Gardens: Womanist Prose* (New York: Harcourt Brace Jovanovich, 1983), xi–xii.
[105]Walker, *In Search of Our Mothers' Gardens*, xi–xii.
[106]Cannon, *Katie's Canon*, 2.

tures and approaches employed to resist and rebel."[107] Revising Cone, the womanist liberationist question remains: "What does it mean to be Black, woman, and Christian?" Womanist theology as a confessional concept and liberationist paradigm undeniably affirms Black women as made in the image of God and recognizes the experiences of Black women at the center of the mission of Jesus Christ and the gospel story, emboldened to confront oppressive systems and powers as Jesus did in Luke 13.

The womanist paradigm has taken shape since the 1980s in multiple academic disciplines including English (African American theorist Clenora Hudson Weems's Africana womanism), literature (Nigerian literary critic Chikwenye Okonjo's African womanism and Afro-politico womanism in African American studies scholar Kalenda Eaton's work), history, theater and film studies, communication and media studies, psychology, anthropology, social work, gender and sexuality studies, architecture, and urban studies, with Walker as starting point for some approaches but not the only point of departure over the last forty years.[108] I argue that womanism sourcing Walker gained its footing most notably in religious studies. Building upon Walker and Cannon, womanist ethicist Stacey Floyd-Thomas frames the womanist paradigm through four central womanist theo-ethical tenets in *Mining the Motherlode: Methods in Womanist Ethics* (2006) and *Deeper Shades of Purple: Womanism in Religion & Society* (2006). First, Floyd-Thomas names *radical subjectivity* as "a process that emerges as Black females in the nascent phase of their identity development come to understand agency as the ability to defy a forced naiveté in an effort to influence the choices made in one's life and how conscientization incites resistance against marginality."[109] Walker's notion of a womanist exercising "outrageous, audacious, or *willful* behavior" and as "responsible, in charge, serious" outlines the self-determination and self-possession of Black women to act and demonstrate agency against oppressive odds.[110] Second, Floyd-Thomas frames *traditional communalism* as

the affirmation of the loving connections and relational bonds formed by Black women—including familial, maternal, platonic, religious, sexual, and spiritual ties. Black women's ability to create, re-member, nurture, protect, sustain, and liberate communities which are marked

---

[107]Cannon, *Katie's Canon*, 5.

[108]See Layli Phillips, ed., *The Womanist Reader* (New York: Routledge, 2006).

[109]Stacey M. Floyd-Thomas, ed., *Deeper Shades of Purple: Womanism in Religion and Society* (New York: NYU Press, 2006), 16.

[110]Walker, *In Search of Our Mothers' Gardens,* xi–xii.

and measured not by those outside of one's own community but by the acts of inclusivity, mutuality, reciprocity, and self-care practiced within it (opposite of the biological deterministic assumption that a woman's role is to serve as nurturer and protector).[111]

Womanists value the intimate and platonic ways of relationality between women, men, and most importantly, the Black community as essential for survival and liberation. Third, Floyd-Thomas identifies *redemptive self-love* as "an assertion of the humanity, customs, and aesthetic value of Black women in contradistinction to the commonly held stereotypes characteristic of white solipsism."[112] Walker's point that a womanist "loves herself, regardless" explicates Black women finding voice, beauty, and admiration in their bodies and the aesthetics they create beyond the white normative gaze and malestream.[113] Fourth, Floyd-Thomas defines *critical engagement* in three essential parts:

> 1) the epistemological privilege of Black women borne of their totalistic experience with the forces of interlocking systems of oppression and strategic options they devised to undermine them. 2) an unequivocal belief that *Black women hold the standard and normative measure for true liberation* [my emphasis]; the capacity of Black women to view things in their true relations or relative importance; and while expected to be among the chief arbiters of accountability, advocacy, and authenticity, they, too, must be faithful to the task of expanding their discourse, knowledge, and skills. 3) a hermeneutical suspicion, cognitive counterbalance, intellectual indictment, and perspectival corrective to those people, ideologies, movements, and institutions that hold a one-dimensional analysis of oppression; an unshakable belief that Black women's survival strategies must entail more than what others have provided as an alternative.[114]

Through critical engagement, womanists pursue the hard questions to break the bonds of misrecognition and misrepresentation of Black women's agency and liberation. Floyd-Thomas contends, "Womanism is revolutionary. Womanism is a paradigm shift wherein Black women no longer look to others for their liberation, but instead look to themselves. The revolu-

---

[111]Floyd-Thomas, *Deeper Shades of Purple*, 78.
[112]Floyd-Thomas, *Deeper Shades of Purple*, 142.
[113]Walker, *In Search of Our Mothers' Gardens,* xi–xii.
[114]Floyd-Thomas, *Deeper Shades of Purple*, 208.

tionaries are Black women scholars, who have armed themselves with pen and paper, not simply to dismantle the master's house, but to do the more important work of building a house of their own."[115] Walker, Cannon, Grant, Williams, Floyd-Thomas, and numerous other Black women theologians, ethicists, biblical scholars, historians, pastoral caregivers, religious leaders in the academy and the church built a solid foundation for a womanist theological house indeed.

Over the last forty years, there is no question that womanist theology and ethics have endured significant and sustained critiques that prompted its own conversion toward multidimensional analysis that included queer experiences and opened space for womanist theological exploration beyond Christianity. I briefly highlight the critiques of Black women religious scholars Cheryl Sanders, Renee L. Hill, and Monica Coleman and ways they each helped to clarify the womanist project.

Christian ethicist Cheryl Sanders, in a 1989 roundtable "Christian Ethics and Theology in Womanist Perspective" in the *Journal of Feminist Studies in Religion*, interrogates whether Walker's term was appropriate for Christian womanists to source, given Alice Walker's 1981 use of the term "womanist" as synonymous with "lesbian" in connection to the narrative of the Black Shaker Rebecca Jackson.[116] Sanders queries,

> In our efforts to tailor Walker's definition to suit our own purposes, have we misconstrued the womanist concept and its meaning? Is the word womanist being co-opted because of its popular appeal and used as a mere title or postscript for whatever black women scholars want to celebrate, criticize or construct? Are we committing a gross conceptual error when we use Walker's descriptive cultural nomenclature as a foundation for the normative discourse of theology and ethics? On what grounds, if any, can womanist authority and authenticity be established in our work? In other words, what is the necessary and sufficient condition for doing womanist scholarship? To be a black woman? A black feminist? A black lesbian?[117]

Sanders questions whether the adoption of "womanist" by Black women theologians to analyze Black women's experiences is fundamentally marred because of Walker's use of the Spirit beyond Christian norms and explicit

[115]Floyd-Thomas, *Deeper Shades of Purple*, 1–2.
[116]Cheryl Jeanne Sanders et al., "Christian Ethics and Theology in Womanist Perspectives," *Journal of Feminist Studies in Religion* 5, no. 2 (1989): 83–91.
[117]Sanders et al., "Christian Ethics and Theology," 85.

acceptance of lesbian sexuality. To answer Sanders's central inquiry, "Does the term womanist provide an appropriate frame of reference for the ethical and theological statements now being generated by black women?"[118] Katie Cannon responds,

> In essence, a womanist liberation theological ethic places Black women at the center of human social relation and ecclesiastical institutions and critiques the images and paradigms that the Black Church uses to promote or exclude women. A womanist theo-ethical critique serves as a model for understanding the silences, limitations, and possibilities of Black women's moral agency, by identifying Afro-Christian cultural patterns and forms, perspectives, doctrines, and values that are unique and peculiar to the Black Church community, in order to assess the dialectical tensions in Black women's past social relations as well as our current participation in the Black Church. A Black womanist liberation Christian ethic is a critique of all human domination in light of Black women's experience, a faith praxis that unmasks whatever threatens the well-being of the poorest women of color.[119]

Womanist ethicist Emilie Townes builds upon Cannon to assert, "The agenda of womanist ethics and theology must articulate an understanding of liberation concerned with human equality and the ever-present, ever-sustaining, judging, and redeeming nature of God. Our additional task is to promote the full partnership of women and men in creation with God—to model and embody inclusivity enveloped by justice. Womanist Christian ethics and theology searches for the possibilities and is so bold as to have the will to grasp them."[120] Cannon and Townes refine womanist theology and ethics beyond essentialist limitations and carve out the universal impetus for womanism as an anti-oppression paradigm that pursues justice and liberation for Black women, the Black community, and all of humanity.

In a related critique, womanist theologian Renee Hill in her 1990 article "Who We Are for Each Other? Sexism, Sexuality, and Womanist Theology" critiqued early womanists' missing engagement with sexuality as an analytical lens—particularly lesbian sexuality. Hill brings an important perspective to the conversation of womanist theology as she addresses the need for lesbian sexuality to join the understanding of Black women's oppression.

---

[118]Sanders et al., "Christian Ethics and Theology," 83, 92.
[119]Sanders et al., "Christian Ethics and Theology," 92–93.
[120]Sanders et al., "Christian Ethics and Theology," 97.

While many first-generation womanist scholars affirmed the tripartite oppression of Black women as racism-sexism-classism, heterosexism and homophobia were initially missing from this continuum. Hill recaptures the essence of Black women gathering sociopolitically, spiritually, and sexually as a means of resistance to a society that devalues their significance, self-determination to create space and conversation where they have been excluded, and necessary self-love to be *who they are* for themselves and for each other.[121] In the introduction of *Sexuality and the Black Church*, systematic theologian Kelly Brown Douglas admits that her colleague Renee Hill's critique of womanist theology coupled with the HIV/AIDS death of a close, gay, male friend impacted her life and theology in ways that she had not imagined.[122] In the 2014 documentary *Journey to Liberation Theology: The Legacy of Womanist Theology*, Douglas tells the story of her friend Lloyd who "loved the Black Church, but it did not love him back."[123] Hill's critique and Lloyd's death convicted Douglas and motivated her inclusion of sexuality in her womanist theological analysis, thus converting womanist theology to a multidimensional analysis of Black women's oppression that includes heterosexism and homophobia.

Process theologian Monica Coleman, in her 2006 article "Must I Be a Womanist?" wonders about the distinctions between Black feminism and womanism and doubts whether she can find a home in womanist religious thought because of its heteronormativity and Christian hegemony. Coleman laments that it took close to a decade for Hill's critique to be embraced by Douglas, and while briefly mentioning gay and lesbian experiences in *Sexuality and the Black Church*, she further conflates queer sexuality with HIV/AIDS. As evidenced throughout this book, womanist religious scholars talk often about God and Jesus. In so doing, Coleman problematizes whether womanists "have often assumed that black women's religious experiences are Christian" and "intentionally or not . . . have created a Christian hegemonic discourse within the field."[124] Though Walker's definition makes Coleman "feel at home," Coleman bemoans that womanist religious scholarship in its

---

[121]Renee Hill, "Who Are We for Each Other? Sexism, Sexuality and Womanist Theology," in *Black Theology: A Documentary History*, ed. James H. Cone and Gayraud S. Wilmore, 2nd ed. rev. (Maryknoll, NY: Orbis Books, 1993), 345–51.

[122]Kelly B. Douglas, *Sexuality and the Black Church: A Womanist Perspective* (Maryknoll, NY: Orbis Books, 1999), 1.

[123]*Journey to Liberation: The Legacy of Womanist Theology*, 2014, https://www.youtube.com/watch?v=PjhtUGqFCWg.

[124]Monica A. Coleman et al., "Roundtable Discussion: Must I Be a Womanist? [with Response]," *Journal of Feminist Studies in Religion* 22, no. 1 (April 1, 2006): 89.

first twenty years "left me in a house without enough furniture. There are not enough chairs, couches, or beds for me or many of the black women I know and love. It isn't a place where we can be who we are in some of the most important ways we live—sexually, spiritually, or politically."[125] Cannon acknowledges Coleman's claims as valid and valuable for pushing the womanist project forward. Cannon resists Coleman's interest to toss away the term "womanist" and evict this house of wisdom. As a master builder,[126] Cannon responds and offers Coleman and the future generations of womanists a charge:

> We officially began constructing this womanist house of wisdom in 1985, and as intellectual laborers we continue to work day in and day out so that our scholarly infrastructure is built on solid rock instead of shifting sand. Let us celebrate this analogous reality by acknowledging that the second generation of womanist scholars has completed the structure of the womanist house of wisdom,[127] and now it is time for Coleman's contemporaries, whom she identifies as the "third wave," to furnish the interior, to provide supportive objects that indicate a readiness for occupancy.[128]

Cannon makes clear there is room for *all* of us, including Black women of diverse sexualities and non-Christian voices, in womanist religious thought. The goal of construction is to build a platform for a multiplicity of voices and perspectives to add their unique contributions.

Melissa Harris-Perry as a political scientist and not a theologian or religious scholar joins this list of critics in *Sister Citizen*. Harris-Perry sees womanism as "the religious academy's attempt to straighten the crooked room by offering black women positive visions of themselves as citizens."[129] However, Harris-Perry is critical of the sourcing of Walker's term "woman-

---

[125]Coleman et al., "Roundtable Discussion," 86.

[126]I discuss in another volume Cannon's constructive vision and clarion call to future generations of womanists to build upon it. See Melanie C. Jones, "The House That Cannon Built and 'The Hinges upon Which the Future Swings,'" in *Walking through the Valley: Womanist Explorations in the Spirit of Katie Geneva Cannon*, ed. Emilie Maureen Townes (Louisville, KY: Westminster John Knox Press, 2022), 27–39.

[127]Cannon points to this coedited article to describe the womanist house of wisdom. Katie Geneva Cannon, Alison P. Gise Johnson, and Angela D. Sims, "Womanist Works in Word," *Journal of Feminist Studies in Religion* 21, no. 2 (2005): 135–46.

[128]Coleman et al., "Roundtable Discussion," 97.

[129]Harris-Perry, *Sister Citizen*, 229.

ist" in the second part of the definition as "traditionally capable." In Harris-Perry's view, the mark of capability carries an undue burden of strength for Black women to save themselves and their communities. Harris-Perry critiques two significant methods of womanism in the religious academy. First, Harris-Perry (like Coleman) addresses the Christian leanings of womanist religious thought, which fall apart as a growing body of womanist religious scholars develop works in religious traditions outside of Christianity including Islam, Buddhism, and African-derived religions.[130] She is skeptical of womanists making connections between the suffering of Black women like Fannie Lou Hamer and the "redemptive suffering" of Christ.[131] Harris-Perry rejects the womanist idea derived from Cannon's affirmation of Black women's agency and resilience noted earlier in *Katie's Canon* that "black women possess an innate capacity to straighten the angles of the crooked room."[132]

Second, Harris-Perry scrutinizes the sourcing of "exceptional" stories of Black women as dynamic moral agents by womanist scholars as "inherently limiting."[133] Harris-Perry notes,

These stories are important to recover, but they can also engender a kind of forgetfulness. They encourage the false belief that black women always face adversity with strength and that their strength is always victorious. But for every Harriet Tubman there are hundreds

---

[130]See a selected list of womanist works beyond Christianity, which is not exhaustive: Debra Majeed, "Womanism Encounters Islam: A Muslim Scholar Considers the Efficacy of a Method Rooted in the Academy and the Church," in *Deeper Shades of Purple: Womanism in Religion and Society*, ed. Stacey M. Floyd-Thomas, Religion, Race, and Ethnicity (New York: NYU Press, 2006), 38–53; Dianne M. Stewart, "Womanist Theology in the Caribbean Context: Critiquing Culture, Rethinking Doctrine, and Expanding Boundaries," *Journal of Feminist Studies in Religion* 20, no. 1 (2004): 61–82; Pamela Ayo Yetunde, "Black Lesbians to the Rescue!: A Brief Correction with Implications for Womanist Christian Theology and Womanist Buddhology," *Religions* 8, no. 9 (September 2017): 1–10, https://doi.org/10.3390/rel8090175; Yetunde, "I Know I've Been Changed: Black Womanist Buddhist and Christian Spiritual Formation and Spiritual Care for a Homicidal White Male Buddhist," in *Navigating Religious Difference in Spiritual Care and Counseling: Essays in Honor of Kathleen J. Greider*, ed. Jill Lynnae Snodgrass and Kathleen J. Greider (Claremont, CA: Claremont Press, 2019), 235–50, https://www.jstor.org/stable/10.2307/j.ctvwrm4c3; Yetunde, *Object Relations, Buddhism, and Relationality in Womanist Practical Theology* (New York: Palgrave Pivot, 2018); Yetunde, *Buddhist-Christian Dialogue, U.S. Religious Freedom Law, and Womanist Public Theology for Transgender Spiritual Care* (New York: Palgrave Macmillan, 2020).

[131]Harris-Perry, *Sister Citizen*, 230.

[132]Harris-Perry, *Sister Citizen*, 232.

[133]Harris-Perry, *Sister Citizen*, 238.

of thousands of black women who died as slaves. For every Sojourner Truth there are hundreds of thousands who were never able to speak publicly about their experiences. For every black woman who remains an independent moral agent in the face of crushing oppression, there are many who are, in fact, crushed.[134]

Harris-Perry chastises womanist religious scholars for the missing perspective of the everydayness of Black women, which is a theme that Townes, in particular, outlines significantly in *Womanist Ethics and the Cultural Production of Evil*, published the same year as Coleman's "Must I Be a Womanist?" and five years before *Sister Citizen*.[135]

Harris-Perry further critiques the "womanist divine imagination" that womanist theologians and ethicists espouse, which calls for Black women to reimagine their identities beyond cultural stereotypes and nurture a sense of inner, divine, or *incarnational* strength to enliven a more just ordering of the world. Harris-Perry argues in a quest to establish a sacred imagination beyond a white savior as articulated in Black theology and male savior as articulated in feminist theology,

> Black women are especially in need of an image of God that assumes divine presence is most available in the most difficult conditions. After all, they point out, it is black women who, like Jesus, bear the cross of racism, sexism, and poverty. It is black women's bodies that, like Jesus' body, were traditionally broken in service of white enslavers or black male abusers. It is black women who, like Jesus with the loaves and fish, manage to feed multitudes despite having few resources. It is black women who, like Jesus, form small groups of intimate friends who try to change to world against impossible odds. Womanists emphasize these similarities of the mission, ministry, and suffering of Jesus to the lived experiences of black women in order to claim that black women have a right and a need to imagine God as looking like and being like them.[136]

For Perry, the womanist theological enterprise falls short if its image of God maintains that Black women must become like God. Perry contends,

---

[134]Harris-Perry, *Sister Citizen*, 230.

[135]Emilie Maureen Townes, *Womanist Ethics and the Cultural Production of Evil* (New York: Palgrave Macmillan, 2006), 159–65.

[136]Harris-Perry, *Sister Citizen*, 242.

Perhaps womanist perspectives are simply another crooked image that
encourages black women to take on yet another role of responsibility for
others [my emphasis]. Perhaps as they imagine a God who is like them,
they see themselves as more like God, and although that imagining
can bolster self-esteem, it might also encourage a level of sacrifice that
is beyond what should be expected of a mere mortal.[137]

Lodged within Harris-Perry's critique is a concern about womanist constructions of theological anthropology as prescriptive in its soteriology.

In contradistinction, I argue that Harris-Perry's critique of the womanist divine imagination misrecognizes womanist theology and ethics on the matter of salvation. Affirmation of Black women's humanity as made in the image of God is in no way a proposal to suggest that Black women should *be* God; neither is it an attempt to encourage Black women to take on the burdens of sacrifice, surrogacy, or strength to save a nation or community. Womanist articulations of Black women's participation in the work of salvation is descriptive at best. Whereas liberation is the ultimate goal, womanist theologian Delores Williams explicitly identifies that the long range of Black women's quest for salvation is survival, as in the narrative of Hagar. Black women's adoption of a radical humanism to survive is not a matter of wanting to bear the weight of salvation, but an awareness that Black women simply cannot wait for another and must work as agents with God. Furthermore, Black women working with the Divine holds promise that Black women will not suffer this yoke alone.

In response to Harris-Perry's second critique of sourcing exceptional Black women, my grandmother's narrative of an ordinary Black woman of faith exposes both the harsh, death-dealing reality of living bent in a crooked world and the hope for embodied transformation (healing-restoration-liberation) for future Black women in life and not in death as her story is remembered. I align with Cannon that "womanism requires that we stress the urgency of the African American women's movement from death to life."[138] My constructive vision in this project is to empower Black women to recognize their power and potential to work with the Divine to confront and release the forces that bend, whether social, political, ecclesial, or doctrinal. Harris-Perry concludes the "God" chapter in *Sister Citizen* by offering some vision of womanist potential. She writes, "Womanism is an approach that may offer more opportunities for accurate recognition of black women. By

---

[137]Harris-Perry, *Sister Citizen*, 251 (emphasis added).
[138]Cannon, *Katie's Canon*, 3.

imagining a God more like themselves, black women might finally find a place to *lay down the heavy mantle of impervious strength* [my emphasis]."[139] I move to explicate the promise of womanist theo-ethical constructions of salvation rooted not in Black women becoming divine but in their co-partnering with God for survival and liberation.

Gonna Lay Down My Burdens: The Promise of Womanist Theologies of Salvation

"She carries the burdens of the Church, and of the school and she bears a great deal more than her economic share in the home," observed Nannie Helen Burroughs.[140] Jacquelyn Grant, Kelly Brown Douglas, Delores Williams, and JoAnne Terrell offer unique perspectives concerning the relationship between sin, suffering, and salvation in Black women's experience that serve as constructive pathways for understanding Black women's mutual liberation and co-partnership with God.

Jacquelyn Grant

Grant begins with Christology as a point of departure to chart a pathway for liberation in " 'Come to My Help Lord for I'm in Trouble': Womanist Jesus and the Mutual Struggle for Liberation." Grant makes clear that Black women hold a deep connection with the human experiences of Jesus, who is God-incarnate. For Grant, the suffering of Black women is identified in the experiences of tripartite oppression: racism, sexism, and classism. Grant uncovers parallel experiences in relation to the "historical imprisonment" of patriarchy, white supremacy, and privilege that restrict and confine Jesus.[141] First, patriarchy, like the crooked room, is a "conceptual trap" that blocks any imagination of a world outside of male ordering.[142] Grant interprets the sin of patriarchy as men using the maleness of Jesus and imaging of God as male to justify the subordination of women (and I would add gender

---

[139]Harris-Perry, *Sister Citizen*, 265 (emphasis added).

[140]Bettye Collier-Thomas, *Jesus, Jobs, and Justice: African American Women and Religion* (New York: Alfred A. Knopf, 2010), 59.

[141]Jacquelyn Grant, " 'Come to My Help Lord for I'm in Trouble': Womanist Jesus and the Mutual Struggle for Liberation," *Journal of Black Theology in South Africa* 8, no. 1 (May 1994): 30.

[142]Grant, "Come to My Help Lord," 23.

minorities) in the church and society. Second, white supremacy represents a racist ideology that justifies white domination and control. Grant identifies the imaging of white Jesus and the construction of a white God in the Western imagination despite historical and biblical inaccuracies as elevating white domination to divine control over oppressed and racially marginalized groups. Third, classist interpretations of Jesus as royal locate Jesus's identity among the rulers and not the servants. Grant outlines the use of servanthood as a Christian duty to serve the powerful and block out the suffering of Jesus as a Jew, born of lowly means, and wrongfully persecuted as a criminal. Jesus Christ can be found in the experiences of Black women because Jesus has also confronted the historical imprisonment of the "sin of patriarchy (sexism), the sin of White supremacy (racism) and the sin of Privilege (classism)."[143] Grant makes the case that Black women as victims of sexism, racism, and classism are three times removed from the image of God in this sinful economy.

Grant raises a theology of mutual liberation between Black women and Jesus Christ. According to Grant, "What we find in the experience of African American Women is a process of mutual liberation: Jesus was liberating or redeeming African American Women as African American Women were liberating or redeeming Jesus."[144] Four models illuminate this mutual liberation: "1) Jesus as Co-Sufferer, 2) Jesus as Equalizer, 3) Jesus means Freedom, and 4) Jesus as Liberator."[145] For Grant, sin is too much service for Black women, which leads to self-destructive behaviors like servitude to religious systems with unequal pay and a belief in Black women's inferiority (i.e., notions of Black women as less fit for leadership, less equal, and presumably less human). Jesus calls Black women to discipleship not servanthood, to equality not inferiority, to freedom not bondage, to liberation not subjugation. Monica Coleman maintains, in Grant's schema, "Salvation, then, is Black women's full participation in church and society."[146] Moreover, "the liberation activities of Jesus empower African American women to be significantly engaged in the process of liberation."[147] Grant cites Sojourner Truth, who put it this way: "When I preaches, I has jest one text to preach from, an I always preaches from this one. My text is, 'When

---

[143]Grant, "Come to My Help Lord," 30.

[144]Grant, "Come to My Help Lord," 30.

[145]Grant, "Come to My Help Lord," 31.

[146]Monica A. Coleman, *Making a Way out of No Way: A Womanist Theology* (Minneapolis: Fortress Press, 2008), 13.

[147]Grant, "Come to My Help Lord," 32.

I found Jesus!' "[148] Jesus provides the ground of mutual liberation for Black women in suffering, solidarity, and salvation.[149]

Kelly Brown Douglas

In her 2006 article "Twenty Years a Womanist: An Affirming Challenge," Douglas admits, "What I have discovered these last twenty years is that I have tried to live into the womanist idea, it is in fact about affirmation—the affirmation of the voices of the weak, the powerless."[150] The womanist theological task, for Douglas, is to rally against all forms of oppression to enliven human wholeness. So, what does a Black Christ mean for Black women? Douglas affirms an ethical responsibility to address the wholeness of a people from her earliest work, *The Black Christ*. Douglas writes, " 'Blackness' must involve more than just being a particular color, or being a particular ethnic group, or identifying with a particular cultural and historical experience. It must include an ethical concern and commitment to the well-being and freedom of all black people."[151] For Douglas, Jesus is found working for the wholeness of the community. Jesus is also a prophet calling out that which seeks to divide and separate the community as a whole.

Refined by Renee Hill and her friend Lloyd in *Sexuality and the Black Church*, Douglas widens the womanist analysis from tripartite to multidimensional oppression. Sin is the multidimensional oppression of Black women that is both sociopolitical and religio-cultural (racism, sexism, classism, heterosexism). According to Douglas, moral accountability and prophetic responsibility go hand in hand. History reveals perpetual cycles of sin "because of the way we deny the past and dismiss the future."[152] As we remember the freedom saga of Black people and face the tragedies of this contemporary moment, Douglas asserts, "I have no doubt until we hold ourselves morally accountable to our past and dare to take prophetic responsibility for our future, then our present realties will continue to be

---

[148]Grant, "Come to My Help Lord," 33.

[149]Grant, "Come to My Help Lord," 33.

[150]Kelly Brown Douglas, "Twenty Years a Womanist: An Affirming Challenge," in *Deeper Shades of Purple: Womanism in Religion and Society,* ed. Stacey Floyd-Thomas (New York: NYU Press, 2006), 156.

[151]Kelly Brown Douglas, *The Black Christ* (Maryknoll, NY: Orbis Books, 1994), 85.

[152]Kelly Brown Douglas, "Moral Accountability, Prophetic Responsibility, and Selma by Kelly Brown Douglas," *Feminism and Religion* (blog), January 20, 2015, https://feminismandreligion.com/2015/01/20/moral-accountability-prophetic-responsibility-and-selma-by-kelly-brown-douglas/.

defined by the worst of who we are and not the best of who God calls us to be."[153] Suffering for Black women is the struggle *against* sociopolitical oppressions that render Black women less than whole.

For Douglas, the Black Christ exists in the faces of Black women and reminds Christians of their responsibility to "imitate Christ" by also calling out social, political, and ecclesial injustice and working toward wholeness. Douglas writes, "For Blacks, it is precisely by imitating Christ that we bring salvation to our community."[154] Black people are called to imitate Christ's prophetic ministry by ridding even an oppressed community from its own oppression. Salvation is the struggle for the wholeness of Black women and the Black community. In this sense, "Salvation is not just the goal of that wholeness, but is found in the *struggle to attain* that wholeness."[155] Salvation is not simply about the saving of souls, but it is also about redeeming bodies and repairing the breach of systems. It is not just benevolence but also empowerment.

Delores Seneva Williams

In *A Troubling in My Soul: Womanist Perspectives on Evil and Suffering*, Williams constructs a womanist perspective of sin from slave songs and ex-slaves' autobiographies of nineteenth-century women as "trouble" that bears weight like "heavy burdens."[156] On the matter of transgression, there are two kinds of moral action: (1) "wrongdoing" and (2) "collective social evil far more serious in its consequence than acts of wrongdoing; this social evil occurs when one dominant group exerts its power in a way that brutalizes another group with less power."[157] Williams, like Cone, identifies sin as social, pointing to collective well-being rather than individual acts. Cone's description of "sin as a society's way of taking people's humanity" aligns with a womanist perspective of sin as any abuse, defilement, or wrong done to the body. Drawing from nineteenth- and early-twentieth-century women's autobiographies of Jarena Lee, Zilpha Elaw, and Julia A. J. Foote

---

[153]Douglas, "Moral Accountability."

[154]Kelly Brown Douglas, "Is Christ a Black Woman? A Womanist Understanding of Christ Is Rooted in Healing Fractured Communities," *Other Side*, April 1994, 8.

[155]Coleman, *Making a Way Out of No Way*, 19.

[156]Delores S. Williams, "A Womanist Perspective on Sin," in *A Troubling in My Soul: Womanist Perspectives on Evil and Suffering*, ed. Emilie Maureen Townes (Maryknoll, NY: Orbis Books, 1993), 130–49.

[157]Williams, "A Womanist Perspective on Sin," 138.

and their profound experiences of "unworthiness," Williams interprets in these women's narratives that "reaching the level of 'somebodiness' amounts to what they see as liberation."[158] Thus, sin is the devaluing of Black women's bodies, sense of self-esteem, and sexuality; the elevation of white woman-hood at the expense of Black womanhood; and the devaluing of Black lesbian sexuality among Black women and within the Black community.[159]

Williams talks at length about suffering for Black women as the burden of surrogacy, which I present in chapter 2.[160] In Williams's view, there is noth-ing redemptive in suffering. According to womanist theologian Stephanie Mitchem, "It is not suffering, surrogacy or defilement that 'saves'" for Wil-liams.[161] The vision of a salvific Jesus is found not in his violent death on the cross, but in his life as Jesus heals, touches, cares, and so forth. Seemingly, salvation is this-worldly for Black women and is present in the "survival and quality of life."[162] Jesus's action and interaction with social outcasts, healing the sick, feeding the hungry, and unsettling the status quo in the Gospel accounts (mostly Luke) say more about redemption than a single event of death. Salvation is the healing and elevation of Black women's self-esteem; rejection of any sacrifice or suffering in the body; establishment of right relationship between Black women, Black men, and the greater society; and the calling out of sin. Black churches and communities can join the work of salvation by revisiting the stories of influential Black figures who helped to combat oppression for Black women and supporting the collective social wellness of Black people to lift the burden of oppression.

JoAnne Marie Terrell

Black women's fight for citizenship marks a bloody battle for recognition, as I narrated in the stories of the Selma March in 1965 and the testimony of Fannie Lou Hamer in chapter 3. JoAnne Terrell sources not an exceptional account of a Black woman, but the story of her mother, an everyday Black woman killed by the hand of an intimate partner in *Power in the Blood?*

---

[158]Williams, "A Womanist Perspective on Sin," 140.

[159]Williams, "A Womanist Perspective on Sin," 146–47.

[160]Delores S. Williams, "Black Women's Surrogacy Experience and the Christian Notion of Redemption," in *Cross Examinations: Readings on the Meaning of the Cross*, ed. Marit Trelstad (Minneapolis: Fortress Press, 2006), 19–32.

[161]Stephanie Y. Mitchem, *Introducing Womanist Theology* (Maryknoll, NY: Orbis Books, 2002), 115.

[162]Delores S. Williams, *Sisters in the Wilderness: The Challenge of Womanist God-Talk* (Maryknoll, NY: Orbis Books, 1993), 6.

Much like Jesus, Black people have endured suffering by violence such as state-sanctioned violence (i.e., torture, incarceration, betrayal, etc.) and, for Black women in particular, intimate partner violence. The cross bears witness to a hermeneutic of sacrifice and a sacramental witness. Jesus died and shed blood "once and for all for the sins of the world."[163] In Terrell's view, Jesus died so that Black women do not have to die to violence. The cross is not significant because of sacrifice, but because of Jesus's blood that is shed. There is power, which is the presence of God, in the blood. Jesus's suffering invites us to consider the extent of God's love. Thus, God loves humanity so that God can be seen in the blood of the suffering.

In Terrell's schema, sin is any form of alienation, whether self-induced or forced; suffering is human estrangement from God. A sacramental take on suffering Black women affirms their blood as sacred and bearing the life force necessary to enliven salvation even in the face of violence. In response to the question "What do womanists want?"—or better, "What do Black women need?"—Terrell constructs a ten-point platform outlining the womanist agenda beginning with this point: "The vigorous promotion of the idea of African women and women of the African Diaspora—black women—as bearing, *as fully as all other persons*, the image and imprimatur of Divine reality."[164] Monica Coleman describes Terrell's vision of salvation this way: "When we see God's presence in the sufferer and learn from the violence, we can be saved. Salvation comes from the lessons learned after instances of suffering. The very life force, the blood, of sufferers is part of the sacred means of pointing us toward salvation."[165] According to Terrell, "Liberation is a long game. And it's God's long game too."

Toward a Womanist Theology of Mutual Liberation and Co-partnership

Monica Coleman describes womanist perspectives of salvation as "making a way out of no way" that point to "(1) God's presentation of unforeseen possibilities; (2) human agency; (3) the goal of justice, survival, and quality of life; and (4) a challenge to the existing order."[166] From womanist

---

[163]JoAnne Marie Terrell, *Power in the Blood? The Cross in the African American Experience* (Eugene, OR: Wipf & Stock, 2005), 1.

[164]Joanne Marie Terrell, "10-Point Platform for a Womanist Agenda (What Womanists Want)," *Union Seminary Quarterly Review* 58, no. 3–4 (2004): 9–12.

[165]Coleman, *Making a Way out of No Way*, 27.

[166]Though Monica Coleman is critical of womanism in her early writings, as discussed

constructions of salvation, I identify the promise of Black women's mutual liberation and co-partnership with God by five major pillars. This five-part formula answers the initial liberationist inquiry about liberation of Black women: to what, for what, by whom, and toward what end as well as the provocative refrain "What must Black women do to be saved?" presented at the beginning of the chapter.

First, salvation for Black women begins with a quest for wholeness. Building on Douglas, salvation for Black women is the struggle for wholeness and the unmitigated gall to call out prophetically that which seeks to divide, separate, and oppress within and outside of Black communities. The quest for wholeness requires a holistic way of living that is concerned with not just the created order (including the environment) but also the past, such as the ancestral world, the present, and the future. According to womanist theologian Karen Baker-Fletcher, "Salvation is possible in the work of healing, sustaining and liberating."[167] This tridimensional work of salvation calls for radical transformation of this world that brings the ancestors, along with Jesus as the greatest ancestor and eternal Spirit, to inform the present and the future.

Second, salvation for Black women requires transformation of self and society. Salvation is Black women rejecting surrogacy as identified by Williams at every turn. It requires the lifting and elevation of Black women's self-esteem and resisting oppressive stereotypes and tropes that malign Black women's bodies, sexuality, and agency. The crooked world as it is known must be transformed. Black women's redemption requires calling out oppression and calling for social salvation of institutions, nations, and even churches.

Third, the salvation of Black women advocates for communal redemption. According to womanist theologian Stephanie Mitchem, "Each person is saved not merely for self, but for community. A person is saved *from* socially constructed limitations, saved *for* the greater good of all people."[168] Walker's second part of the womanist definition affirms and celebrates the value of community and salvation as a communal good. Grant draws on

---

earlier, Coleman does glean the womanist wisdom of first- and second-generation womanist voices to cast a postmodern womanist theological vision of Black women's salvation. Coleman's *Making a Way out of No Way* provides a thorough analysis of Black womanist perspectives of salvation, which adds value to my engagement with these thinkers. Coleman, *Making a Way out of No Way,* 33.

[167]Coleman, *Making a Way out of No Way,* 33.
[168]Mitchem, *Introducing Womanist Theology,* 111.

Harriet Tubman, who went back to the South to retrieve her kin because freedom "just can't be kept to yourself. Yes, freedom experienced is indeed freedom shared."[169]

Fourth, the salvation of Black women necessitates a realized eschatology. Black women cannot wait for some otherworldly cosmic redemption. Salvation is necessary in the here and now. The quest to do the work of salvation in a womanist paradigm is not a move to become God or take on superhuman divine abilities that bear more burden than promise, as Harris-Perry suggests, but to work *with* God toward liberation.

Fifth, the salvation of Black women fosters co-partnership between God and Black women. God partners with Black women; Black women partner with God. Womanist theologian M. Shawn Copeland makes this plain in "Wading through Many Sorrows": "A womanist theology of suffering is *redemptive*. In their narratives, Black women invite God to partner them in the redemption of Black people. They make meaning of their suffering."[170] The narrative of Hagar is a ripe example, as Williams demonstrated. God does not provide immediate salvation but empowers Hagar with the tools and skills through "survival and quality of life" to seek her own redemption. The New Testament example of Luke 13:10–17 and the doubly bent woman illuminates Jesus's healing of her eighteen-year-long suffering as a prophetic move to expose the crooked characters of an oppressive sociopolitical and religio-cultural order. Coretta Scott King's attempt to "wade through the many sorrows" of the loss of her beloved husband with God on her side called America to greater accountability of its citizens and its morals. God works with Black women toward a redemptive present and future. There is meaning in both the suffering and the liberation. A womanist understanding of salvation is not cheap or immediate but requires Black women to work with the Divine to enliven transformation for ourselves and communities.

And We Are Not Yet Saved?

In the Black Baptist tradition, once saved, always saved! Salvation requires an initial confession of Jesus Christ as Lord who walked this Earth, died for the sins of humanity, and abides as a risen savior to grant believers the right

---

[169]Grant, "Come to My Help Lord for I'm in Trouble," 4.

[170]M. Shawn Copeland, " 'Wading through Many Sorrows': Toward a Theology of Suffering in Womanist Perspective," in *A Troubling in My Soul: Womanist Perspectives on Evil and Suffering*, ed. Emilie Maureen Townes (Maryknoll, NY: Orbis Books, 1993), 124.

to eternal life. Nothing a person does can shake this confession of faith. Like clockwork, on numerous occasions, I remember sitting in church with my grandmother during the altar call or invitation and watching her approach the altar in search of salvation and redemption. For Baptist congregations, this act was unnerving with clergy and laity often repeating the line to her, "You are *already* saved." Ministers who appeased her journey to the altar "again" often prayed over her for healing, but eventually sent her back to her seat still wanting. In fact, as a Black woman domestic she was the one charged with saving homes, by picking up the dirt of messy lives. She was doubly assigned this role as a Black churchwoman expected to care for people who needed mothering. Yes, my grandmother had confessed Christ again and again. She was one of Jesus's most faithful followers, but there was something unfulfilled about her experience of salvation—something that could not be simply glossed over or ignored. It was not just a physical and spiritual healing that she longed for. Like the woman with a bent condition in Luke 13:10–17, I imagine that she was looking to work out her body and soul salvation by working with God to confront and release the political and religious forces that bend.

The salvific potential within Black women does not preclude the Divine. A womanist reckoning with the existential reality that our saviors are ourselves does not affirm that Black women must bear alone the burdens of both a crooked world and salvation of a bent condition. A liberating God through Jesus Christ recognizes Black women's bodies and agency and works with us in efforts toward wholeness. The story of my grandmother further illuminates Black women remaining faithful to the very end of their struggles and the enduring need of both human agency and divine power to realize salvation. My womanist reading of Luke 13:10–17, developed in chapter 6, provides a glimpse of the Resurrection hope of Black women that salvation and redemption can ultimately be seen with God through Jesus.

5

"Hitting a Straight Lick with a Crooked Stick"

A Womanist Reading of Luke 13:10–17

"De nigger woman is de mule uh de world so fur as Ah can see."
—Zora Neale Hurston[1]

Mule

*she scowls all the time 'cause her shoulders bow underneath all
      that work and worry*
*and get nothin' in return that's why her feet are planted in stubborn
      stance that's why*
*she don't move, when others around her say move sometimes all a
      woman's got is her push & pull against the grain and that's how
      she survives how she plods underneath the*
*pack & load she carries she carves out rows with determined grit
      if she likes you you might get a taste of her metallic wit flashing
      like silver starlight every now and again if*
*she don't like you she will give you nothin' but raised hand and back
      turned attitude if you're wise you'll escape the eyes that rapier
      glare more serrated than words if you're*
*smart you'll know better than to get into a kicking contest with a
      mule you'll see that she's had it tough in this world the same
      world that will never love her and see that*
she's a jewel—will never recognize that black diamond gleam she

---

[1]Zora Neale Hurston, *Their Eyes Were Watching God* (New York: PerfectBound, 2004), 17.

brings to the world you'll know what she knows the world only
wants her for her sweat—step and groan

Glenis Redmond[2]

Nobody captures the experience of the Black woman more than the inimitable Zora Neale Hurston, the most prolific Black woman writer, folklorist, anthropologist, and thinker of the twentieth century.[3] In her American classic *Their Eyes Were Watching God*, Hurston narrates the experience of Black women's subordination and subjugation in a white supremacist capitalist heteropatriarchal world. Hurston opines,

> Honey, de white man is de ruler of everything as fur as Ah been able tuh find out. Maybe it's some place way off in de ocean where de black man is in power, but we don't know nothin' but what we see. So de white man throw down de load and tell de nigger man tuh pick it up. He pick it up because he have to, but he don't tote it. He hand it to his womenfolks. De nigger woman is de mule uh de world so fur as Ah can see.[4]

As the furthest away from the white, able-bodied male norm and the last on the totem pole, Hurston frames the bendedness of Black women as akin to the mules of the world who suffer as "beast of burden" with the task of carrying heavy loads.[5] Building upon Hurston, Katie Cannon frames the Black womanist liberation task as "hitting a straight lick with a crooked stick," which is "to debunk, unmask, and disentangle the historically conditioned value judgments and power relations that undergird the particularities of race, sex, and class oppression."[6] Womanists discern ways that Black women

---

[2]Glenis Redmond, "Mule," *Meridians* 11, no. 2 (March 1, 2013): 25–26, https://doi.org/10.2979/meridians.11.2.25.

[3]This phrase is derived from African American folk language. Black folklorist Zora Neale Hurston refers to this expression in her writings to identify the challenging task Black people face when up against race, gender, and class oppression. Womanist progenitor Katie Cannon names her article with this phrase to identify the daunting undertaking of womanist ethicists to articulate a Black liberation ethic. My title for this chapter is a riff on this folk saying. See Katie Geneva Cannon, *Katie's Canon: Womanism and the Soul of the Black Community*, rev. and exp. 25th anniversary ed. (Minneapolis: Fortress Press, 2021), 59–66.

[4]Hurston, *Their Eyes Were Watching God*, 16.

[5]Hurston is the quintessential womanist muse, inspiring the works of Alice Walker and Katie Geneva Cannon.

[6]Cannon, *Katie's Canon*, 59.

are excluded from traditional inquiries of theological ethics and biblical interpretation while employing critical analyses to write Black women's experiences and stories back into the canon of these traditions.

The death of my grandmother in 2013 awakened my womanist sensibilities to the theo-ethical implications of bendedness for Black women. Though my grandmother lived with a bent condition for close to twenty years, her struggle was misrecognized. In a moment and the twinkling of an eye, I watched my grandmother's body transform from bent to redeemed, signaling healing, release, restoration, and liberation from the multidimensional forces that bent her over as a poor, Black, divorced mother and migrant, and domestic who was a faithful follower of Jesus.

My womanist aim here is to employ this narrative from my grandmother's garden, but also to ground an interpretation of Luke 13:10–17 with a backdrop of the experiences of an everyday Black woman and to expose the thick location of the problem of bendedness for Black women at a multilayered level. As a womanist theological ethicist, I frame human agency as the starting place for the "doing of ethics" and narrative as a valuable tool for engaging questions of embodiment. The hermeneutic of parallel/biblical appropriation in the female tradition of survival that comes out of Delores Williams's *Sisters in the Wilderness: The Challenge of Womanist God-Talk* encourages womanist interpreters to read the biblical text alongside Black women's experiences. Williams does this by starting with the biblical text and exegesis of the narrative of Hagar and then moves into analyzing Black women's stories and lives. I do the reverse in this book by starting with a narrative of an everyday Black woman and then exploring biblical exegesis and textual interpretation of Luke 13:10–17.

While Black women continue to read and return to the narrative of the bent woman through proclamation and sacred rhetoric in many Black Church traditions and cultures, no womanist biblical scholar has yet given serious attention to reading this text for liberation.[7] Without my grandmother's story, the popular correlation between Black women and the Luke 13 woman may only be linked through a theology of contempt for Black women espoused most notably by Bishop T. D. Jakes and the Woman Thou Art Loosed movement as described in chapter 4. Black feminist religious

---

[7]See Alyson Diane Browne, "Straighten Up!," in *This Is My Story: Testimonies and Sermons of Black Women in Ministry*, ed. Cleophus James LaRue (Louisville, KY: Westminster John Knox Press, 2005), 68–71; Gina Stewart, "The Fierce Urgency of Now," in *Those Sisters Can Preach! 22 Pearls of Wisdom, Virtue, and Hope*, ed. Vashti M. McKenzie (Cleveland: Pilgrim Press, 2013), 113–19.

critic Tamura Lomax in *Jezebel Unhinged* provides a sustained critique of
Jakes and WTAL misinterpreting this passage, but Lomax does not rein-
terpret the text to engage constructive readings of it. My grandmother's
narrative is a framing story for the project and layered throughout the book
in each chapter to inform a womanist theo-ethical reading of the problem
of bendedness for Black women in their enduring quest for liberation and
redemption.

I raise the narrative of the bent woman in Luke 13:10–17 as ripe for
womanist theo-ethical analysis because it brings to center stage the woman's
body and her subjectivity/agency. Furthermore, I think the bent woman's
narrative parallels with the story of my grandmother and the broader
historical and contemporary narratives of the Black female body bent by
pervasive historical, social, and religious threats seeking to stifle her survival that are inextricably linked to attacks against Black women's moral
agency.[8] Utilizing a womanist hermeneutic of appropriation and parallel,[9]
I aim to read and interpret this text through a bent body politic. I use the
concept of body politic to name two overlapping ideas concerning Black
women's bodies. First, the term "body politic" articulates the Black female
body's representation as a site of multidimensional oppression bearing the
weight of thick discursive inscriptions. Drawing from feminist phrasing, the
personal is political as the presence of Black women's bodies opens dialogue
for broader sociopolitical realities. Second, "body politic" addresses the
lived experiences of the Black female body as a primary source to combat
corrupt societal norms. Here, the political becomes prophetic as Black
women's bodies (e.g., aesthetics) and experiences (feelings, weeping, rage/
anger/fury, erotica, suspicion, etc.) transform into powerful, divine weap-
onry to self-protect and rally against interlocking systems of oppression.

My womanist reading of Luke 13:10–17 engages the unnamed woman's
bent body and restoration that uncovers the crookedness of the religious
leaders' orthodoxy and dogma surrounding the Sabbath. Similar to my
grandmother's story, the wrong done to the woman's body causes the woman
to bend and not her weak character. Utilizing Katie Cannon's canonical
virtues, including *invisible dignity, quiet grace,* and *unshouted courage*
that illuminate moral wisdom of Black women, I argue that the unnamed

---

[8]In the words of Audre Lorde, Black women were never meant to survive! See Audre
Lorde, "A Litany for Survival," in *The Collected Poems of Audre Lorde* (New York: W. W.
Norton, 1997), 255–56.

[9]I am drawing this from Williams's *Sisters in the Wilderness* and her parallel of Black
women's experiences alongside Hagar's story in Genesis 16 and 21.

woman's body acts with virtue by seeing and being seen in the public eye, speaking and commanding her healing from Jesus, and confronting and disrupting the crooked characters of the synagogue leaders and hypocritical members of the crowd seeking to discredit this woman's healing. Despite her bent condition, these *body acts* signify the woman's virtuous, upright character. Through rereading this text, I encourage Black women to reveal their bodies, listen and attune to their body language, and "tell the truth while shaming the devil" by prophesying to corrupt social and religious powers of the day with the evidence of their bent bodies. Reclaiming these acts, in my view, affirms and forms the virtuous moral agency of Black women and their bodies.

The Gospel according to Luke

The Book of Luke, the third book in the New Testament, a member of the Synoptic Gospels, presents Jesus as the Savior of the World. The date of Luke's writing is approximately 80–95 CE, as the Lukan writer is aware of the destruction of Jerusalem, which happened in 70 CE. The Book of Luke is written by a second- or third-generation Gentile Christian who was "well informed about and deeply committed to the God, Scriptures, and community of the Jewish people."[10] Luke is likely educated in Hellenistic Greek and familiar with the Hebrew Scriptures in Greek. Luke code switches from common to sophisticated Greek to "vary the style of expression to suit speaker and occasion."[11] Luke's linguistic abilities expose the author's belonging to a high social status with access to education and resources. Luke writes to Theophilus, who was likely a Roman governor, in Luke 1:1–4 and Acts 1:1–2, but whose name means lover of God; therefore, this book is presumably written to those who are friends of God and among the beloved. Unlike the other Gospel accounts, the Book of Luke has a narrative pair or a sequel that continues the Lukan lesson in the Book of Acts.[12]

Lukan theology, among other themes, presents Jesus as a Savior who is concerned for and stands with oppressed and marginalized people. According to New Testament scholar John Carroll, "Salvation is a central concern

---

[10] John T. Carroll, *Jesus and the Gospels: An Introduction* (Louisville, KY: Westminster John Knox Press, 2016), 141.

[11] Carroll, *Jesus and the Gospels*, 141.

[12] Narrative pairs reflect the form and content of the book of Luke. Luke 13:10–17 belongs to a doublet narrative of man healed on the Sabbath in Luke 14: 1–6.

of Luke and Acts. In these two books, Luke tells the story of God's decisive intervention in the world to bring salvation to Israel and to the whole earth—all in fulfillment of ancient promise."[13] Most notably, Luke's Gospel utilizes women as disenfranchised folk whom Jesus restores to full humanity and reclaims their place in the community. The Acts of the Apostles continued Luke's theology in the forging of community by the apostles, which presents new challenges for the presence of women in carrying out Luke's Jesus mission.

Feminists and womanist theologians have gravitated to Luke-Acts because of Luke's emphasis on women while also questioning whether Luke's Gospel values actual women's lives and experiences in relation to other New Testament biblical writers (i.e., Mark, Matthew, John, or Paul). There are forty-two passages about women in Luke, of which twenty-three are peculiar to Luke's Gospel (L Source). Most biblical scholars affirm that Luke relied on earlier traditions and Gospel accounts (i.e., Mark and Q sources). Examples of narratives of women that overlap with other Gospel accounts are as follows: Simon's mother-in-law (Lk 4:38–39); the woman with an issue of blood (Lk 8); Jairus's daughter (Lk 8); woman baking bread (Lk 13:20–21); a widow who gives her all (Lk 21:1–4); the Galilean women who witness Jesus's death and burial (Lk 23:49, 55–56) and discover an empty tomb (Lk 24:1–12). Following source criticism, the L source represents Lukan material peculiar to Luke's Gospel that features many of the women's narratives in Luke: "Infancy Narrative"—Elizabeth, Mary, and Anna (Lk 1–2); "Jesus's ministry in Galilee"—the raising of the son of the widow of Nain (Lk 7:12–17); the city woman who anoints Jesus (Lk 7:36–50); Galilean women as followers of Jesus (Lk 8:1–3); "Jesus's journey to Jerusalem" with Martha and Mary (Lk 10:38–42); the woman crying out from the crowd (Lk 11:27–28); the woman bent double (Lk 13:10–17); the parable of the sweeping woman who searches for a lost coin (Lk 15:8–10), the parable of the persistent widow (Lk 18:1–8); and "The Passion Narrative" with women preparing spices (Lk 23:56). In many ways, the presence of women in Luke does not support the idea that the writer of Luke was a feminist; nor does it suggest that Luke valued the voices and perspectives of women more than other Gospel writers (i.e., was more gynocentric).[14]

---

[13] John T. Carroll, "Bodies Restored, Communities Fractured?: Luke and Salvation Revisited," *Currents in Theology and Mission* 45, no. 4 (2018): 18.

[14] Carol A. Newsom, Sharon H. Ringe, and Jacqueline E. Lapsley, eds., *Women's Bible Commentary*, 3rd ed., 20th anniversary ed. (Louisville, KY: Westminster John Knox Press, 2012).

What is critical for biblical interpretation is not the number of stories of women in Luke but what these women are doing (not doing) or saying (not saying) that become important for analyzing Jesus's ministry to women and Luke's rhetorical strategy. Women are considered members of the Jesus and early Christian movement; however, their roles are often supportive and receiving in Luke. Two challenges emerge in Luke: (1) Lukan silence—Luke presents women's narratives in the Gospel but often silences their voices; (2) Lukan ambiguity—Luke introduces the stories of women, but some narratives are cut off and incomplete with no names, origins, and so on, which leaves ambiguity around their purpose and function. Feminist New Testament scholar Frances Taylor Gench suggests that Luke has a double message. "While women are more visible in Luke, they are prescribed to circumscribed roles."[15] Luke often undercuts or undermines women's agency in these narratives. Because of these restricted roles, Luke's Gospel is prime for critical interpretation. As a result of silence and ambiguity, biblical interpreters are left to read and interpret these stories through imaginative lenses to open the world of the text and recognize the agency of these characters.

Framing the Text: The Story of a Body-Bent Woman in Luke 13:10–17

ἦν δὲ διδάσκων ἐν μιᾷ τῶν συναγωγῶν ἐν τοῖς σάββασιν καὶ ἰδοὺ γυνὴ πνεῦμα ἔχουσα ἀσθενείας ἔτη δεκαοκτὼ καὶ ἦν συγκύπτουσα καὶ μὴ δυναμένη ἀνακύψαι εἰς τὸ παντελές ἰδὼν δὲ αὐτὴν ὁ Ἰησοῦς προσεφώνησεν καὶ εἶπεν αὐτῇ γύναι ἀπολέλυσαι τῆς ἀσθενείας σου καὶ ἐπέθηκεν αὐτῇ τὰς χεῖρας καὶ παραχρῆμα ἀνωρθώθη καὶ ἐδόξαζεν τὸν θεόν ἀποκριθεὶς δὲ ὁ ἀρχισυνάγωγος ἀγανακτῶν ὅτι τῷ σαββάτῳ ἐθεράπευσεν ὁ Ἰησοῦς ἔλεγεν τῷ ὄχλῳ ὅτι ἓξ ἡμέραι εἰσὶν ἐν αἷς δεῖ ἐργάζεσθαι ἐν αὐταῖς οὖν ἐρχόμενοι θεραπεύεσθε καὶ μὴ τῇ ἡμέρᾳ τοῦ σαββάτου ἀπεκρίθη δὲ αὐτῷ ὁ κύριος καὶ εἶπεν ὑποκριταί ἕκαστος ὑμῶν τῷ σαββάτῳ οὐ λύει τὸν βοῦν αὐτοῦ ἢ τὸν ὄνον ἀπὸ τῆς φάτνης καὶ ἀπαγαγὼν ποτίζει ταύτην δὲ θυγατέρα Ἀβραὰμ οὖσαν ἣν ἔδησεν ὁ Σατανᾶς ἰδοὺ δέκα καὶ ὀκτὼ ἔτη οὐκ ἔδει λυθῆναι ἀπὸ τοῦ δεσμοῦ τούτου τῇ ἡμέρᾳ τοῦ σαββάτου καὶ ταῦτα λέγοντος αὐτοῦ κατῃσχύνοντο πάντες οἱ ἀντικείμενοι αὐτῷ καὶ πᾶς ὁ ὄχλος ἔχαιρεν ἐπὶ πᾶσιν τοῖς ἐνδόξοις τοῖς γινομένοις ὑπ' αὐτοῦ (Luke 13:10–17, mGNT)

---

[15]See Frances Taylor Gench, *Back to the Well: Women's Encounters with Jesus in the Gospels* (Louisville, KY: Westminster John Knox Press, 2004).

Jesus was teaching in one of the synagogues on the Sabbath. A woman was there who had been disabled by a spirit for eighteen years. She was bent over and couldn't stand up straight. When he saw her, Jesus called her to him and said, "Woman, you are set free from your sickness." He placed his hands on her and she straightened up at once and praised God. The synagogue leader, incensed that Jesus had healed on the Sabbath, responded, "There are six days during which work is permitted. Come and be healed on those days, not on the Sabbath day." The Lord replied, "Hypocrites! Don't each of you on the Sabbath untie your ox or donkey from its stall and lead it out to get a drink? Then isn't it necessary that this woman, a daughter of Abraham, bound by Satan for eighteen long years, be set free from her bondage on the Sabbath day?" When he said these things, all his opponents were put to shame, but all those in the crowd rejoiced at all the extraordinary things he was doing. (Luke 13:10–17 CEB)

The story of Luke 13:10–17 is peculiar to Luke's Gospel. For New Testament source critics, this text belongs to the "L" source, featuring particular material that does not emerge in Mark's or Matthew's writings. The story is closely associated with a Lukan double account of a man healed on the Sabbath in Luke 14:1–6. Though the overlaps between the stories are quite exact, with Jesus approaching the woman and man to heal and the reference to an ox, the difference between this female-male pair is that the woman's account precedes the male narrative, extends in greater length, and elaborates more about the healing scene.[16] The woman's healing is the second of three stories about healings on the Sabbath (Lk 6:6–11; 13:10–17; 14:1–6) and the third account of Luke's five major miracle stories (Lk 5:1–11; 7:11–17; 13:10–17; 14:1–6; 17:11–19).[17] This narrative is Luke's last "woman healing/healing woman" account, which may be linked to the severity of her bent condition for eighteen years.[18] The story functions within Luke's overarching message of Jesus as a savior of the world that is "accessible to all people."[19] Womanist

---

[16]Elizabeth V. Dowling, *Taking away the Pound: Women, Theology and the Parable of the Pounds in the Gospel of Luke* (London: T&T Clark, 2007), 167.

[17]David Arthur DeSilva, *An Introduction to the New Testament: Contexts, Methods & Ministry Formation*, 2nd ed. (Downers Grove, IL: InterVarsity Press, 2018), 315.

[18]Elaine Mary Wainwright, *Women Healing/Healing Women: The Genderization of Healing in Early Christianity*, BibleWorld (London: Equinox Pub, 2006), 176.

[19]Stephanie R. Buckhanon Crowder, "The Gospel of Luke," in *True to Our Native Land: An African American New Testament Commentary*, ed. Brian K. Blount et al. (Minneapolis: Fortress Press, 2007), 158.

biblical scholar Stephanie Buckhanon Crowder, in her commentary on Luke in *True to Our Native Land*, argues, "Women, the lame, the hungry, and those deemed 'other' are brought to the forefront by Luke presenting Jesus as one of and for the oppressed. Lukan theology is grounded in a Jesus who comes not just to offer compassion to those who are wounded but to speak to the evil of those who wound."[20] As prophesied in Luke 4:18–19, Luke's Jesus is divinely anointed to "bring good news to the poor, proclaim release to the captives, recovery of sight to the blind, and to let the oppressed go free." Luke 13:10–17 is double-edged because it addresses the woman whose bent body signals her oppression and a bent religious system that excludes the othered, thus denying restoration and liberation.

The story begins in the synagogue, when Jesus is teaching on the Sabbath. By describing Jesus's activities on the Sabbath in Luke 13:10, it seems that the narrator is pointing to Jesus doing something out of the norm for this community but also continuing a lesson of "liberating the oppressed" that is taught by the miraculous activities Jesus performs on the Sabbath.[21] In Luke's Gospel, the setting of the Sabbath, a place of assembly where people from all walks of life gather and convene, signaled that Jesus was likely shifting the religious order through a miraculous healing. The fact that Jesus was teaching in the synagogue on the Sabbath is a continuation of a Lukan lesson that Jesus is the Lord of the Sabbath who has come to shift socio-religious norms by doing the necessary work of healing and liberation for a sustaining gospel.

Jesus was a traveling itinerant preacher, so a large crowd likely came to witness his ministry from in town and out of town. Some people in the crowd surrounding Jesus were likely standing, watching, and listening. The juxtaposition of some audience members standing and the women bent over may have given Jesus notice of the woman's presence. There is no description by the narrator of the woman's name, place of origin, or religious pietism. The woman is present in the crowd and is described only by the narrator in Luke 13:10 as "disabled by a spirit" (CEB) or possessing a "spirit of infirmity" for an extended timespan of eighteen years even before her physically bent condition is mentioned in Luke 13:11a. As I discuss

---

[20]Crowder, "The Gospel of Luke," 158.

[21]This narrative of a woman healed on the Sabbath follows the Sabbath healing of the man with a withered hand in Luke 6:6–11 and precedes the Lukan double of the man healed on the Sabbath in Luke 14:1–6. Jesus's mission, as pronounced in Luke 4:18, is to set the captive free, and this narrative follows suit with Jesus fulfilling this mission, especially on the Sabbath.

later, in physiognomic readings, the woman's primary identity marker as spirit possession has often been misinterpreted as a weak, feeble, feminine character that has bent her body.[22]

The crookedness of her body is described twice in Luke 13:11b as "bent over" and "unable to stand upright." Jesus looks into the audience and notices the woman who is συγκύπτω (*sygkyptō*), meaning bent completely forward or bent over double. She is not a stranger to the community or the gathered. Though she has likely been present in the crowd for a while, she is looked over or misrecognized until her body signals Jesus's eye. Jesus noticing this woman is significant because Jesus recognizes her bendedness.

Upon seeing her, Jesus summons the woman to him and says in Luke 13:12, "Woman, you are set free from your ailment." "Ailment" represents a chronic, persistent condition that is causing her bodily injury. The Greek term ἀσθένεια (*asthenia*) opens inquiry to question what spiritual force may be at work against her body, including religious, social, political, and economic evils of oppression.[23] In Luke 13:12, Jesus seems to be speaking first to the spiritual force enacted upon her body rather than her bent physical condition. Thus, Jesus recognizes the evil spirit bending her body and signals her freedom.

Not only was the woman bent, but she could not stand up straight, meaning she was bent over double. Jesus's second act of touching her body in Luke 13:13 leads to a miraculous straightening of her physical form.[24] According to Crowder, "Jesus restores her humanity by calling her to him and by touching her, thereby symbolically drawing an 'untouchable' once again into community."[25] The narrator is ambiguous about whether the woman desired to be touched physically. However, the narrator does cue that Jesus's "laying hands" on the woman was less of an invasion and more about restoration as she praises God.

New Testament scholar John Carroll makes the case that this narrative of the bent woman aligns with the larger Lukan theme of salvation that incites release based on the condition of the need. Carroll argues,

---

[22]Mikeal Carl Parsons, *Body and Character in Luke and Acts: The Subversion of Physiognomy in Early Christianity* (Grand Rapids: Baker Academic, 2006), 86.

[23]Parsons, *Body and Character in Luke and Acts*, 86.

[24]The woman's straightening is not her healing, but the liberation from her oppression symbolizes her restored humanity. Jesus's touching the woman is more meaningful here than a straightening.

[25]Crowder, "The Gospel of Luke," 172.

For those who are bound or oppressed (e.g., by demonic spirits), salvation means "release"; these persons are saved by being liberated. For those whose lives are marked as sinful (thus estranged from both God and the community), salvation means forgiveness. For those who suffer from economic marginalization through accumulated debts, salvation means economic liberation. For those who experience disability (physical impairment together with its social-relational limitations) or who experience sickness and disease, salvation means bodily restoration or wholeness—healing. Salvation in these varying dimensions is a prominent concern in Luke's narrative (both the Gospel and Acts). It is personal, yet much more than an individual affair. Release—whether from demonic control, sin, impairment, sickness, or debt—carries with it restoration to community, to a fuller participation in the community and its relations. At the same time, however, Luke's narrative also profiles ways in which varying forms of release can disrupt and destabilize—indeed, fracture—communities. When a person moves toward wholeness, there are effects on the larger social system (whether household, village, or synagogue) whose equilibrium has been affected.

Carroll makes clear that Luke's Jesus brings salvation, but it often causes conflict by disrupting the status and shifting the power dynamics to reestablish the community. The bent woman in Luke 13 falls within this construct, as the synagogue leader and the crowd contest her release. Jesus responds by extending the woman's individual release to a cause for the sociopolitical liberation of this community.[26]

At this point in the narrative, the reader expects that the woman's voice will be heard.[27] However, the voice of the presumably male synagogue leader emerges in Luke 13:14 with outrage that the woman's healing has taken place on the Sabbath. The synagogue leader retorts, "There are six days on which work ought to be done; come on those days and be cured, and not on the Sabbath day." The tone of the male voice is unsympathetic to the woman's condition and reflects a strict orthodoxy regarding the Sabbath, a holy day of observance and ritual refrain from labor.[28] Furthermore, the synagogue leader's words participate in misrecognizing the woman yet

---

[26]Carroll, "Bodies Restored, Communities Fractured?," 18.

[27]Dowling, *Taking away the Pound*, 168.

[28]Perhaps the synagogue leader's indignation is a response to being cast out by Jesus for his perpetuation of the marginalization that once bent the woman's body.

again by overlooking her body and need for liberation. The narrator shifts names from Jesus to Lord to highlight Jesus's authoritative response to the synagogue leader's outburst.

It is striking that Jesus calls the crowd "Hypocrites!" in the plural form and not just the synagogue leader who has just spoken. This may suggest that an entire community questioned Jesus's actions or dismissed the woman's desire for restoration. Luke's Jesus in Luke 13:15 lists domestic, routine chores that the crowd would have likely participated in on the Sabbath that could be classified as "unnecessary work," such as untying an ox or donkey from its stall to get a drink or receive sustenance. The narrator uses this as a rhetorical strategy to emphasize the "necessary" task of restoring and liberating the woman who has suffered in bondage for a sustained and severe eighteen years.

In Luke 13:16, Jesus does something unusual again by describing the woman not by her bent condition but by her belonging to the community of the liberated as *a daughter of Abraham*. Feminist biblical scholar Turid Karlsen Seim, in her commentary titled "The Gospel of Luke," contends, "The woman is Abraham's daughter; she does not become one. It is one of the premises of healing, not a consequence of it, but it is not a statement about great piety on the woman's part."[29] I disagree with Seim that it is not clear by the description of the daughter of Abraham of the woman's religious pietism. In Luke 13:13, the woman's immediate response to Jesus's touch is to praise God, which gives some sense that the woman at least knew who Jesus was and likely was a follower of Jesus's ministry to show up on this day of Jesus's teaching. The distinction "daughter of Abraham" describes the woman's restoration to a community she belongs to by ethnic and spiritual heritage, which has misrecognized her virtue. No other woman in the biblical canon is named as a daughter of Abraham in this way, which illuminates Jesus's raising of this woman's extraordinary virtue.

Most Christian interpreters know Abraham had many sons because the patriarchal lineage sustained throughout the biblical canon consistently mentions the God of Abraham, Isaac, and Jacob. The biblical accounts of Genesis 21 point to Abraham's firstborn, Ishmael, being evicted from Abraham's household with his mother, Hagar, and the tumultuous failed sacrifice of Isaac, the promised son, in Genesis 22. What do we know about Abraham's

---

[29]Turid Karlsen Seim, "The Gospel of Luke," in *Searching the Scriptures*, vol. 2, ed. Elisabeth Schüssler Fiorenza, Shelly Matthews, and Ann Graham Brock (New York: Crossroad, 1993), 736.

daughters? Though the stories of Abraham's many sons are prolific in the Hebrew Bible, the names and stories of Abraham's daughters are hidden or incomplete, especially in relation to his lesser wives following Hagar's dismissal and Sarah's death. Abraham did have six children with his third wife, Keturah, appearing in Genesis 25:1, whose gender identities cannot be determined by their names alone. Womanist Hebrew Bible scholar Kimberly Russaw writes a comprehensive critical analysis of *Daughters in the Hebrew Bible* that identifies a daughter as a "female member of the household who is not yet a mother."[30] She further argues that "biblical daughters may be read as more than foils for the males in their narratives; daughters execute particular tactics to navigate antagonistic systems of power in their worlds."[31] The Lukan ambiguity around the woman's origins conceals her age and status as a mother or wife; however, readers may assume by her condition that she is older than eighteen years of age and likely an adult woman. Interpreters may read the woman in Luke 13:16 as a daughter of Abraham who defies the powers of her day through her body and whose story matters as much as those of the male counterparts in the text.

The use of the term "shame" (καταισχύνω) in Luke 13:17 to describe the synagogue leader and dissenters reveals the woman as a daughter of Abraham and a more virtuous character in the passage than the crooked characters who oppose her healing. Biblical scholar James Arlandsen highlights the rhetorical use of this shame motif in *Women, Class and Society in Early Christianity*. Arlandsen asserts,

> Despite the remarkable gains women were making in the first century, they still lived by at least one cultural value that differed from that of men. A sense of shame was absolutely appropriate for, and indeed required of, women. It was tied to modesty, restraint, discretion, and purity, all of which are inward qualities. Shamelessness spelled ruin for women. . . . Powerful women were not required to show deference for every man, as slaves or peasants were. But one thing is certain: poor and lowly women (and men) had to defer in the presence of wealthy and powerful men (and women).[32]

---

[30] Kimberly D. Russaw, *Daughters in the Hebrew Bible* (Minneapolis: Fortress Academic, 2020), 1.

[31] Russaw, *Daughters of the Hebrew Bible*, 20.

[32] James Malcolm Arlandson, *Women, Class, and Society in Early Christianity: Models from Luke-Acts* (Peabody, MA: Hendrickson, 1997), 156.

Jesus's priority with this bent woman on the Sabbath rather than the male synagogue leader and more powerful members of the community is the source of the conflict in this passage. In Luke 13:17, Jesus exposes and re-bukes the crooked characters of the synagogue leaders and dissenters, thus unearthing the noble virtue of the woman's unashamed character. Elisabeth Schüssler Fiorenza cautions feminist interpreters from celebrating Jesus's dismissal of the synagogue leaders and the "revelatory authority of this text as liberating" while sustaining dualistic anti-Jewish tendencies.[33] This pas-sage is significant because Jesus exposes the evil of systems that hinder the most vulnerable from belonging to God's vision of salvation and inclusive community, which is indeed a Christian predicament and, as presented throughout this book, an enduring problem within the Black Church.

The text ends with the crowd rejoicing and praising God *with* the liber-ated woman because her *body acts* enable Jesus to fulfill his prophetic mis-sion of liberating the oppressed, as described in Luke 4. The bent woman is restored as a disciple who "fully functions in the Jesus movement" and "carries on the work of the Jesus movement."[34] By the end of the passage, the woman is miraculously healed, restored to her community, and liberated from a context that misrecognizes her virtue, thus fulfilling her embodied transformation (healing-restoration-liberation). In the next section, I turn my attention toward the interplay of the woman's body and subjectivity/agency that intersect with theories of the body related to physiognomy and misogyny.

Physiognomy and Misogyny in Luke

New Testament scholar Mikael Parsons, in his salient work *Body and Character in Luke-Acts: The Subversion of Physiognomy in Early Christian-ity,* lays the groundwork for the origin of physiognomy and its relationship to ancient literature and Western thought. According to Parsons, it was popular in ancient literature for physiognomy to be used in literary works where descriptions of the body gave inquiry into the soul. Parsons notes, "Throughout history it has been commonplace to associate outer physical characteristics with inner qualities; it was assumed that you can, as it were,

[33]Elisabeth Schussler Fiorenza, "Lk 13:10–17: Interpretation for Liberation and Trans-formation," *Theological Digest* 36 (1989): 308.

[34]Wainwright, *Women Healing/Healing Women,* 179.

judge a book by its cover. The study of the relationship between the physical and the moral was known as physiognomy."[35] Drawing from Western constructions influenced by Aristotle, the soul and body are intimately related and can alter each other. In this sense, the soul can "change the form of the body" and vice versa.[36] Physiognomy was also widely used as a rhetorical device in ancient literature, including writings on the Greco-Roman world and Jewish and Christian literature.[37] Parsons notes that one example of a physiognomic tradition in Jewish literature is the Levitical description of the priest's physical body as unblemished (Lv 21:16–18), which is often linked to the expectation of the priest to be morally blameless.[38] Physiognomic influences persist in early Christian literature with the work of Paul. For example, in Parsons's view, Paul's reference throughout his writings (e.g., Gal 4:13–14; 1 Cor 2:3; 2 Cor 10:1) to his own infirmity or physical weakness is often interpreted as a moral failure or tragic flaw that makes Paul "ashamed and vulnerable to his opponents."[39]

Patristic writers follow suit by making judgments based on body characteristics. Parsons introduces Ambrose, who based moral character on bodily movements and even declined ordination to persons because of repeated body gestures and unusual tone of voice.[40] From Parsons's analysis, it is clear that physiognomy was used not only in Jewish and Christian literature but that these texts also criticized the use of physiognomy or perceiving the body to judge moral character. One example from the Hebrew Testament is David's narrative as a scrawny, young shepherd boy in 1 Samuel 16 who is more fit for king among his physically attractive elder brothers and morally astute than the reigning Saul.[41] In Pauline literature, Paul's glorification of the body in 1 Corinthians 12 articulates the spiritual and moral uprightness of the community in relation to Christ and the bringing together of multiple parts to form one Lord, one Spirit, one Baptism, and one Body that critiques judgments of a detached body by what is visual to the naked eye.

It is Parsons's primary claim that Luke's use of physiognomy is not to simply accept its exterior judgment on inner character, but to destabilize its influence, especially as it relates to the inclusive eschatological commu-

---

[35]Parsons, *Body and Character in Luke and Acts,* 9.

[36]Parsons, *Body and Character in Luke and Acts,* 10.

[37]Parsons, *Body and Character in Luke and Acts,* 28.

[38]Parsons, *Body and Character in Luke and Acts,* 40–41.

[39]Parsons, *Body and Character in Luke and Acts,* 48.

[40]Parsons, *Body and Character in Luke and Acts,* 59.

[41]Parsons, *Body and Character in Luke and Acts,* 61.

nity of the Abrahamic covenant.⁴² Parsons suggests that the use of the bent
woman as daughter and Zacchaeus as son of Abraham shape Luke's rhetorical argument that abnormal bodies, misfits, and outcasts exercise great
courage, hospitality, and moral virtue in the line of Abraham and belong
to the Abrahamic covenant community. The healing of the bent woman in
Luke 13:10–17, for Parsons, is Luke's first attempt to subvert the characterization of the body by its exterior. When read in light of a physiognomic
tradition, the woman's body as bent or crooked signals character inferiority
and feminine weakness that is harshly misogynistic. In physiognomic literature, a straight, upright back demonstrates a strong male character, and
a bent/crooked spine suggests a weak female character. Parsons contends,

> According to physiognomic traditions, the bent woman's problem is
> best understood as moral. Her bent back results from a feeble character,
> even an evil disposition. This characterization sheds light on Luke's
> description of the woman as having a spirit of weakness, which, accord-
> ing to the physiognomic handbooks, is a characteristically feminine
> problem. . . . In physiognomic thinking, women are weaker in moral
> character than men and are therefore more prone to bent backs: no
> crooked man walking a crooked mile here, only bent women. In fact,
> the woman's crooked stature was also to indicate, as pseudo-Aristotle
> suggests, an "evil disposition," and it would have been apparent to the
> Lukan Jesus that this was a physical manifestation of a satanic posses-
> sion, the bonds of which Jesus decided to break.⁴³

Jesus's naming of the woman as "daughter of Abraham" reinforces the
woman's virtuous character in relation to Abraham's faithfulness and
noncanonical Maccabean writings (4 Mc 15:28) of a mother who endured
the brutal death of her sons with incredible strength and was also called
"daughter of Abraham."⁴⁴

Parsons also points out that Jesus's reference to the animals of ox (or
cattle) and donkeys may link to Luke's knowledge of zoological physiognomy that claimed mules as "stupid, lazy, or insolent" because of the
size of their eyes, head, and tone of voice.⁴⁵ Parsons writes, "Not only are
Jesus's opponents more willing to aid an animal than a woman, but they

---

⁴²Parsons, *Body and Character in Luke and Acts,* 14.
⁴³Parsons, *Body and Character in Luke and Acts,* 86.
⁴⁴Parsons, *Body and Character in Luke and Acts,* 87.
⁴⁵Parsons, *Body and Character in Luke and Acts,* 89.

are also more willing to aid those animals who symbolize such negative traits as cowardice, sluggish-ness, stupidity, laziness or insolence than to help a daughter of Abraham whose status is masked, not reflected by her physical condition."[46] The priority of these animals on the Sabbath over the woman may be another sign of dehumanizing the woman and degrading her character based on outward appearance. Finally, for Parsons, Luke's Jesus overthrows the physiognomy by healing the woman on the Sabbath, releasing the Satanic bond, and exposing the woman's strong moral virtue.

Though Parsons's breakdown is quite convincing, I do not incorporate his work on physiognomy and misogyny in such great length to affirm simply his premise of Luke's rhetorical strategy of subversion. I include Parsons's work to illustrate the Western intellectual and ancient literary tradition of interpreting and judging women's character solely based on how female bodies look or are seen. Moreover, the woman's virtue is discredited solely based on her bent appearance. Though Luke's narrative validates the woman's moral character with Jesus's describing her as a "daughter of Abraham" and shifting the shame away from her and toward the religious dissemblers, her moral virtue is concealed by her captivity. At this point, the narrative of the woman with a bent body in Luke 13:10–17 intersects with Black women's historical and contemporary realities.

Of Mules and Women

There is no question that the Euro-American gaze upon the Black body since Europeans' first encounters on African soil illuminate the enduring problem of Black physiognomy. The distinctiveness of Black skin marked Black bodies as heathen that spawned European preoccupation with and obsession for control of Black people, Black identity, and Black culture in the Western imagination. The social construct of race and racism remains hinged on physiognomic assertions that blackness deems subservience. I have raised in this book the political nature of Black women's bodies facing mischaracterization from the auction block to the voting booth that denied full humanity and equal citizenship in this nation. On the one end, Black women's bodies are marked by their utility to produce and reproduce, as evidenced in the case of Henrietta Lacks, whose HeLa cells were extracted from her reproductive organs without consent but continue to be useful

---

[46]Parsons, *Body and Character in Luke and Acts,* 89.

for the advancement of medical research and experimentation today.[47] On the other, Black women's bodies, through stereotyping and typifying, locate the moral virtue of Black women as vicious in a bent world.

In this regard, the opening quote of this chapter raises Zora Neale Hurston's characterization of Black women as the mules of the world. Jesus in Luke 13 makes an interesting parallel between a community that misrecognizes this woman but pays more attention to the "mules" or cattle that maintain the community's work. The bent woman's value in Luke 13 appears less than a mule until Jesus recognizes her. Similarly, the problem of misrecognition restricts Black women's agency and conceals Black women's moral virtue.

"Reading the Bible Her Way" and Womanist Biblical Interpretation

From Alice Walker's four-part definition in *In Search of Our Mothers' Gardens: Womanist Prose*, womanism was born in religious studies and theological education as a critical approach to taking seriously the lived experiences of struggle and survival of African American women against multiple forces of oppression (race, class, gender, sexuality, etc.). I articulate womanist scholarship with four primary motifs. First, it promotes the liberation and survival of Black women and the entire African American people while also advocating against all forms of oppression.[48] Second, it reclaims Black women's experiences, history, bodies, aesthetics, literature, and so on as primary sources for theological reflection and biblical interpretation. Third, it maintains that God/Jesus/Spirit identifies with the oppressed "least of these" in their quest for justice and wholeness. Fourth, it encourages intergenerational bonds between girls and women in order to strengthen relationships and transfer survival tools. Womanist biblical interpretation follows suit with the quadruple aim identified above: African American female biblical scholars and theologians who confess womanist convictions read and interpret biblical texts.

---

[47]See Rebecca Skloot, *The Immortal Life of Henrietta Lacks* (New York: Broadway Paperbacks, 2011).

[48]Raquel St. Clair, "Womanist Biblical Interpretation," in *True to Our Native Land: An African American New Testament Commentary*, ed. Brian K. Blount et al. (Minneapolis: Fortress Press, 2007), 59.

Drawing from the work of New Testament womanist scholar Angela Parker, I define womanist biblical interpretation by seven defining principles:

1. Womanist biblical interpretation is "grounded in the lived experience and concrete realities and artifacts of Black women."
2. Womanist biblical interpretation "prioritizes intersectionality in its analysis of biblical texts" with an eye toward addressing the multidimensionality of Black women's oppression.
3. Womanist biblical interpretation "questions the objectivity of historical-critical methods" and revalues the social location of the interpreter.
4. Womanist biblical interpretation is "inextricably linked to Womanist theology and Christology," offering survivalist and liberative visions of the intimate, human connection to the Divine through story and text.
5. Womanist biblical interpretation is an anti-oppressionist paradigm that "seeks to eradicate multiple oppressions" not just for Black women, but for all of us.
6. Womanist biblical interpretation "seeks to 'name' and give voice to the 'least of these,'" while amplifying the voices of the marginalized that may not always be intoned in a feminine key.
7. Womanist biblical interpretation is "regularly multidimensional, multidialogical, collaborative and/or multi-contextual."[49]

More particularly, womanist biblical interpreters across the tradition and academy draw on a range of varied approaches, among which are the following:

1. Hermeneutics of storytelling and rereading for liberation (Renita Weems)[50]
2. Hermeneutics of suspicion, liberation, resistance, and hope (Clarice Martin)[51]

---

[49]Angela N. Parker, "Bodies, Violence, and Emotions: A Womanist Study of Σῶμα and Πτῶμα in the Gospel of Mark" (PhD diss., Chicago Theological Seminary, 2014), 18.

[50]See Renita J. Weems, *Just a Sister Away: A Womanist Vision of Women's Relationships in the Bible* (San Diego, CA: LuraMedia, 1988); Weems, "Reading Her Way through the Struggle: African American Women and the Bible," in *Stony the Road We Trod: African American Biblical Interpretation*, ed. Cain Hope Felder (Minneapolis: Fortress Press, 1991), 57–79.

[51]See Clarice J. Martin, "The Haustafeln (Household Codes) in African American Biblical

3. Sociolinguistic approach and hermeneutics of wholeness (Raquel St. Clair Lettsome)[52]
4. Maternal thought (Stephanie Buckhanon Crowder)[53]
5. Reading darkly (Margaret Aymer)
6. reading against victimization, toward integrity and wholeness (Koala Jones-Warsaw)[54]
7. Reconstructionist and Midrashic interpretations (Wil Gafney)[55]
8. Lens of intersectionality and inter(con)textuality (Mitzi Smith)[56]
9. Postcolonial womanist approach, hermeneutics of ambi*veil*ance (Shanell Smith)[57]
10. Subversive philological, social-scientific, and cross-cultural readings (Kimberly Russaw)
11. Multioppositional consciousness (Angela Parker)

Though not exhaustive, this womanist biblical litany qualifies the multivocal nature of womanist biblical interpretation. Black women in biblical studies carve out a womanist biblical tradition for Black women to write their stories back into the history of salvation.[58]

Interpretation: 'Free Slaves' and 'Subordinate Women,' " in *Stony the Road We Trod: African American Biblical Interpretation*, ed. Cain Hope Felder (Minneapolis: Fortress Press, 1991), 206–31.

[52]See Raquel St. Clair, "Womanist Biblical Interpretation," in *True to Our Native Land: An African American New Testament Commentary*, ed. Brian K. Blount et al. (Minneapolis: Fortress Press, 2007), 54–62.

[53]See Stephanie R. Crowder, "BMW: Biblical Mother Working/Wrecking, Black Mother Working/Wrecking," in *Mother Goose, Mother Jones, Mommie Dearest: Biblical Mothers and Their Children*, ed. Cheryl A. Kirk-Duggan and Tina Pippin (Leiden: Brill, 2010), 157–69; Crowder, *When Momma Speaks*.

[54]See Koala Jones-Warsaw, "Toward a Womanist Hermeneutic: A Reading of Judges 19–21," *The Journal of the Interdenominational Theological Center* 22, no. 1 (1994): 18–35.

[55]See Wilda Gafney, *Womanist Midrash: A Reintroduction to the Women of the Torah and the Throne* (Louisville, KY: Westminster John Knox Press, 2017).

[56]Mitzi J. Smith, "Race, Gender, and the Politics of 'Sass': Reading Mark 7:24–30 through a Womanist Lens of Intersectionality and Inter(Con)Textuality," in *Womanist Interpretations of the Bible: Expanding the Discourse*, ed. Gay L. Byron and Vanessa Lovelace, Semeia Studies 85 (Atlanta: SBL Press, 2016), 95–112.

[57]See Shanell T. Smith, *The Woman Babylon and the Marks of Empire: Reading Revelation with a Postcolonial Womanist Hermeneutics of Ambiveilence* (Minneapolis: Fortress Press, 2014).

[58]For a fuller treatment, see Gay L. Byron and Vanessa Lovelace, eds., *Womanist Interpretations of the Bible: Expanding the Discourse*, Semeia Studies, number 85 (Atlanta: SBL Press,

First-generation womanist biblicist Renita Weems is known to many as the first Black woman to earn the doctor of philosophy in Hebrew Bible from Princeton Theological Seminary in 1988. Weems's first book, *Just a Sister Away*, published thirty-five years ago, demonstrates a hunger, thirst, and urgency for womanist biblical interpretation in the early 1980s as few writings moved beyond the male tensions in the texts (e.g., Cain and Abel, Jacob and Esau, Elijah and Elisha) and recentered women's stories. Moreover, even fewer writings integrated Black women's perspectives in the reading of the biblical stories of women. In the late 1980s, Weems began to write (and continues to write) for Black women whose "souls have remained starved for a new revelation on the role of women in salvation history," and those who know, as Weems, contend that "surely, God did not mean for us to be a footnote to redemption."[59] While Weems holds the distinction as the trailblazing first, she admits that Katie Geneva Cannon was the first Black woman doctoral student in Hebrew Bible at Union Theological Seminary of New York in the 1980s, but the racist, anti-Black politics of the biblical academy resulted in Cannon's dismissal from the program. According to Weems, "The biblical field's loss was ethics' gain," as Cannon faced the challenge of locating her "very existence within the discipline" and introducing an unintelligible subject before 1985, Black women, into the field of Christian ethics.[60] Cannon's story proves the womanist ethical dilemma in what she describes as a "noncanonical other." Cannon writes,

> The dilemma of the Black woman ethicist as the noncanonical other is defined as working in opposition to the academic establishment yet building upon it. The liberation ethicist works both within and outside the guild. The Black womanist scholar receives the preestablished disciplinary structures of intellectual inquiry in the field of ethics and tries to balance the paradigms and assumptions of this intellectual tradition with a new set of questions arising from the context of Black women's lives. The tension is found in the balancing act of simultaneously trying to raise the questions appropriate to the discipline while

---

2016).; Mitzi J. Smith, ed., *I Found God in Me: A Womanist Biblical Hermeneutics Reader* (Eugene, OR: Cascade Books, 2015).

[59]Weems, *Just a Sister Away*, viii.

[60]Renita J. Weems, "The Biblical Field's Loss Was Womanist Ethics' Gain," in *Walking through the Valley: Womanist Explorations in the Spirit of Katie Geneva Cannon*, ed. Emilie Maureen Townes (Louisville, KY: Westminster John Knox Press, 2022), 3–11.

also trying to understand what emphasis ought properly to be placed
on the various determinants influencing the situation of Black women.
In order to work toward an inclusive ethic, the womanist struggles
to restructure the categories so that the presuppositions more readily
include the ethical realities of Black women.[61]

In this sense, womanism is a prophetic move to reclaim Black women's
moral wit, wisdom, and agency.

Though Cannon earned the distinction as the first Black woman to earn
the doctor of philosophy at Union Theological Seminary in the field of ethics,
Cannon never left the Bible or literary and textual analysis. In fact, Cannon's
1985 article "The Emergence of the Black Feminist Consciousness," which
first sourced Alice Walker's term "womanist," also argued the centrality of
the Bible for Black women. According to Cannon,

> The Bible is the highest source of authority for most Black women. In
> its pages, Black women have learned how to refute the stereotypes that
> depict Black people as minstrels or vindictive militants, mere ciphers
> who react only to omnipresent racial oppression. . . . Understanding
> the prophetic tradition of the Bible empowers Black women to fashion
> a set of values on their own terms, as well as mastering, radicalizing,
> and sometimes destroying the pervasive negative orientations imposed
> by the larger society. Also, they articulate possibilities for decisions
> and action that address forthrightly the circumstances that inescap-
> ably color and shape Black life. Black women serve as contemporary
> prophets, calling other women forth so that they can break away from
> the oppressive ideologies and belief systems that presume to define
> their reality.

The Black womanist tradition functions as an "interpretive principle," according to Cannon, "to chip away at oppressive structures bit by bit." Black
women rereading and reinterpreting the Bible represents a life-affirming
pathway for strategic action in the face of a death-dealing and hostile world.
Cannon affirms, "Often compelled to act or to refrain from acting in ac-
cordance with the powers and principalities of the external world, Black
womanists search the Scriptures to learn how to dispel the threat of death

---

[61]Cannon, *Katie's Canon*, 62.

in order to seize the present life."[62] The task of womanist biblical interpreters and scholars is to analyze texts in meaningful ways that ground the experience of Black women and open possibilities for uncovering Black women's virtues and pathways to liberation.

A Womanist Hermeneutics of Appropriation and Parallel

In her classic work *Sisters in the Wilderness: The Challenge of Womanist God-Talk*, womanist theologian Delores Williams constructs a hermeneutics of appropriation and parallel wherein she places the lived realities of Black women alongside Hagar in Genesis 16 and 21. Williams writes, "I selected from Hagar's story those issues that had, simultaneously, personal, social, and religious significance for black women and for the African-American community: the predicament of motherhood, the character of surrogacy, the problem of ethnicity, and the meaning and significance of wilderness experience for women and for the community."[63] Though Williams embraces a Hebrew Bible account, I adopt Williams's hermeneutic of appropriation and parallel as a womanist pathway to place Black women's lived experiences in dialogue with the New Testament narrative of the bent woman in Luke 13:10–17. Here, my articulation of a double-sided Black women's body-bent politic comes into closer view. The discursive inscriptions enacted upon the Black female body as well as lived realities bear weight on Black women and bend Black women's bodies. From a more panoramic view of Black women's lived realities, I understand Black women's bodies in a metaphorical sense as bent by the interconnected systems of oppression including, but not limited to, racism, sexism, classism/poverty, homophobia, transphobia, ableism, and so on. Whereas early womanist scholars initially noted Black women's existence as trapped in the forces of the tripartite oppression of race, gender, and class,[64] I join contemporary womanist scholarship to argue that Black women face multidimensional oppression that is intersecting and interlocking. In this sense, a Black woman is likely bent double, triple, quadruple, and more as her body exists further away from the white, male,

---

[62]Katie G. Cannon, "The Emergence of a Black Feminist Consciousness," in *Katie's Canon: Womanism and the Soul of the Black Community*, revised and exp. 25th anniversary ed. (Minneapolis: Fortress Press, 2021), 30.

[63]Delores S. Williams, *Sisters in the Wilderness: The Challenge of Womanist God-Talk* (Maryknoll, NY: Orbis Books, 1993), 9.

[64]Katie G. Cannon, *Black Womanist Ethics* (Atlanta: Scholars Press, 1988), 7.

able-bodied norm. I also want to make the case that Black women's bodies face character assassination often, even before they are seen in a white supremacist capitalist heteropatriarchal world. Much like the bent woman in Luke, evil systems trap Black women's bodies and often conceal Black women's moral wisdom.

My grandmother's narrative, layered throughout the book, illustrates the familial, social, political, economic, environmental, and medical pressures that participated in physically bending her back. Though she was not born with a crooked spine in the sense of genetics, my grandmother's body may be identified as a crooked or bent body because she was unable to stand straight, and her functionality and mobility were altered for a sustained length of time. Perhaps this bent positioning could have given her a different way of seeing the world—from the bottom up or from the side in. Parallel to the woman in Luke, the abilities of crooked bodies may be limited in some aspects, but they may also be understood as more gifted or virtuous than other able bodies. Disability theorist Rosemarie Garland-Thomson makes this case by identifying the disabled body as an "extraordinary" body.[65] In this sense, disabled bodies may carry extra or counter abilities than able-bodied counterparts. Whereas a curved Black female body's appearance may depict a lower standing than other erect forms, this does not reflect the moral respectability that Black women and their bodies truly possess. I would argue here that my grandmother held more respect in my family and her community in bent form during her elder years than her younger years of more upright standing. Such recognition could have been earned because of her bent body. In other words, she received greater admiration because of the sight of her bent body, which demonstrated to onlookers' incredible virtue and wisdom to survive the weight of multidimensional entrapment as a poor, domestic, migrant, Black churchwoman in America.

The physical bending of the Black female body may also be categorized in terms of the battered or wounded body. This suggests that women face bending of the body from the physical, emotional, and spiritual scarring and abuse that come with battering. Doubly bent bodies are battered bodies who face the violence of both private acute battering in intimate partner violence and public sustained battering against Black women in a imperialistic capitalistic white supremacist heteropatriarchal world. Moreover,

---

[65]See Rosemarie Garland-Thomson, *Extraordinary Bodies: Figuring Physical Disability in American Culture and Literature*, 20th anniversary ed. (New York: Columbia University Press, 2017).

Black women often experience battering alone and in silence. The statistical data of domestic violence in relation to Black women are grossly misleading because so many cases go unreported. In *Wounds of the Spirit: Black Women, Violence, and Resistance Ethics*, Black feminist ethicist Traci West makes the argument that Black women victim-survivors live in the liminal space of intimate violence, "exacting their silence" and sparking "defiance of silence."[66] In West's calculation, Black women suffer from being "*not heard, not listened to, not permitted to speak out*, and *censored to the point of losing one's sense of self*."[67] Much like the woman in Luke 13:10–17, Black women face silencing and victimization when battered and bent that strip her voice, creating such a "noisy silence" that Black women's cries go unheard.[68] Womanist practical theologian Sharon Ellis Davis argues that "self-love, regardless," to borrow from Walker, rightly names a necessary anecdote to gender entrapment for battered Black women.[69]

Though the narrator in Luke 13:10–17 does not permit the woman to speak in this account, this example of Lukan silence and ambiguity does not mean the woman failed to speak or even, as I introduce in the next section, that her body language does not speak out on her behalf to Jesus. Whereas the appearance of a battered body that is bent may illustrate that Black women willfully give in to battering, this display erases Black women's relentless resistance and bellowing calls for help. Historically, the battering that enslaved African women underwent in slave fields from the whippings and beatings of white male overseers bent their backs but did not bow their fortitude. In today's contemporary society, there are numerous examples of bodies that make visible a physical bending of the Black female body, including but not limited to the dark body, the pornographic body, the fat body, the queer body, and the wilderness/unhoused body. Though outside the scope of this chapter, I raise these lived contemporary realities of Black women to articulate the appearance of multiple othered Black female bodies that often disguise the true moral virtues belonging to these women. I shift the conversation toward Black women's moral wisdom and *body acts*.

---

[66] Traci C. West, *Wounds of the Spirit: Black Women, Violence, and Resistance Ethics* (New York: NYU Press, 1999), 11.

[67] West, *Wounds of the Spirit*, 11–12.

[68] West, *Wounds of the Spirit*, 12.

[69] See Sharon Ellis Davis, *The Trauma of Sexual and Domestic Violence: Navigating My Way through Individuals, Religion, Policing, and the Courts* (Eugene, OR: Cascade Books, 2022).

Body Acts, Body Language, and Moral Agency

"I'm speaking," vice presidential candidate Kamala Harris said.[70]

Katie Cannon remains the leading figure in womanist constructive virtue ethics. Her salient work, *Black Womanist Ethics*, traces the moral agency of Black women from the antebellum period (as early as 1619) to the latter half of the twentieth century (roughly the 1980s). Her central thesis in this work is to frame "how Black women live out a moral wisdom in their real-lived context that does not appeal to the fixed rules or absolute principles of the white-oriented, male-structured society."[71] For Cannon, Black women are the oppressed of the oppressed, representing the "most vulnerable and the most exploited members of the American society."[72] Cannon takes up Black women's literary tradition as a re/source to engage the "living space" of Black women's complex and dynamic moral agency as well as her struggle for survival amid the tripartite oppression of racism/white supremacy, sexism, and classism/poverty.[73] By analyzing Zora Neale Hurston's life and literature, Cannon identifies three ethical virtues that describe the moral wisdom of the Black community in the nineteenth and twentieth centuries: *invisible dignity*, *quiet grace*, and *unshouted courage*. The passing down of these moral virtues for future generations models what womanist ethicist Melanie Harris identifies as "womanist moral wisdom."[74]

First, invisible dignity characterizes the sagacious discretion that a Black woman maintains in the face of systemic and persistent threats against her survival. Cannon writes, "Virtue is not the experiencing of suffering, nor in the survival techniques for enduring. Rather, the quality of moral good is that which allows Black people to maintain a feistiness about life that nobody can wipe out, no matter how hard they try."[75] It is Black women's invisible dignity that exposes the racist, sexist, classist, homophobic, ableist . . . societal norms that often render her Black female body othered and unintelligible.[76]

---

[70]Vice presidential debate between Mike Pence and Kamala Harris, Salt Lake City, UT, 2020, https://www.youtube.com/watch?v=t_G0ia3JOVs, October 7, 2020.

[71]Cannon, *Black Womanist Ethics*, 4.

[72]Cannon, *Black Womanist Ethics*, 4.

[73]Cannon, *Black Womanist Ethics*, 7.

[74]Melanie Harris, *Gifts of Virtue, Alice Walker, and Womanist Ethics* (New York: Palgrave Macmillan, 2013).

[75]Cannon, *Black Womanist Ethics*, 104.

[76]The ellipsis here is my attempt to include the destabilization of false norms and ideals

Second, quiet grace represents the virtue of Black womanhood to deal with the truth of her reality, often without the sound of a mumbling word.[77] In Cannon's view, Black women have "*never practiced grace*: the quality of being dainty, luxurious and feeble in constitution, characterized by modesty with an extreme respect for protocol."[78] Simply put, Black women were never afforded the privilege of a weak character in American society. Black women maintaining quiet grace is not the affirmation that Black women remain silent and submissive, but the recognition that Black women have utilized a wide range of unconventional strategies to navigate an oppressed reality and search for truth.

Third, unshouted courage is "the quality of steadfastness, akin to fortitude, in the face of formidable oppression."[79] Unshouted courage is the unrelenting gall to pursue freedom despite the powers and principalities in high and low places. Cannon notes, "Unshouted courage as a virtue is the often unacknowledged inner conviction that keeps one's appetite whet for freedom. The ethical speculation is that courage is the staying power of the Black community wherein individuals act, affirming their humanity, in spite of continued fear of institutionalized aggression."[80] Even when situations are out of their control, Black women act prophetically or demonstrate moral resilience by making "a way out of no way" and transforming the temporal into the spiritual in order to survive. In Cannon's framework, these three ethical virtues that constitute Black women's moral wisdom "does not rescue Black women from the bewildering pressures and perplexities of institutionalized social evils but rather exposes those ethical assumptions which are inimical to the ongoing survival of Black womanhood."[81] Despite cultural tropes of Black women as devious Jezebels, angry Sapphires, and

---

in relation to Black women that exist outside the scope of this chapter.

[77]In the Black Church tradition, it is often said, "Jesus never said a mumblin' word." The notion that Jesus never said a mumbling word during his trial and crucifixion points to Jesus's virtue of acting responsibly and completing his task without complaint or a fit of rage. It is clear that many Black churches are familiar with the Gospel accounts of Jesus speaking during his time of crucifixion because they hold Seven Last Words services during the Lenten Season and Good Friday services ritually. The juxtaposition of Jesus never saying a mumblin' word during a pinnacle moment of terror and the ritual storytelling held annually retelling what Jesus said during his final moments on the cross give a clue that the former is pointing to something different than speech, but perhaps his character.

[78]Cannon, *Black Womanist Ethics*, 125–26.

[79]Cannon, *Black Womanist Ethics*, 144.

[80]Cannon, *Black Womanist Ethics*, 144.

[81]Cannon, *Black Womanist Ethics*, 5.

complacent Mammies, Cannon's work proves that it takes moral virtue in order for Black women to exist and survive in the American context.

Cannon's womanist wisdom virtues form basic building blocks for contemporary Black women to build upon. As a fourth-wave Black millennial womanist ethicist, I seek to mine ancestral womanist wisdom to imagine and cultivate counterhegemonic methods for flourishing womanist futures where Black women exist as whole and free. I amend Cannon's terms with a slash line in/visible dignity and un/shouted courage as a rhetorical play on the challenge of visibility versus invisibility, quiet versus loud, and un-shouted versus shouted courage while paralleling the bent woman in Luke 13 with virtue strategies for Black women to thrive. Contemporary Black women are in search of recognition that values our visibility, voice, and virtue in religion and society.

It is the woman's body in Luke 13:10–17, not her ethnic heritage or place of origin, that relates directly to the lived experiences of Black women. Whereas the appearance of the woman's body as bent conceals her moral virtue, interpreters may also read this narrative with the framing that the woman's body *acts* as a moral agent that makes her encounter with Jesus possible and enables her restoration. Bringing forward a hermeneutics of parallel and appropriation, I argue that the woman's body in Luke 13:10–17 exercises Cannon's three ethical virtues of in/visible dignity by placing one-self in a position to see and be seen by Jesus, quiet grace by speaking and listening to Jesus, and un/shouted courage by prophetically disrupting the social order and deconstructing the crooked exclusivity of the synagogue leader and crowd. Furthermore, the woman's body, as a wise teacher, avows proverbial ethical learnings for Black women to employ in order to navigate a corrupt and crooked world, which invite Black women to show up, speak up, and never shut up about the injustices they endure.

Show Up: This Is My Body!

In the case of the virtuous woman in Luke 13:10–17, the woman's body acts with in/visible dignity that sees Jesus, but also positions the woman in place to be seen by Jesus and others. The narrator does not suggest that the woman comes to Jesus verbally requesting to be healed. Instead, the woman places her body before Jesus and Jesus recognizes her body, which prompts her restoration. This woman's bodily virtue is that she does not hide her crookedness. She exercises in/visible dignity as her body stands "slumped over." The woman's body catching the eye of Jesus demonstrates her power of presence in a crowd that has overlooked her for a while. Though the woman's voice is silenced, her body's in/visible dignity articulates a tenacious persistence to be unmoved until she is restored. The ethical learning Black women can adopt is to show their bodies "as is" because the presence of bent bodies gives more indication of what bends their bodies than words will ever be able to reveal. For battered Black women who are less likely to speak up about domestic violence and abuse, the body exposes the wrong done to it by freely exposing the scars, bruises, or marks of battering rather than hiding them. Simply showing up is the first act of this woman in Luke 13 that places her in a position to receive necessary liberation even amid the noisy silence.

Speak Up: Practice Body Talk!

In the case of the virtuous woman in Luke 13:10–17, the woman's body acts with quiet grace by participating in body talk with Jesus that requires both speaking and listening in order to enliven truth. The woman's body commands Jesus to grant her liberation by establishing her presence, and she listens to Jesus's command to cast out the oppressive forces bending her body. The woman's body speaks the truth of not just her individual crookedness but also the reality of a larger structural and systemic crooked system that bends her body. With a hushed boldness, the woman's body declares a bent body language that Jesus hears and gives a double response of voice and touch. The woman's bent body also seeks and receives liberation for its needs and the broader community. The woman's body allows the community to become more inclusive and inviting to other bodies who are looked over, misrecognized, or rendered "untouchable."[82] The ethical learning that Black women can extract is to listen to the body's signs, language, and truths that may be speaking the unspoken. The body seeks its own liberation by telling the raw truth of the wrong done to it.

Never Shut Up: Dare to Be Different!

In the case of the virtuous woman in Luke 13:10–17, the woman's body acts with un/shouted courage by disrupting the scene and deconstructing the strict religious orthodoxy. The presence of the woman's bent body is a disruption both to Jesus's teaching and the synagogue. On the one hand,

---

[82]Crowder, "The Gospel of Luke," 172.

Jesus is teaching the crowd, but the woman's body performs the lesson. The woman's body disrupts the order and deconstructs strict adherence to religious observances that prohibit liberation and restoration. Although the narrator does not qualify how the woman praised God, praise is a bodily act. The woman does not leave the scene after her restoration, but her praises continue in the community. The woman's body displays un/shouted courage by showing up to a scene where she is overlooked and remaining present even when the synagogue leader and powerful members of the crowd treat her harshly. The presence of the woman's body clarifies something is wrong not with the woman but with the male leader and powerful members assembled who display crooked characters, excluding the woman from the community to which she belongs. The woman's body participates in the prophetic fulfillment of Jesus by experiencing liberation and exposing the moral degeneration of exclusivism of all manners and forms. The ethical learning that emerges for Black women is that outlawed, othered, battered, bent bodies are perhaps more virtuous than other acceptable body forms because they expose the evil realities that create their otherness. Reclaiming bent bodies can be seen as an act of resistance and restoration that straightens faulty systems and casts out the "unbearable weights" that bend bodies.

The Bent Body Tells the Story

Luke 13:10–17 is a classic text that warns interpreters to be careful about who is cast aside based on appearance or condition because the person on the margins might just be the most noble. This text probes religious leaders to question their alignment with a crooked social gospel of doctrinal hypocrisy and religious exclusion, which denies or delays the healing and transformation of the most vulnerable. This text reminds all Christian believers to sit with the question "Whose liberation have we hindered or suppressed by our bent and jaded assumptions and biases?" Jesus heals the woman but confronts a broken religious system by speaking truth to the powerful. Jesus healed the woman and restored the woman doubly to a more noble, transformed position of virtuous distinction within the community. Although this woman had been shamed for eighteen years, Jesus flipped the social program yet again by raising this bent woman's stature and putting her dissenters to shame. For it is Jesus who lifts up the lowly and humbles the proud. Jesus and the bent woman work together as co-partners in mutual liberation as she represents the fulfillment of Jesus's mission, and

Jesus confronts the power players/crooked character in the text who seek to enact double harm by misrecognizing her and restricting her opportunities for restoration. Perhaps this story of Jesus and the bent woman working together as co-partners is liberation in living color.

The narrative of the bent woman in Luke 13:10–17 provides parallels with Black women and offers a wise lesson that pronounces and reclaims Black women's moral agency and bodily virtue in light of a bent condition. This Lukan account pushes against physiognomic thought and exposes the lie that the exterior represents the interior or how a person looks denotes the quality of their character. Through a womanist hermeneutics of parallel, the Lukan woman's bent body and my grandmother's crooked body tell more truth about the wrong done to their bodies than words can muster. Together, these stories and lived experiences represent an embodied virtue that becomes more visible upon liberation from the oppressive forces that bent these bodies and restoration to their rightful designation as women of noble character and members of God's beloved community. Father Abraham had many sons, but the gospel of Jesus Christ is revealed through the *body acts* of this noble daughter.

6

Turning the World
Right Side Up

I end this book exactly where I began: with my grandmother's story. After completing my first year of coursework, my grandmother's death on May 6, 2013, shifted my entire world, including my discipline interest from religious history to theological ethics and the subject of this project. Something happened in that Chicago hospital room as I gazed upon her straightened body for the first time in twenty years that gave me profound clarity that Jesus touched my grandmother. Furthermore, she also encountered healing, restoration, and transformation before my eyes. Since that very moment, my aim to bring recognition to the problem of bendedness for Black women and to construct life-abundant pathways for Black women's salvation and redemption remains at the core of my doctoral research and this project.

As a third-generation Black preaching woman, I know the power of story. In the Black preaching tradition, there is value in telling the story, that is, framing the gospel in a way that captures the fragility of the human condition and enlivens the reign of God for the most vulnerable. Katie Cannon describes the Black preacher as the "moral arbiter"[1] for the Black community and sacred texts skilled in "telling of the old, old, story."[2] This book's promise is rooted in the narrative of an everyday Black churchwoman who faced bendedness by a crooked society and a woman with a bent condition revealed in Luke 13:10–17. I join the chorus of womanist scholars who return to the hard questions of the Christian faith because of the faith of their grandmothers. I find resonance with Katie Cannon's story of her grandmother as she begins *Katie's Canon*. Cannon writes,

---

[1] Katie G. Cannon, *Katie's Canon: Womanism and the Soul of the Black Community*, rev. and exp. 25th anniversary ed. (Minneapolis: Fortress Press, 2021), 75.

[2] Cannon, *Katie's Canon*, 82.

My grandmother, Rosa Cornelia White Lytle, was the "gatekeeper in the land of counterpain." She was always available with salves, hot towels, and liniments to cure physical aches and spiritual ills. As a charismatic healer, Grandma Rosie's practice consisted of diagnosis, treatment, and prevention in the maintenance of overall wholeness. Many days my soul struggled with whether to go to school or stay home and be healed from the injuries of the world inflicted unknowingly. In 1983, womanism became the new gatekeeper in my land of counterpain.[3]

I am confident that my womanish proclivities were cultivated during my nascent girlhood developmental stages as a young Black preacher's kid in urban metropolitan Chicago in the late 1980s and 1990s. My mother's backhand scoldings to shut my mouth because I had too much to say too soon revealed I had been "acting grown" and "taking charge" for a long time. Although womanism is a confessional and scholarly identity, my entry point began as an undergraduate at Howard University and later cultivated in graduate coursework with womanist scholars at Vanderbilt University Divinity School and Chicago Theological Seminary. My grandmother's passing sharpened my womanist sensibilities, providing me with tools and language to make meaning of her suffering and "move from death to life" by drawing from the timeless wisdom of her story.[4]

Methodologically speaking, this book is not the product of history but utilizes "emancipatory historiography" as a womanist methodology to trace the social landscape of Black women's struggles in the American context.[5] As a Black Chicagoan with Southern roots, this book includes the undertold story of Black migrants from the South navigating the Midwest and the struggle for freedom under the guise of better economic opportunities in the North. The failed promises Black people encountered during the Great Migration impacted Black women's labor while contributing to the burdens of service, surrogacy, and strength injuring Black women's lives. Womanist theologian Yolanda Pierce notes, "The Black Church coordinated the migration efforts of African Americans leaving the South in search of the American dream. These same churches then provided havens when the dream was replaced with the reality of the American nightmare."[6] Black migrants like

---

[3]Cannon, *Katie's Canon*, 1.

[4]Cannon, *Katie's Canon*, 3.

[5]Stacey M. Floyd-Thomas, *Mining the Motherlode: Methods in Womanist Ethics* (Cleveland: Pilgrim Press, 2006), 106.

[6]Yolanda Nicole Pierce, *In My Grandmother's House: Black Women, Faith, and the Stories*

my grandmother found the Black Church as often the only institution to offer comfort and care, which gives context to why migrant Black women cling to the convictions of their Black faith and why they stayed with Jesus, like the women near the cross, even in the most terror-laden times.

The cross is a culmination point for many Christians, but this book bears witness to this salvation history as a point of departure. Any rigorous discussion of Christology and the cross in contemporary theology is incomplete without serious engagement with womanist theologies. Jacquelyn Grant, Kelly Brown Douglas, Delores Williams, and JoAnne Terrell provide mystical nuances to this work and develop my understanding of what it meant to bury my grandmother proverbially near the cross.

Much like the story of the doubly bent woman, I approached this work with a clear conviction that the bendedness that Black women face is double-sided, with political damages in the American landscape and spiritual hypocrisy in the Black Church. Black women belong at the center of any discussion about the political mapping of America in its quest to pursue democracy and the prophetic witness of the Black Church in its attempt to redeem the soul of America. As a daughter of the Black Church and a womanist theological ethicist, my conception of the Black Church is double-edged. The Black Church has operated as a resting place to survive the harsh realities of a heteropatriarchal capitalist white supremacist world, yet the Black Church itself perpetuates oppressive theologies that deny the bodies and souls of its most faithful members. As a countercultural resistance movement that once valued *somebodiness* against a hostile white world, the Black Church now misrecognizes Black women's bodies and character.

In line with Cone, the Black Church must undergo conversion for its sin-sick soul to be redeemed. Pierce contends, "The Black Church has replicated the worst of patriarchal structures, misogyny, and discrimination. It has been the house of God for some even as it has failed to be a safe haven for many others. And I am left living in the tension: gratitude for what I have inherited, sadness at the unfinished work of what we can be."[7] The distorted Black Church mission that is invested in the business of *saving* Black women as popularized by T. D. Jakes and the Woman Thou Art Loosed movement and countless others expose gaping fissures in its moral fabric. The prophetic talkback of womanist theology casts a vision of liberation for all of us and calls the Black Church to accountability that, if

---

We Inherit (Minneapolis: Broadleaf Books, 2021), 148.

[7]Pierce, *In My Grandmother's House*, 150.

heeded, will redeem the soul of the Black Church. In preaching, teaching, and sacred popular rhetoric, Black women resonate with and return again and again to the Lukan text of the bent woman. My reading of this passage is to move the scripting of the bent woman beyond the jaded theologies of contempt espoused most notably by T. D. Jakes and WTAL. I return to the text for my grandmother's sake, illustrating that salvation and redemption go hand in hand. Finally, I return to the biblical text because Black womanists continue to see these passages, especially the Jesus stories, as primary texts to, in Cannon's view, "search the Scriptures to dispel the threat of death in order to seize the present life."[8] The oppressive powers that bend in society and religion must be interrogated to recognize and redeem the embodied virtue of Black women.

In "Listen, Lord: A Prayer," poet and activist James Weldon Johnson illuminates the prayers of the saints of old in *God's Trombones* in a posture of coming to God with "knee-bowed and body-bent."[9] For a brief period during elementary school, I remember my grandmother living with my family. My grandmother made my whole world better. Every day, she cleaned the house to perfection. Every evening, she prepared a fresh homemade meal. Her sheer presence and grace-filled company brought excitement to our daily routines. Every season, my grandmother's wisdom and healing gave my family footing for the journey ahead. Like Pierce's *In My Grandmother's House: Black Women, Faith, and the Stories We Inherit*, this work is a product of grandmother theology.[10]

The second part of Walker's womanism, "Mama, I'm walking to Canada," illuminates the necessity of intergenerational bonds between girls and women to transfer survival tools and map a path to liberation. Remembering my grandmother's story gives meaning to her suffering and womanist wisdom to forge a way to wholeness. After a restless night of playing video games until the wee hours of the morning, I vividly remember tiptoeing to the kitchen to grab a snack and overhearing my grandmother downstairs "knee-bowed and body-bent" praying for me, my future, our family, and our church.

My grandmother prayed for me.

Grandma's prayers protected me from getting too involved with the wrong crowd. Grandma's prayers humbled me when my attitude grew bigger than

---

[8]Cannon, *Katie's Canon*, 29.

[9]James Weldon Johnson and Henry Louis Gates, *God's Trombones: Seven Negro Sermons in Verse*, rev. ed. (New York: Penguin Books, 2008).

[10]Pierce, *In My Grandmother's House*, xvii.

my altitude. Grandma's prayers kept the disappointments of my past from dimming the brightness of my future. Grandma's prayers carried me through school and traveled with me around the globe. My grandmother prayed for me then, and I am confident that this book is a product of her answered prayers. Indeed, this book belongs to my ancestors' wildest dreams.

Index